Assessment in Counselling

Assessment in Counselling

Theory, Process and Decision-Making

JUDITH MILNER
and
PATRICK O'BYRNE

Consultant editor

JO CAMPLING

First published 2004 by
PALGRAVE MACMILLAN
Houndmills, Basingstoke, Hampshire RG21 6XS and
175 Fifth Avenue, New York, N.Y. 10010
Companies and representatives throughout the world

PALGRAVE MACMILLAN is the global academic imprint of the Palgrave Macmillan division of St. Martin's Press, LLC and of Palgrave Macmillan Ltd. Macmillan® is a registered trademark in the United States, United Kingdom and other countries. Palgrave is a registered trademark in the European Union and other countries.

ISBN 1–4039–0429–4

This book is printed on paper suitable for recycling and made from fully managed and sustained forest sources.

A catalogue record for this book is available from the British Library.

Library of Congress Cataloging-in-Publication Data
  Milner, Judith, senior lecturer.
    Assessment in counselling: theory, process, and decision-making/Judith Milner and Patrick O'Byrne; consultant editor, Jo Campling.
      p. cm.
    Includes bibliographical references and index.
    ISBN 1–4039–0429–4 (pbk.)
    1. Counseling. I. O'Byrne, Patrick. II. Campling, Jo. III. Title.
    BF637.C6M5249 2003
    158'3—dc22
                                                          2003058118

10   9   8   7   6   5   4   3   2   1
13   12   11   10   09   08   07   06   05   04

Typeset by Cambrian Typesetters, Frimley, Surrey

Printed in China

Contents

List of Tables and Figures

Preface

We all make assessments of clients and others every working day. These include evaluations of qualities, needs, abilities – the list could be endless. In counselling with clients, understandings and decisions may be central but these are influenced not only by the clients and how they are, but also by the work context and by our own theoretical perspectives, beliefs about people and philosophies of life.

Our fascination with the question of what is good practice in assessment has been longstanding. For many years we lectured on counselling methods, theory and skills, as well as aspects of psychology, sociology and human growth and development. But it is in our current counselling experience, where clients deserve the most respectful and effective help, that our thoughts have been focused on evaluating the world of theory in order to examine the usefulness of various approaches in practice, their advantages and disadvantages in understanding people's predicaments and helping clients to deal with them effectively. We have taken a view that the best understanding/assessment/analysis of a problem is one that leads to the best outcome for the client. This pragmatic view will appear throughout the book.

Our practice is mainly based at the Northorpe Hall Child and Family Trust in Mirfield, West Yorkshire, although Judith is also involved in freelance training and Patrick is also a family mediator. The people who come to Northorpe Hall include children and young people of all ages, many referred by Social Services, doctors, police and schools, although there are also self-referrals. Children and parents are worked with, in a variety of approaches, and the problems addressed are as diverse as families are – they include abusive relationships, depression, addictions, behavioural and relationship difficulties.

As well as teaching the subject, we have been discussing how we make our assessments and looking at how assessment is addressed in government guidelines and agency policies and at how, in this age of audits and managerialism, assessment is often a sheet of tick boxes or form-filling that goes no further than data collection. The interesting question for us has been what use is made of the data? Is it used for decision-making and, if so, what decisions and how are they made?

Sometimes the search for the cause of the problem is raised, sometimes not. Sometimes the only decision is whether to offer counselling or not. Some counsellors see it as important to develop a
formulation; sometimes this is based on appropriate theory and
borders on being a diagnosis, other times it simply records client
complaints. The use made of theory in assessment is often opaque;
theory shows up much more clearly in interventions.

The lengthy reference list in this book is indicative of our searches
in the literature, where little is available on assessment, but more useful
still was our mini-research – our semi-structured interviews and
conversations with 18 respondents, all colleagues and contacts in
counselling practice. In doing this research we were influenced by
McLeod (1998), who suggests that counselling has an oral tradition as
much as a written one, and that implicit knowledge of the former
strongly influences practice (this research is reported in detail in the
journal *Counselling and Psychotherapy Research*, June 2003). We were
impressed by the care our respondents take in deciding whether to
offer counselling to people and in trying to reach shared understandings with them. However, the ways by which they approached assessment, especially in coming to a formulation, varied according to the
theoretical orientation they acquired in training – sometimes with the
addition of skills learned after training. Apart from counselling
psychologists, many of the counsellors we met did not develop
formulations as such, even when their preferred theory could easily
have helped them to do so. Their theoretical backgrounds varied and
the spectrum was wider than that of the six approaches we discuss in
this book. This helped us greatly in examining the approaches we
have presented, some of which we seldom draw on in our own practice. We will be referring to the views of those we consulted as we
work through the book, offering a blend of theory and practice
wisdom with a view to helping counsellors making assessments identify their theoretical underpinning as well as a pragmatic usefulness.
Our own main approaches are solution-focused and narrative, as
presented in Chapters 8 and 9 (see also Milner and O'Byrne, 2002a).

Our aim throughout is to be explicit about our own philosophy of
social constructionism and how it provides our particular perspective
on theory (Chapter 1); to explore the assessment relationship with its
power differences and potential for oppression (Chapter 2); to examine various types of assessment and data collection (Chapter 3); and
seek to make six of the main theoretical methods, or theoretical
'maps', and their implications for assessment, accessible not only for

colleagues but especially for students and those training for counselling (Chapters 4 to 9). We also discuss the problems for assessment
of integrating methods (Chapter 10), and finally (in Chapter 11) the
decision-making process, particularly the difficulties in keeping an
open mind and avoiding bias, as well as the effects on clients of written assessments and records.

We hope you will read this book as an invitation to reexamine the
issues involved in assessment and to visit, or revisit, some of the theory
underpinning your preferred method so as to be able to make more
use of it in your decision-making and in planning your work. We
hope you will find our various metaphors for summing up ideas
useful, as well as the notion that all theory is but metaphor for the
unseen processes that we discuss in counselling. In particular we invite
you to contribute to the oral tradition in counselling by discussing
your own practice and approaches with colleagues and perhaps in
group supervision.

JUDITH MILNER
PATRICK O'BYRNE

Acknowledgements

We owe much to the many friends and colleagues who have helped and encouraged us in writing this book, in particular Jo Campling for inviting us to consider the project, and Magenta Lampson and Andrew McAleer at Palgrave Macmillan for their generous assistance.

We want to mention especially those who not only allowed us to interview them in our research, but also gave generously of their time as ongoing consultants: Chris Atha, Brenda Atkinson, David Broadbent, Anne Clarke, Rob Cannon, Andrew Duggan, Jackie Emmett, Jean Goad, Sue Greaves, Julie Hall, Naseem Ijaz, Steve Myers, Paula Partington-Utley, Nicky Ryden, Rene Smith, Karen Squillino, Doreen Ward and Nigel White. Anne, Sue, Julie, Paula, Nicky, Rene and Doreen also provided us with useful feedback on drafts of chapters.

Thanks are also due to the staff at Northorpe Hall for putting up with us in their customary supportive way.

Lastly we acknowledge the unfailing support that we have had from our families at all times.

JUDITH MILNER
PATRICK O'BYRNE

1

Introduction:
Assessment Complexities

In this chapter we will begin by putting our interest in assessment into context and discussing briefly our research for the book. Then the influence of the process of assessment is discussed along with the interplay between this and counsellors' theoretical homes and common techniques. The chapter will end with an explanation of what we see as 'waves' of theory, of what we call the theoretical 'maps' that appear in Chapters 4 to 9, and of our social-constructionist philosophy.

In our practice at Northorpe Hall, the client is given a choice of counsellor in terms of ethnicity and gender and, within these preferences, the counselling coordinator makes an initial decision to allocate client to counsellor on the basis of the age of the client and type of problem, matching these to the known preferences and skills of the counsellor. An assessment interview is undertaken, after which the counsellor has the option of referring the client to another counsellor; the client can request a change of counsellor; or counselling can proceed on the basis that both parties are satisfied with the original 'match'. Additionally the counsellor can at any time bring in another member of the team or the client can request a change of counsellor. The latter is facilitated by the client being made aware that they do not have to give a reason for wanting to change, they only need to ring the counselling coordinator. Neither are they expected to 'work through' their rejection of a counsellor.

Thus assessment of clients' needs, preferences and suitability for counselling is taken particularly seriously, as is the suitability of the counsellors and the counselling approaches that are available. This led us to think that a good starting point for the preparation of this book would be informal discussion with our colleagues about both the purpose and content of assessment in counselling. Our assumption

1

that the purpose of assessment was universally understood turned out to be naive. It was not necessarily that there was a lack of consensus (although there are obvious differences in how counsellors view assessment, dependent on their theoretical orientation, see for example Ruddell and Curwen, 1997; Merry, 1999), rather it was to do with the lack of a coherent framework, a common comment being that assessment was dealt with on training courses as a hotly debated subject, constructed to fit the particular needs of each counselling model. By constructed we mean based on a language, a set of metaphors developed to enable people to talk or write about aspects of living, particularly when living includes difficulties and behaviours that someone, not necessarily the client, wants to change.

In order to unpick these constructions, we stepped back from our informal conversations and arranged a number of research interviews with counsellors using different models over a range of settings. We gave each respondent our interview schedule and a counselling scenario well in advance of the actual interview so that they had time to think about the how and why of assessment, one outcome being that respondents found the opportunity to reflect on assessment useful. Indeed, the initial research interview has led in several instances to ongoing dialogue, encouraging us to believe that the subject is ripe for exploration and debate.

We were successful in interviewing 18 counsellors (12 women and 6 men) from a range of settings, several of whom are also supervisors, working for agencies, or privately, or a combination. All were experienced counsellors, counselling psychologists and psychologists, using a range of counselling media, including art, play and writing therapies as well as 'talking'. The age range of clients covered the whole lifespan. Our intention to interview two people from each methodological orientation was less successful. Counsellors turn out not to be what colleagues think they are – or even what they initially say about themselves. One counsellor, for example, regularly accepted referrals for cognitive behavioural work but saw herself primarily as TA/psychotherapeutic in orientation. Apart from those with a Freudian orientation, the others were much more eclectic or integrated; for example, 'I am basically person centred but integrate other theories I have found useful; a tiny bit of solution focused, a lot of TA, and a little cognitive behavioural if the case needed it.' We discuss eclecticism and integration in a later chapter but here we outline some of the complexities that emerged from counsellors' thinking about assessment and briefly review what is said about assessment in the counselling literature.

Remarkably little is written about assessment in comparison with 'middles' and 'endings'. We suspect that it is easier to talk about the process of counselling after it has begun than the rationale for beginning it, the purpose of assessment depending on the purpose of counselling – and that is contested, ambiguous and fluid.

Purpose of counselling and the influence of this on assessment

Because of its emphasis on the facilitation of personal change, the purpose of counselling must necessarily be highly individual, and therefore endlessly variable, making it difficult to define its purpose. McLeod cites Feltham and Dryden's (1993) definition of counselling:

> A principled relationship characterised by the application of one or more psychological theories and a recognised set of communication skills, modified by experience, intuition and other interpersonal factors, to clients' intimate concerns, problems and aspirations. Its predominant ethos is one of facilitation rather than advice giving or coercion. (McLeod, 1998, p. 3)

But, of course, it is not this simple. Counselling is not just something that happens between two people, the counselling encounter involves but one small section of a complex set of relationships. These include:

- The client's home. The counsellor has no direct experience of the client's extended family and community relationships, which are filtered through the client's narrative, shaped by the counsellor's questions.
- The counsellor's theoretical home. The relationships here consist of the relationship the counsellor has with her or his own values and beliefs, choice of psychological theory, and experiences. Counsellors' degrees of comfortableness in their theoretical homes will affect their confidence in shaping clients' narratives through the sort of questions asked and the interpretations made. As the counsellor also has a relationship with his or her supervisor – who has no direct experience of the client – the narrative may be further shaped by this encounter. The client has no direct experience of this relationship, nor of its potential to influence what will seem an intensely personal and private relationship between counsellor and client.
- The counsellor's agency home. The counsellor's relationship with the employing agency affects how assessments are undertaken.

Respondents who worked solely for agencies found that they had assessment formats imposed on them, particularly in regard to risk assessment. They also complained that the number of sessions permitted restricted the assessment, even though this ranged from six sessions that were not time-limited to weekly sessions over two years. The respondents in private practice were similarly restricted by their relationships with referrers – few clients actually paid directly for their own counselling.

• Counselling's political home. This includes the relationship between counselling and society more widely, the legitimisation of counselling as a social institution. Paradoxically the most enduring feature of the societal context of counselling is the one that is most vague, what McLeod (1998) refers to as the liminal role of both counsellor and client:

> Counsellors are rarely managers or executives who hold power in colleges, businesses or communities. Counsellors, instead, have a more 'liminal' role, being employed at the edge of these institutions to deal with those in danger of falling off or falling out (McLeod, 1998, p. 7).

Implicit in this is that counselling provides the basis for 'climbing back', although the grey area of the counselling space means that this cannot be an explicit part of the process, a possible rationale for assessment. This is essentially a political issue, which we discuss further in the following chapter. Here we simply wish to make the point that the therapeutic relationship has many hidden facets, all of which complicate assessment purposes and procedures. We have in mind the analogy of Green's (1994) approach to the analysis of ancient drama. Literary analysts can, and do, flit backwards and forwards through the pages of a text, just as counsellor and supervisor can flit through the counsellor's copy of the text. This will yield a detailed and subtle analysis but not one that says anything about the way the performance was received or the influence it had. Just as theatrical performance involves interplay with the expectations of an audience created in the theatre as much as the players, so too do counselling genres shift to meet the needs of both particular individuals and particular times. Thus it is important to remember that the bedrock of counselling, the therapeutic relationship, does not exist as an entity in itself. Like a play, the counsellors (actors) will give different performances depending on decisions made about methods (production style), client (audience) reactions, and cultural shifts (fashions). The difficulty in examining all these variations has, we suggest, led to a preoccupation with process (the text) at the expense of rationale – what we are assessing for and why. As one counsellor said to us, the theoretical home of the counsellor is a matter of personal experience, in-depth training and reflexive practice, not a matter of understanding in an abstract way.

This is a 'hands-off' statement, one that has resonance with McLeod's introductory comment that counselling is a practice that can only be grasped through the experience of doing it (1998, p. xvii), and with comments made in our interviews. Respondents frequently mentioned the 'feeling' factor and often assessed for their own 'comfortableness' with a client as much as the client's 'comfortableness' with them. This was related to them seeing the major component of assessment as beginning a journey with the client. The only difference being that some saw this as a journey towards finding the 'truth' about a problem, while others viewed this in terms of journeying towards the client's goals. Must we accept that abstraction is impossible, that clients must trust us sufficiently to try an introductory session so that they can see how it *feels* rather than have an introductory explanation about the purpose and method so that they can evaluate the feeling content of that first session within a *thinking* framework? We believe that the latter is only fair, it being the responsibility of counsellors to try to make sense of their practice, even if it does occupy a liminal space.

And we consider it important that counsellors make explicit their methodological approach rather than leave it up to the client to test their experience of it – what is not infrequently referred to in the literature as the 'flavouring' element of the first session (see, for example Tantum, 1995). Not least is our concern with dropout rates, which McLeod estimates at one-third, but also the issue of counsellor socialisation and indoctrination into particular methods. Somewhere between assessment and intervention, a *formulation* is made (Tillett, 1996; McDougall and Reade, 1993), where information is processed within some sort of theoretical framework, the counsellor's reality:

> An essential part of becoming a counsellor is to choose a version of reality that makes sense, that can be lived in. But no matter what version is selected, it needs to be understood that it is only one among several possibilities. (McLeod, 1998, p. 29)

A 'version of reality' can be said to be a story written from a particular perspective and drawing on metaphors and insights of that perspective. There is evidence that these formulations, particular theoretical versions of the client story, are subject to a number of errors and biases which can lead to prematurely fixed conclusions. These are often influenced by theory indoctrination and in-depth professional training (Dumonte and Lecomte, 1987), proving resistant to reflexive practice as the supervisor chosen is usually one who has been subjected to similar socialisation processes.

We make a plea, therefore, for more abstraction, for a greater critical examination of our theoretical homes and the influence of these on our assessment frameworks. We do not exempt ourselves from this process; we, too, recognise that we favour a particular model of counselling (a combination of solution-focused and narrative approaches), so we will be equally critical of our preferred approaches. We are aware of our indoctrination and the danger in being practised in deconstructing and reconstructing realities that may lead us to be dismissive of the contributions of other approaches. We hope to illustrate that different methods, and the assessment implications of these, do not necessarily lead to certainty; merely that our chosen reality is made explicit to clients at the assessment stage and has the potential to be helpful to each client who engages with us in a therapeutic relationship. As Holmes (1995) points out, the word assessment is derived from the Latin *assidere* – to sit beside – which underpins the 'empathic attempt to grasp the nature of the patient's predicament', but there is always another strand to assessment: 'a more distanced effort to calculate the likelihood of therapeutic success' (p. 28). The majority of our respondents' criteria for taking a case depended on assessing for psychological-mindedness and the existence of resilience factors in the client, excluding those with serious, long-standing problems – what one counsellor referred to as 'the hot-potato client' who is referred from agency to agency. This has counselling access implications for clients under severe social stress, a consideration we discuss in more detail in Chapter 2, but, here, we emphasise the need for a more detailed and explicit attempt to assess client suitability for counselling; the suitability of different forms of counselling for different clients and/or client concerns, problems and aspirations; how long it is likely to take; and, how we will measure effectiveness.

Bayne *et al.* (1994, pp. 9–10) contend that whatever a counsellor's theoretical orientation, there are six main objectives of assessment. We aim, below, to examine these objectives in the light of the previous discussion, demonstrating that they could perhaps be better termed the subjectivities of assessment.

1 'To help you and your client understand the nature of the client's presenting problem and related issues'

The main barrier to assessment here is that unless the counsellor makes their theoretical framework explicit, clients will not know how to present these concerns, other than from information about counselling gleaned from previous direct experience or indirectly from media accounts. Neither is all that likely to fit the counsellor's expectations. The client, or referrer, may well also couch these problems within what they know about your agency's criteria for acceptance for counselling, so the presenting problem may bear little relation to the actual problem, which may in itself be held back due to a number of possible reasons such as shame, embarrassment, distrust and so on. Additionally the counsellor is involved in assessing the characteristics and emotions of clients, all of which defy accurate measurement because of the intensely personal nature and fluidity of the concepts underlying them. For example, self-esteem – that cornerstone of much counselling practice – is impossible to assess, intervene in, and measure progress in development, as there is lack of consensus on what it is (see, for example, Whiston, 2000). It is largely context-specific rather than a fixed trait, there being no 'objective' ways of measuring it.

We ask you to consider many questions, some of which may appear to be pedestrian; for example, what are the initial tasks of assessment? At this stage, assessment has many questions to ask:

- If the client has had counselling before, do we need to establish what was and what was not helpful then and in what ways the counselling approach currently offered will differ from the previous experience? Selekman (2002), for example, asks 'You have seen a lot of therapists before me, what did they miss or overlook in your situation that it is important for me to know?', and 'Has there been anything that any of your past therapists tried with you that you found to be most helpful?' (pp. 40–1).
- How do we consider what ideas about counselling the client has gathered from other sources, such as friends, the media and so on, and how do these differ from the counsellor's understanding?
- How do we decide what needs to happen in this session for it to be useful to the client who, having turned up, is surely eager for

something helpful and should not therefore be assumed to be resistant if they have difficulty articulating their concerns?
• Where the agency places restrictions on the number of sessions
  available to the client, how can the counsellor establish what is the
  least that needs to happen to make a difference for the client?

2 'To identify factors that may be associated with the problem and the client's experience or behaviour'

Any one problem has a whole range of factors that may be associated
with it but causal relationships between the two are less easy to establish. Depending largely on a counsellor's theoretical home (which will
influence what research findings are deemed most relevant), a counsellor will filter the 'factors' through her own understanding of problem causality. This will influence whether the questions asked to elicit
associated factors are about internal states, interpersonal relationships,
external factors, or a combination of any of these. Even where our
respondents had some sort of assessment structure imposed on them,
they still structured their assessment questions to meet the requirements of their particular model of working. They knew what they
were looking for: the Freudian, TA and some of the person-centred
counsellors were most interested in exploring the internal worlds of
their clients; the solution-focused, narrative and some person-centred
counsellors were most interested in client strengths; and the CBT
counsellors wanted a clear understanding of the problem: 'I want to
assess how they think, behave, feel physically, and what sort of
emotions go along with this'.

Without an explanation of the counsellor's understanding of the
nature of people, this will at best puzzle the client and at worst insult
them. For example, the mother of a child exploited as a prostitute and
murdered at the age of 17 reported that when she sought help in
coping with her daughter at the age of 14, a psychologist suggested
that the situation was a product of rebellion in the context of a liberal
household. The mother thought the questions about the interpersonal
nature of her relationship with her daughter were not relevant to her
concern that her 14-year-old daughter was being sexually abused by
a 32-year-old man (cited in Weir, 2002, p. 9). Similarly, some clients
can perceive solution-focused approaches as 'solution-forced'
(O'Connell, 2001).

The accurate assessment of associated factors is a major problem.
Piper *et al.* (1995) point out that the more transference interpretations

are made during brief (less than 20 sessions) psychotherapy, the worse the therapeutic alliance and the treatment outcome. Similarly, the high drop-out rate from counselling may be a result of inappropriate associated factor search. The search for possible associated factors presumes a causal connection that may well not be necessary; there is ample evidence that solutions do not necessarily link to problems (de Shazer *et al.*, 1986). The questions arising at this stage of assessment include:

- How to describe briefly the counsellor's understanding of the nature of people and explain the purpose of the questions asked?
- Before embarking on eliciting a long history, how to decide with the client how much you need to know?
- How to check with the client that questions, or encouragement to say more about a particular topic, has some meaning for the client?
- How appropriate it is to ask questions about internal states when attending too much to the irrational dimension of the relationship is demonstrably counterproductive?
- What strengths and abilities does the client possess that counter concerns and problems, or enable them to be endured?

3 'To determine client expectations and desired outcomes'

This is not as straightforward as it seems because, although counselling has 'emerged from a long historical journey in the direction of *self-contained individualism*' (McLeod, our emphasis), the client may well have expectations that others, too, will be influenced by the counselling. These 'others' are not easily visible to the counsellor, as McLeod warns us:

> The client experiences counselling as one facet of a life that may encompass many other relationships; the counsellor has no first-hand involvement into these other relationships and is limited to his or her experience of the actual sessions. The two types of experience therefore have quite different horizons. (1998, pp. 27–8)

What we do know is that client expectations about counselling *before* they enter it have very little influence on eventual outcomes, but the expectations they build *during* initial sessions have significant influence on outcomes (Sexton and Whiston, 1997). The initial session is therefore critical to the effectiveness of overall counselling as this is the opportunity to build positive expectations about the process. The non-specific factors, particularly the ability to develop a therapeutic relationship (see, for example, Atkinson *et al.*, 1993; McLeod, 1998), are essential at this stage of the assessment process. These are not all to do with factors such as warmth, unconditional regard, trustworthiness and so on, but also relatively simple things which will increase the counsellor's credibility. Initial client perceptions of counsellors account for 31 per cent of variance in favourable therapeutic outcomes (Heppner and Claiborn, 1989), such as instilled optimism (Lambert, 1992) and attractiveness (LaCross, 1980). Wheeler (1995) recommends that counsellors dress appropriately for fee-paying clients in order 'to present themselves in a way that will inspire confidence' (p. 117), but surely all counsellors could be aware of the non-verbal statement their dress code makes?

Questions asked at this stage of the assessment process aim to help the client clarify their expectations, with opportunities to enlarge on these to include their aspirations as well as their concerns. Such questions might include:

- What needs to happen in this hour to make your coming here today worthwhile?
- If we were to meet in a year's time and all the problems that had brought you here today had been solved, what would be different in your life?
- What is your biggest concern?
- What is your wildest dream?
- Anything else? We suggest that a counsellor can hardly ask this question too often as it prevents premature formulation.

4 'To collect baseline information that can be compared with subsequent data to evaluate progress'

With increased pressure for counsellors to provide accountability information on their own effectiveness for third-party payers and administrators, and for legal reasons as well as the professional development of the counsellor, collecting baseline information becomes even more important. The problem is whether this data can be standardised so that effectiveness can be measured across clients and/or client concerns. As counselling is essentially preoccupied with individuals, all of whom have their own individual problems and solutions, it is rarely possible to translate data from one client into a larger population. Although there are common areas of information collected at this stage, such as presenting problem, previous treatment, personal history and symptomatology (Tillett, 1996; Waddington-Jones, 1996), how this is collected and the emphasis given to it varies. Partington (1997), for example, found that clinical psychologists were most likely to use standardised questionnaires, counselling psychologists rather less so, and counsellors used them on relatively few occasions, echoing Dryden and Feltham's comment that formal assessment procedures and instruments are not popular with counsellors who fear that formal data-gathering exercises lead to clients being labelled or treated as objects or specimens of pathology (1994, p. 99). However, underestimating problem severity has been found to be a major factor in negative outcomes (Mohr, 1995); how then is it to be assessed accurately?

The data collected has to relate to each client's unique situation rather than fit into the agency schedule, or the counsellor's knowledge about the possible cause of problems, if progress is to be measured in a way that is meaningful for the client. It is therefore essential to collect data about the severity of the problem, what the client can and can't do at this stage, and what they hope to be able to do in the future. An emphasis on emotional states will make measurement difficult but, equally, an emphasis on behavioural indicators may limit progress to small sets of behaviour that have little meaning for the client. To add to these complexities, the first session can be too late a time to collect baseline data, many clients having been shown to have made significant progress between the time of making the appointment and arriving for the first session – what Berg and Reuss (1998) refer to as 'pre-session change'.

Regardless of theoretical orientation, many counsellors use scaled questions to elicit baseline data at the first session, using numbers not to measure severity *per se*, but to measure progress later. Thus one client may rate the severity of the problem as 1 out of 10 while another may rate it at 8, but the counsellor is largely interested in movement from 1 to 2 and 8 to 9 rather than considering what the numbers mean. Thus responses to scaled questions cannot be used to compare different clients' progress. Scaled questions aimed at collecting baseline data include:

- If 1 is how the problem was affecting you when you made the appointment and 10 is the problem has been completely solved, where are you on this scale today?

- Think of the best person you could be and give that person 100 points. Where are you on this scale today?
- If 1 is 'the pits' and 10 is perfect happiness, where would you place yourself on this scale?
- On a scale of 1–10 (where 1 is 'not at all well' and 10 is 'very well'), how well do feel you are doing at the moment?

These questions can be tailored to each client's individual problems, related concerns and aspirations; for example, the counsellor can devise a drinking or depression scale. Similarly they can be used to assess risk:

- At this point, how much more do you feel you can cope with?
- How often recently have you felt you are getting completely to the end of your tether?
- How close do you feel, right now, to ending your own life?

5 'To facilitate the client's learning and motivation by sharing the counsellor's view of the problem. This in itself may contribute to therapeutic change through increasing self-awareness'

In order to facilitate the client's learning, their learning style must first be understood. For example, Holmes (1995) suggests that psychological-mindedness is an indicator for psychoanalytic psychotherapy, and therefore he would be assessing clients' ability to accept trial inter-pretations, the capacity to see self from the outside, to reflect on one's inner world, tolerate psychic pain, regress in the service of the ego, autobiographical competence, and fluidity of thought. However, not all clients learn from insight or reflecting; they may be pragmatic and prefer to learn from trying out new ideas, or they may prefer to theo-rise and analyse. Dryden and Feltham (1992) make the important point that client temperament is often not well-understood by coun-sellors and tends to be overlooked. Nevertheless, assessing learning style is an important part of the assessment process and 'a good coun-sellor will adapt to fit the clients with different problem-solving styles' (O'Connell, 2001, p. 11).

Equally important is the need to assess motivation, it being well-established that veterans of counselling, for example, are less likely to make smooth progress. Where a client lacks motivation to change, counsellors have to ask themselves whether counselling can help the client, what Leigh (1998) refers to as 'the bottom line', although counsellors do have a responsibility for setting the scene so that moti-vation can be improved (see, for example, Turnell and Edwards, 1999). Prochaska and Di Clemente (1992) suggest that recovery weaves back and forth through five stages; pre-contemplation, contemplation, preparation, action and maintenance, and it is useful to assess where the client is at in terms of willingness to change as well as overall emotional states. Questions which have the potential to aid the assess-ment of willingness, confidence and capacity to change will vary depending on the theoretical orientation of the counsellor, but there are some basic scaled questions which can be used at this stage of the assessment process:

- On a scale of 1–10 (1 being you having no confidence at all that you can reach your goal and 10 being you knowing, tough though it may be, that you definitely will), where do you see yourself now?
- On a scale of 1–10 (1 being very dissatisfied and 10 very satisfied), how happy are you with your score on [the problem severity rating] scale?
- On a scale of 1–10 (1 being not at all bothered about the way that things are and 10 being you knowing that this is the most signifi-cant thing facing you at the moment which has got to change), where are you at the moment?
- On a scale of 1–10 (1 being you knowing that you would not be willing to do anything different to resolve this situation and 10 being knowing that you would whatever it takes to sort this out), where do you see yourself right now?
- What don't you want to change about your life?

6 'To produce an initial assessment (formulation) which provides the counsellor with the basis for making the first decision about whether to offer a counselling contract, to initiate referral and to suggest that coun-selling would not be appropriate, and second to provide the basis for developing a therapeutic or counselling plan, including the length of the contract'

Although humanistically inclined counsellors see the assessment process as less to do with dynamic formulation and more as an oppor-tunity for the counsellor and client to decide whether to embark on the relationship (see, for example, Merry, 1999; King, 2001), they do make assessments – even if only whether to carry on with sessions. The argument between the various theoretical orientations is more to do with *how* formulations are made and the therapeutic relationship established. The counsellor has to decide not only if the client can benefit from counselling, but also if the client can benefit from that counsellor's type of counselling. Establishing psychological mindedness is a two-way process through which both parties decide whether or not to carry on, albeit explicit in the case of the counsellor and implicit – dropping out – on the part of the client.

This is not simply a matter of waiting for the client's responses to various questions, but of explaining why they were asked – the theoretical frame. Less clients might drop out after trial interpretations (Piper, 1995) if the counsellor was explicit about the reasons for making them. For example, Holmes (1995) makes a psychoanalytic formulation by looking at the triangle of the person – the current difficulty, the transferential situation and the infantile or childhood constellation of conflict or difficulty but Segal *et al.* (1995) would make a cognitive-behavioural formulation by looking for a circumscribed chief complaint, which they find most likely to benefit from this approach. Both are working from an 'expert', scientist-practitioner-led model and searching for compatibility with their therapeutic rationale. Humanistic and narrative counsellors would be more likely to see their assessment style as client-led, through encouraging the client to tell their story and defining the problem through agreement (see, for example, Merry, 1999; Payne, 2000), but their beliefs about the nature of problems (and solutions) would be implicit in that they, too, were looking for compatibility with their therapeutic rationale. This is individually problem-based in the case of the former, whilst the latter encourages the client to consider the problem as located in factors influencing the client rather than as intrinsic to the client or as symptoms of deficit.

This makes 'flavouring', the tasting of counselling offered to the client at the first session, a central issue. What is interesting is that counsellors do not frequently refer clients to other counsellors; perhaps because the therapeutic relationship has begun and the counsellor feels an investment in continuing. An additional factor may be that as counsellors do not always make it any more clear to colleagues than to clients what their particular expertise is, they are not in a position to make accurate referrals to each other – an interesting finding from our small-scale research project was that only four of the respondents actually worked in the way they were most usually viewed by their colleagues. Rose (2000) suggests, more cynically, that some counsellors are more interested in cherishing their own beliefs, related to the theoretical orientation they adhere to, than taking into account the best interests of their clients.

As counsellors do make formulations, and this remains a central purpose of assessment, it behoves them to ensure that these formulations are both tentative and partial, so that they can be revised in the light of later information and made explicit to clients. Thus we would expect all counsellors to summarise what they heard at the end of the first session and check with the client that this is agreed. Additionally they can build-in checks to their formulations by asking questions such as:

- Have I got this right – or have I got it completely wrong?
- Is there something important that I have missed?
- Has this session been what you expected, or was it different?
- Has what we have been doing here today been at all helpful?
- How could I have been more helpful?
- Will it be helpful to have more sessions?
- How long would you like it to be before we meet again?

Waves of theory

From the early work of Freud to theorists of the present day, there has been a succession of theories, some linked to previous theories, some outright opposite theories, but all embraced by those who found them useful in both understanding and helping clients. We find it useful to group theories in 'waves' that have arrived over the years.

Beginning with the *first wave* of counselling theory – this included the essentialist and realist approaches, based on the idea that people are determined by essences, virtually hardwired into our psyches, and that inner processes can be known as facts. This led to a belief in the power of science to locate *pathology* in the inner structures of the mind, believing in a modernity that could find the true cause of problems and put them right, as in the medical tradition. This wave includes the various psychodynamic approaches and methods based on them – transactional analysis, for example – that focused mainly on emotional disturbances.

The *second wave* focused more on the cognitive and learning powers of people and on how 'thinking makes it so'. It saw problems as created by unhelpful habits of thought that affected perceptions of life and led to states such as depression and anxiety.

Dysfunctional thinking was analysed and categorised, and treatment consisted of replacing irrational beliefs with rational ones, so as to eliminate the problem. This wave includes cognitive-behavioural counselling and rational emotive therapy, and possibly person-centred counselling, although the latter overlaps as waves sometimes do with aspects of the first wave as well as the human-potential aspects of the third wave.

The *third wave* was pushed along by social constructionism which moved away from the 'modernist', 'grand theories' towards a more personally constructed approach to knowledge as we moved into the postmodern era. Social constructionism holds that language not only describes what there is, but is constitutive of social/political/psychological 'realities'. It sees people making sense of experience through their own local narratives, although dominant narratives may oppress or impoverish them greatly. The power of language is considered central; talking constructs life and meaning and many truths, therefore words can be used not only to oppress but to liberate, to construct solutions without needing to understand problems. This wave includes solution-focused brief therapy, solution-orientated approaches as well as narrative approaches that consider how people are 'invited' into problem stories in various ways but are capable of being helped through re-storying their lives and inviting them to co-construct a new empowering story that speaks of heroism and strength.

Method maps

Rather than seeing the various theories as competing for the truth about people, relationships and situations, we find we can embrace them all when we see them as metaphors for different truths, as versions of the story of people and minds rather than as real discoveries of what really is. What 'is' is created by the talking and, further, what is thus created is not fixed. For example, Freud is said to have commented that what he first meant by 'melancholia' was not the same as what he meant by it in later years. Maps are versions of a territory – they are not the territory. We like the map metaphor because it conveys the sense of help with a journey. Assessment is a journey, undertaken with the client, hoping to find the best route towards a goal. Many different maps are more or less useful, depending on the method of travel, be it by land, sea or air, for example.

Professional formulations (explanations of difficulties) involve the use of one or more theoretical maps to give meaning and interpretation to data that have been collected, to find pointers to what is the matter and what can be done. Each map raises a different set of questions, the replies to which give direction to the work. Theories provide a language for the writing of assessments, signposts to meaning-making and to decision-making. We take the pragmatic view that the theory with the most 'truth' is that which leads to the most satisfactory outcome for the client.

Summary

Denman (1995) says that formulation act as a lens which can focus the details of a case into a coherent vision and this gives the client powerful evidence of being listened to, but *whose* coherent vision is being presented – the client's or the counsellor's? As all models of counselling are based on a set of ideas about the nature of people, the counsellor will inevitably be listening for particular things and, as eclecticism is the most popular model, there is a danger of muddle. McLeod (1998) suggests that counsellors are influenced by their initial training in a single approach but acquire ideas and skills from other approaches, a finding confirmed in our interviews. Whether or not the newer ideas and skills fit with the original model depends, he says, on whether or not they consist of higher or lower-level constructs and concepts. The former cannot easily be taken out of context of their parent theoretical model, whilst the latter can be borrowed without confusion. For example, there is no problem in a humanist counsellor using *techniques* from solution-focused approaches, but the *philosophies* of both approaches are entirely different. The humanist approach is a problem-solving one, and the solution-focused approach is a solution-finding one.

We have introduced the notion of 'waves', each with a different philosophy, and 'maps' with their different techniques. Table 1.1 overleaf best sums them up.

McLeod argues that counsellors 'can enhance the practical value of their theory by ensuring that it is consistent, coherent and comprehensive' (1998, p. 201). We hope the 'maps' chapters will help readers achieve this, but first we discuss power, values and ethics in Chapter 2, before introducing the types of assessment and our overarching framework for assessment in Chapter 3.

Table 1.1 Waves and maps

Waves	Philosophical focus	Cause of problem	Methods/ maps
1: Pathology-based	The way it is (science)	Result of early life experiences	Psychodynamic – The map of the ocean Transactional Analysis – The games map
2: Problem-based (problem-focused)	The way it is seen	Behaviour and thought habits (learned)	Cognitive – Handy road maps Person-centered – The growth map
3: Solution-based	The way it can be (socially constructed)	It just happens, or there are invitations that constrain choice	Solution-focused – The navigator's map Narrative approach – The forecast map

2

The Climate of Counselling

In this chapter we attempt to lift counselling practice from its general context in order to examine the political aspects that affect the specific contexts in which the therapeutic relationship takes place; in particular, various aspects of power and the potential abuses of power, and the implication of these for assessment. Generally, abuses of power are assumed to be avoidable if the counsellor holds the 'right' values and adheres to a desirable set of ethical principles. Although aspects of counsellor values and principles will be discussed at various points in this chapter, we do not intend to promote a particular code of practice, largely on the grounds that '. . . the client is typically less concerned with these personal abstractions [values and principles] than with the *personal and moral qualities* of the practitioner offering the service' (Ashcroft, 2001, p. 11, our emphasis).

Ethical principles such as respect for client autonomy, non-malificence, justice, reliability and confidentiality, are experienced by the client as trustworthiness. As personal integrity is a property of the person, not the model, no code of ethics can instil this should it be absent. King (2001) points out that codes of ethics are not legally enforceable, they can only be morally binding. Additionally:

> It is as futile as it is impossible to expand the Codes to take account of every eventuality; it undermines the ethic of responsibility that the codes were designed to promote and on which the safety of the client must ultimately rest. (Barden, 2001, pp. 42–3)

Whilst we cannot legislate for the unprincipled counsellor, we can look at the ways in which we may *unintentionally* abuse the power we hold in the therapeutic relationship. Kearney (1996, p. 3) comments that we cannot easily accept that the process of counselling may have consequences for some clients which are other than we intend; our good intentions prevent us from examining power relationships, thus

19

making the ideology of counselling less apparent to both ourselves and clients than perhaps is desirable.

Power is a complex and pervasive concept in our lives generally, being a significant element in every relationship and a main motivating influence. Indeed all relationships, whether between one individual and another, between one group and another, or between rulers and subjects, can be said to be the result of power. In counselling, power may be used legitimately to empower others in anti-oppressive practice or illegitimately to oppress others in malpractice. Power is also an element in the competitiveness of life, of the struggle for resources, employment and education. Counsellors, too, can experience a lack of power, not least being the commonly expressed frustration at having the number of sessions available for each client dictated by agency requirements rather than client needs, and this can help them to understand the powerlessness experienced by clients. In work with marginalised people seeking to counteract negative images of life, negative life experiences, blocked opportunities and unrelenting physical and emotional distress, it is essential to recognise how power links to the personal:

> counselling does not take place in a social or ideological vacuum, it is a product of its time and place, as much as any other cultural product, and if this is the case, it follows that counselling itself will reflect the political ideas of the present. (Kearney, 1996, p. 88)

Below we examine how power is inevitably distributed unequally between counsellor and client, and how this has the potential to disempower the client regardless of the benevolent intentions of the counsellor.

Power and the therapeutic relationship

A major factor obscuring the ideology of counselling arises from the liminal role the counsellor occupies. Although counsellors do not occupy positions in social institutions overtly recognised as powerful, the very fact that they are dealing with people 'in danger of falling off or falling out' (McLeod, 1998, p. 7) means that their role is to assist people to fit back into society's institutions as they are *currently constituted*. Counselling may offer people a way of being known and being heard, but on society's terms. Thus the central role of counselling is that of promoting the *status quo*, be this encouraging children to go back to school, or adults to think twice before having an abortion or assisted conception, or learn to forgive cruel parents. Counsellors are, therefore, political agents, however much they may disavow this:

> We choose whether to become aware of our political framework of ideas or avoid doing this . . . The choice of being non-political or a-political is simply not available to us as counsellors, however much we might want it to be so. (Kearney, 1996, p. 77)

This means that the *status quo* counsellor has an inbuilt tendency towards oppressive practice. At best this has the capacity to limit client choice and potential where experiences of structural inequality are not listened to fully because the counsellor believes this to be outside her realm of action. At worst it biases assessments towards locating the problem within the person rather than seeing clients as people with problems and thus seeking solutions within the person rather than in social structures, encouraging people to 'come to terms' with their difficulties, regardless of inequality of opportunity. Some counselling models do have an explicit political dimension – narrative therapies, for example, are centrally concerned with power – but most models sidestep political issues. It is important not to neglect these effects when making assessments, not least in deciding whether or not to accept a client. For example, one of us was asked to see a boy whose 'early experiences of sexual abuse are exhibiting as behavioural problems in school'. This boy had a number of problems at home and school – he was soiling, becoming aggressive towards his younger brother, and refusing to go to school. However he was also being seriously bullied at school – other pupils kicking and beating him as well as extorting money from him. The political question here is whether or not he should be accepted for counselling before his school environment was made safe. Some clients may not even be aware of their oppression; women, particularly, are likely to seek help with managing their interpersonal relationships more successfully and it behoves the counsellor to say honestly that it is not their job to help a woman become, for example, a 'better adjusted' battered wife.

The second major way in which counselling has the potential to be oppressive is the use counsellors make of the concepts that underpin their understanding of the nature of people – their practice theories. These theories are not neutral; they reflect the power relationships that exist between us all. It is naive to underestimate the difficulties in operationalising empowerment strategies as powerful people resist yielding power not only through their overt power as managers but also through their capacity to develop powerful theories and methods of intervention which support their *status quo* – what Foucault (1980) refers to as self-regulation and Ingleby (1995) as a total institution without walls. As the most powerful people in our society are men-as-a-group, the theories used by counsellors to understand not only how people are but also how they should ideally be, have not been objectively arrived at, despite their seemingly scientific basis. They are biased towards white, male, healthy, employed, Western men's understanding of their position in the world.

If a major task of counselling is to offer clients a coherent framework that makes sense of their lives, it also makes sense for counsellors to consider how adequate their practice theory is for each client. The central notion in counselling of the person as a bounded, autonomous self with infinite, albeit perhaps unrealised, capacity for self-transformation is not such a liberating idea when one ponders on the origins of what we consider to be emotional health. For example, Bowlby's theory of attachment, a secure base from which to explore and return to at times of stress, has more to do with the creation of an emotionally satisfying world for men, with little consideration of the possible detrimental effects on mothers' and wives' emotional health and well-being imposed by the implicit demands that they will provide that secure base – despite any hardships they may experience. It is worth noting also that Bowlby's ideas are historically situated within particular power relationships, fitting neatly with men's needs to reclaim jobs occupied by women at the end of the Second World War. Our current notions about sensitive mothering and babies' emotional growth are entirely absent from prewar baby books (see, for example, Gibbens, 1946, which contains only one paragraph on the growth of emotions, pp. 41–2, but a whole chapter on fathers' responsibilities, pp. 15–22). Even the counselling models that eschew theorising in favour of developing the therapeutic process, for example solution focused and person centred approaches, do so by concentrating on personal choice and personal responsibility – a focus on individualism that stories the person as living in a social and political vacuum.

The counsellor's expertise to channel how a client's story emerges in the assessment stage of counselling through the provision of a framework for understanding the nature of people, and the counsellor's power to channel the client's development in a particular direction through the use of interpretations, insights and challenges, has the potential to disempower as well as empower. McLeod (1998) suggests that counsellors could profitably develop critiques of mainstream majority theories, but this ignores the fact that a firm belief in individual responsibility and capacity for growth leaves this for the individual counsellor to discover. Training programmes are thus exempted from a collective responsibility to develop critiques although they retain the power as educators to formulate and promote particular theories uncritically:

> It is ironic that whilst most models insist on therapists developing a reflective awareness of self in the therapeutic encounter, this reflectivity has been accorded less priority in the actual teaching of theory itself. (Pollard, 2001, p. 14)

This means that beginning counsellors set out with little critical awareness of the appropriateness or otherwise of their model for each client. For example, how does a belief in individualism accommodate the complexities and pressures of women's lives; how does psychodynamic theorising equate homosexuality and emotional well-being within a gay affirmative belief framework? That a lack of critical awareness can bias assessments and silence clients is evident in much of the literature, perhaps most notably in Jacob's (1988) reframing of 'Hannah's' opening comment that she had expected to see a woman counsellor as a hidden anxiety about her sexuality. Here his use of practice theory led him to discount what many would see as a reasonable expectation. We find that where clients are given the choice of a male or female counsellor there is a tendency to choose a woman counsellor. This may well tell us more about clients' theories about the nature of women counsellors than it does about practice outcomes, but whose theory should have most salience – the counsellor's or the client's?

An uncritical awareness of our practice theories means that we also run the risk of not recognising the limitations of our models for particular clients, resulting in less referring-on than may be desirable. As one respondent in our survey commented:

> No-one ever said to me in training, we talked about contracts, but we never discussed the appropriateness of an individual client situation for the agency or our model and I think person centred, in particular, has a rather arrogant view that we can meet the needs of all clients. We never discussed that in training.

Another problem with an overemphasis on the person as a bounded, autonomous self, with a resulting preoccupation on issues to do with individual identity and self-esteem, is that because individuals are actually social beings, identity and self-esteem are really context-specific and influenced by different power relationships. Foucault questions the relevance of ideas about power as primarily repressive by counterposing the idea of power as productive (see, for example, Sawicki, 1991). Powerfulness is not necessarily expressed in terms of easily identifiable oppressive groups. Neither is powerlessness necessarily expressed in terms of easily defined oppressed groups; it is much more diverse and complex, with people experiencing power in some situations and powerlessness in others. Men, for example, are easily identified as powerful as a result of patriarchal power (or, more properly, virarchy), but men individually exhibit a wide range of masculine behaviours depending on the social situation. Messerschmidt (2000) demonstrates how male teenagers can have hegemonic, oppositional and subordinated masculinities simultaneously, but that these different identities are manifested according to their power positioning within the home, school and peer group. Ignoring the social content of clients' lives through the application of theories of individual growth and development runs the risk of psychological reductionism, which is in itself as oppressive as sociological reductionism: 'Conversational therapy can't be truly neutral, respectful, and non-hierarchical, or exist in some free zone in society, untainted by social context' (Goldner, 1992).

The artificiality of the therapeutic free zone – the counselling session that is established *for* the client – is another place where unequal power relationships exist. The counsellor is the person who knows the rules, dictating the space and pace by deciding on the length of the session, using her expertise to assess how many sessions will be needed and presenting a contract. This latter is despite evidence that clients often prefer to dip in and out of counselling. By virtue of simply being a client who lacks the power to frame the therapeutic encounter and, through having their judgements about themselves and their needs seen as inferior to those of counsellors, there is a danger of clientism developing. Paradoxically, clientism is more likely to occur as a result of the very measures taken by counsellors to prevent it – the increased professionalisation and accreditation aimed at protecting clients by ensuring a basic level of ethical practice. As we suggested earlier, trustworthiness is a personal characteristic, whereas a code of ethics offers more protection to counsellors than clients.

Kearney goes further in her discussion of increasing professionalisation, suggesting that it has more to do with social and political pressures on counsellors:

> the image of concern for the protection of the client, public concern and
> altruism and the ostensibly disinterested practice of counselling is an ideology
> which may be used to protect and justify higher prestige and to prevent
> encroachment by other members in the area of work. (Kearney, 1996, p. 97)

Similarly, Skynner regrets the different motivation emerging in
psychoanalysis:

> a wish to use the knowledge gained to earn a living and a respected place in
> the world. At this point, people would build a 'camp' or 'institute', the object
> being to train selected people in the therapeutic method who satisfy their
> criteria, and exclude others who do not. (Skynner, 1997, pp. 5–6)

Thus accreditation rules out large groups of people who have been
found to be effective as professional helpers: see, for example, Durlak's
(1979) comparison of professional and paraprofessional helpers,
restricting client choice of counsellor. The need to keep records for
several years during the accreditation period also means that clients'
ownership of their new-found competence is threatened. And the
expertise accredited further reduces client autonomy in that it
becomes increasingly used as a rationale for allocating scarce
resources. Major social institutions are already consulting counsellors
for an expert diagnosis that will confirm particular clients' 'neediness'.
This leads to counsellors storying clients as individually vulnerable
when they may well be competent but subject to unfair practices. For
example, we received a plea from a previous client to support her
housing application which spoke of her frustration: 'I don't have an
eating disorder now, or sleeping problems, but I can't get a house
unless I can prove I'm depressed'.

There is an important legacy left by powerlessness that includes
lethargy, despair and listlessness – 'learned helplessness' – and, as Friere
(1972) called it, a culture of silence in which there is an apparent
acceptance of servitude and dependence. Marginalised people
subscribe to the myth that they get what they deserve, internalise, and
are oppressed by feelings of alienation and worthlessness. This is
hardly the most profitable way of setting in train a therapeutic process
which has the intention of actualising a client's potential for growth
and reducing dependency. How this particular power imbalance is

addressed varies according to the counselling model used, with some embracing it as an essential part of the therapeutic process. Psychodynamic counselling, for example, takes issue with arguments for more equal communication on the grounds that it discourages regression:

> With many patients the experience of dependency is absolutely crucial for any healing to take place . . . Far from being an exercise in power, it often makes the therapist who can meet their patient on a feeling level feel power-less themselves. (Bravesmith, 2001, p. 509)

However, most models of counselling aim to discourage dependency, particularly the brief therapies (see, for example, Barrett-Kruse, 1994, pp.109–15; Dryden, 1998, pp. 143–4), but few address power imbalances at the assessment stage. This is largely because informed consent is difficult for the client to exercise until they have experienced a taste of counselling, although solution-focused approaches emphasise giving clients honest, uninhibited feedback and designates them as experts in their own lives (see, for example, O'Connell, 2001, p. 5).

Josselson (1996) suggests that a useful way of addressing the ethical issues arising from power imbalances in the creation of a therapeutic relationship is to embark on it in the same way as one would in qual-itative research which, similarly, has the potential to intrude on people's intimate lives. The links between the ethical imperatives of both qualitative research and counselling are addressed further in Chapter 3 where we outline a possible framework for assessment, but here we make the point that the main ethical consideration is to make values explicit. Counsellors actively look for psychological-mindedness – checking for similarities in values – but when counsel-lors put their 'selves' on the back burner in order to give space to the client there is a danger that they will forget to explore important differences between themselves and clients which may affect under-standing. Differences and similarities involve complex power relation-ships, the source of the various 'isms'.

The 'isms'

It is clear that some 'isms' are more powerful than others at various times. Although counsellors will be aware of the oppressions affecting them personally, we would suspect that in relation to other 'isms' they are most likely to have undertaken race-awareness training – most of the counsellors we interviewed said that race/culture would be a consideration in their assessment of the client outlined in the scenario, but none mentioned any other possible difference between them and the client/s that might affect their assessment. One reason for this situation could, perhaps, be that black men have much more in common with the most easily identifiable powerful group in our society – white men. There are suggestions that masculine solidarity will make blackness the most important issue, deflecting attention away from male power, there being more that 'joins men across class and disability, and even race and sexual orientation, than divides them' (Cordery and Whitehead, 1991, p. 29).

Feminist critiques have placed gender more centrally in the anti-oppressive debate, (see, for example, Miller, 1973; Elliott, 1997), with counselling practice incorporating notions that are pro-feminist. Not only is it potentially oppressive to promote any particular 'ism' in that it creates a hierarchy of oppression that elevates one form of discrimination above another, but it ignores the interrelatedness and complexities of the various 'isms', most notably, race, gender, class, age, disability and sexual orientation. More recently linguistic oppression has also received attention (see, for example, Thompson, 2003). We examine each 'ism' in turn below to highlight briefly the particulars of each 'difference' and suggest possible ways in which counsellors can more readily engage in exploring difference. Then we return to the interrelatedness of the 'isms', demonstrating how both similarities and differences can be negotiated to avoid clientism.

Ethnicity and culture

Black people, whether male or female, have to negotiate at least three different social contexts: *mainstream* (white) processes, in which they also constitute a *minority*, with a potential for experiencing racism; and, within that minority context, they also have to negotiate a *black cultural* agenda, which can be as diverse as Rastafarianism or Seventh Day Adventism. The difficulties of living as a minority ethnic group in a white society are most easily understood by counsellors who are only too aware of the danger of overpathologising black people in mental-health assessments, but perhaps not always clear that 'blackness' is not the only feature in the overdiagnosis of black people as psychotic. Race, gender and class interrelate powerfully in assessments, with younger, single black men *and* older, white women being more likely to be constructed as subjects of psychiatric narratives and admitted to hospital compulsorily (Audini and Lelliott, 2001). Similarly, black male pupils are more likely than white or black female pupils to be excluded from school, but both parents and pupils see class as important determinant of teachers' treatment of them (Blair, 1996). There is a need, therefore, for counsellors to be aware of the complexities of black masculinity, black men being 'over-gendered' and exoticised, and their physicality unduly emphasised (see, for example, Westwood, 1996).

More subtly, counsellors may be unconsciously racist through the cultural values underpinning much counselling practice – independence, self-sufficiency, assertiveness and competitiveness. In a discussion of working cross-culturally, Rayner asks 'Was it possible I privileged these values over those such as interdependence, harmony, and cooperation in relationship?' (2000, pp. 8–12). If differences in values are not recognised, then the counsellor risks failing to identify clients' sources of strength that black people have developed to alleviate their oppression.

Not all the strategies for negotiating the different social contexts of race will always be displayed in power and oppression terms, the mainstream processes having to be negotiated *in lieu of* minority and black cultural agendas. These agenda clearly conflict with the mainstream one and, for that matter, also *with each other*. Hussain (2001) illustrates the complexities involved in her discussion of the limitations of cultural consultancy in working with Bangladeshi families where each family has a unique culture and each family member also holds different versions of cultural stories. She finds multiple, and competing, stories emerging which are difficult to accommodate:

> The dilemma for me is not which story to work with but when stories within a family become competitive or when a family's stories conflict with the therapist's story. This often leaves little scope for the therapeutic story to emerge. (2001, pp. 15–6)

Hussain is talking about cultural/religious understanding which has different meanings not only within an ethnic group, but also dependent on the degree of acculturisation within the mainstream context. Although it is important not to forget that 'blackness' is the most visible aspect of many people from ethnic minorities, it is not the only aspect of their lives to be taken into consideration. A study of Asian users of counselling services (Netto *et al.,* 2001) found that although there was a low level of take up, those who did found it beneficial;

they were able to use the Western psychological model, valued being 'heard' with respect, and preferred a choice of counsellor – not always wanting a counsellor of the same ethnicity. Being heard with respect means allowing them to tell their stories, to set their own frame of reference, and to have their values and spirituality appreciated (hooks, 1993). Rather than seek a single cultural consultant as expert, counsellors can extend their reflective practice by establishing community links with groups whose experience and insights are useful to their work, and work towards maximising the range of experience within their staff group. Tamasese and Waldegrave (1996) refer to this as 'just therapy', countering both individual and institutional discrimination through making one's own work accountable to subjugated groups by consulting always with local communities or colleagues who have more similarity with the client. Burnham and Harris (1996) set out guidelines for counselling those whose ethnicity and culture are different from the counsellor:

- Culture and ethnicity are always important and not always obvious.
- People who are different [from you] are not necessarily the same [as each other].
- Ethnicity and culture are socially constructed.
- Be willing to suspend both your belief and disbelief.
- Be clumsy rather than clever.
- Do not use clients with different cultural backgrounds as an education lesson for the professional.
- Be sensitive, not superficial.
- The list is always emerging, so what would you add to it?

We would add that this list is a useful set of practice pointers for work with all clients as there as many cultural stories as there are people.

Gender

In our so-called post-feminist era, it may not seem necessary to detail the effects of sexism – the inequalities of opportunity in every sphere of life which women have experienced and, to a lesser extent, still do. Not only have there been many feminist critiques of counselling theory (see, for example, Mitchell, 1974; Gilligan, 1982) and the development of pro-feminist counselling (see, for example, Miller, 1973; Kaplan, 1987), but men, too, have applied masculinist critiques (see, for example, Hearn, 1996; McLean *et al.*, 1996). All of these have attempted to integrate political and social issues into counselling. However, there remains a powerful legacy from years of male psychologising about the nature of people that continues to place women centrally in the emotional development of families. We may no longer subscribe to Freud's oedipal theorising which implies inferior moral development for women, but newer thinking has often had the effect of merely tinkering with mainstream counselling theory in a sort of 'add-on' way. Women's social contexts remain limited to the immediate family through the strength of narratives about secure attachments as essential for the healthy emotional growth of the individual, the bounded, autonomous self. For example: 'Attachment explains the differential development of resilient and mentally healthy personalities, and also of personalities prone to anxiety and depression, or to developing a false self or some other form of vulnerability to mental health' (Bowlby, 1988, p. 132).

Expecting women to be sensitive mothers who provide their children with a secure base, thus making them responsible for the emotional tone of the whole family without taking into account the conditions of very real hardship under which they may perform this role, actually places them in a position of powerless responsibility (Rich, 1977). Although the 'good-mothering' narrative grew out of psychologising and was supported by counselling, it has been internalised by clients through advice in baby books and the media as having meaning in describing their lives. In Foucault's terms, this means that women will regulate themselves according to the dominant cultural narrative about mothering. In White's (1995) and Freeman *et al*'s (1997) terms, the 'good-mothering' narrative story has mass and considerable evidence to support its momentum, so that proposing an alternative story as the 'counterplot' suggested by feminist and masculinist theorising is all too easily discounted.

This has implications for assessment as power differences in families will not always be apparent when counsellor and client subscribe to the same dominant story about family life. This is despite the fact that counsellors are more likely to see children accompanied by their mothers than their fathers, even though they are as likely to be working. Women who come to counselling are much more likely than men to have internalised their problems, are more devastated by destruction of relationships, have a sense of lack of control over their lives, tend to blame themselves for everything that has gone wrong in their families, and take responsibility beyond what is reasonable and realistic (see, for example, Berg and Reuss, 1998; Milner and

O'Byrne, 2002). Men, on the other hand, subscribe to notions that they are expected to be calm and cool, take the lead, solve problems in a rational way, be a success outside the family, are devastated by the destruction of relationships (not necessarily because they have a sense of failure but rather a sense of loss of the one person with whom they can express themselves emotionally), and feeling that they are not cared for enough, that their efforts are not appreciated, and with threats to their self-esteem (see, for example, Jenkins, 1990; Milner and Jessop, 2003). Accepting their concerns at face value ignores the social and political realities that shape their expectations about responsibility-taking within the family and community.

Evans (1995) holds that this has advantages for women in that they can possess a superior and more accurate knowing derived from their experiences of subordination, active parenting and nurturing responsibilities. And it could be said that men are disadvantaged in counselling if they are emotionally inarticulate, although they should benefit from couples work as we know that part of women's emotional responsibility in everyday conversation is to support and sustain conversation while men have the power to control and define who speaks and what gets talked about (Fishman, 1978; West, 1990). However, there is some evidence, albeit small scale, that shows important gender differences in how counsellors respond to clients, particularly the use they make of interruptions.

Counsellors, male or female, are conversational experts who have an obligation to exercise this power appropriately to ensure that things get talked about, that people are heard, and therefore we would expect their interruptions to be entirely therapeutic and free from gender bias. This is not demonstrated to be true in the research. Stratford's (1998) study of four family therapists showed that although both male and female therapists interrupted both male and female clients, the male therapists used interruptions three times more frequently than female therapists. They also interrupted female clients three times more frequently than male clients. Their explanations for interrupting showed a gender bias too; a male therapist described his interrupting as a way of controlling a talkative female client, whilst a female therapist explained it as a means of protecting a male client from distressing information. In a larger study (Werner-Wilson *et al.*, 1997), both male and female therapists interrupted female clients approximately three times more frequently than male clients. This was not connected to the amount of talk by female clients so was not related to encouraging men who are quiet or controlling talkative women.

The implication is that women are silenced in counselling, although it would be interesting to research counselling models which are more explicitly gender-aware, such as narrative approaches (see for example, McLean *et al.,* 1996; Gosling and Zingari,1996). Counsellors using more traditional models, particularly psychodynamic ones, could usefully remember that these models do not easily accommodate gender issues that influence both men and women in counselling. Neither is person-centred counselling free from criticism; Waterhouse (1993) points out that the emphasis on personal responsibility pays insufficient attention to the social and political realities of women's lives.

The easiest way a counsellor can ensure that they are not overinterrupting is to say 'Tell me more, is there anything else?' This is essential for both women and men clients as the latter may be silenced when the counsellor rescues them from talk that is emotionally laden. The main distinction between questions for men and women could profitably be geared towards reducing women's unrealistic responsibility-taking; such as, 'do you expect too much from yourself; could your difficulties be more due to lack of resources than ability; what supports do you have?'; whilst men could be encouraged to take on more responsibility; such as, 'can you tell me about the times you have been caring; how, as a man, as a father, do you handle these issues?'

Class

Improvement in family incomes over the last 30 years has changed traditional ideas about class, particularly blurring distinctions between the working and middle classes. Although there has been a large increase in the real annual income of the *average* household, this conceals its unequal distribution. Forty per cent of the increase is enjoyed by the richest 20 per cent, whilst the income of the poorest 20 per cent has actually fallen. The implications for counselling are that the divide between largely middle-class counsellors and their working-class clients is now wider in terms of everyday living experiences as well as recognised differences in terms of how they view the world and express themselves.

For assessment purposes the counsellor has to consider whether empowerment is possible when clients are under multiple stresses arising to a large degree from chronic poverty and little control over their lives, both of which severely limit their choices. Poverty contributes to high levels of stress in families, which may well, for example, affect children's behaviour and performance at school. The referrals to counsellors by teachers of their pupils are often framed in behavioural or emotional terms, although the referrer is also influenced by the political realities of school performance indicators. The political and social realities of children's home circumstances are further hidden under the 'psychological story' – one study found that a family on income support could not afford the diet fed to children in a Bethnal Green workhouse in 1876 (NCH, 1994). Similarly, child-protection social workers increasingly refer family members for counselling, but add 'strings' in that there is a covert secondary goal that may conflict with the process of counselling, and these social workers may not welcome any ensuing empowerment. For example, mothers are referred for help to come to terms with earlier experiences of sexual abuse – but have to achieve this within a time limit if their children are not to be removed; looked-after children are referred for assistance in getting in touch with their feelings – but have to achieve this so that they no longer display 'acting-out' behaviour which is preventing a foster placement; abusive men are referred for help in coming to terms with earlier attachment experiences – but the subtext is managing their aggressive behaviour. And, there is always the hidden housing application, thus all these seemingly specific emotional and behavioural problems are embedded in a legal as well as a social context that severely limits the client's capacity for growth at a pace that is appropriate. The question for the counsellor at this stage is what form of counselling is appropriate for low-income families, especially those who are referred by other agencies.

The evidence is that such clients prefer practical, goal-oriented counselling provided on a drop-in, drop-out basis (for an overview, see McLeod, 1998, pp. 248–9), but the reality is that they tend not to get counselling at all. Holmes and Lindley (1989) found that they were less likely to be offered brief counselling on the grounds that they had long-term difficulties and most long-term counselling rules out clients with chronicity of problems and verbal inarticulacy (see, for example, Jacobs, 1988, p. 53). The issue of inarticulacy has been considerably debated in the counselling literature; most notably by Bromley (1983), who suggested that working-class language does not lend itself to psychotherapy where insight is central. The respondents in our survey who were optimistic about the effectiveness of their models for a very wide variety of clients qualified this by adding that effectiveness was linked to resilience factors, motivation and the absence of serious problems – factors most likely to be present for low-income clients.

Conversational harmony is an important determinant of acceptance for counselling but, in ruling out clients who are not psychologically-minded enough, counsellors are adding to clients' existing oppressions. There is evidence, for example, that parents who fail to conform verbally and agree a plausible explanation in child-protection assessments are less likely to form a positive relationship with the assessing social worker and more likely to have their children removed from their care (Holland, 2000). Kearney (1996) maintains that it is difficult for a counsellor to develop a meaningful conversation with some lower-income clients because of the counsellors' use of empathy, it being difficult to identify accurately what it feels like to be 'in the client's shoes':

> A particular response I often have difficulty with when working with a working class client is descriptions of feelings that are so general that I can't get a sense of how important a feeling is because the client is using words which are very general and could apply to a whole range of emotions. When this happens, I not only don't know how important the feeling might be, I am often even not sure what the specific feeling is. (Kearney, 1996, p. 41)

The low-income client who is ground down by experience of multiple stress and lack of opportunity is likely to have developed the attributional style of learned helplessness (Seligman, 1992), one where the perception of uncontrollability is more important than the uncontrollability itself and is manifested in lack of hope about the future and a tendency to attribute improvements to luck rather than individual effort. It is more relevant in these instances for the counsellor to ask questions that open out the unrealistically negative view of the self rather than reach out for feelings that may well have become blunted or attempt to 'fill the gaps empathically from his/her own meaning structures' (Kearney, 1996, p. 39). At the very least, says Rapp (2001), it is important that the counsellor does not psychologise what may be unmet social, physical or political needs. For example, Bowlby (1988, p. 153) suggests asking a client who disparages therapy or misses a session why they are afraid to express their feelings openly and what their childhood experiences may have been to account for the distrust, when a more likely, and respectful, hypothesis would be that the client is perceiving the therapy as unhelpful in the first instance, and lacks money for the bus fare in the second.

In attempting to bridge differences between counsellors and low-income clients it is imperative to use the assessment stage to ensure that these clients have access to counselling by opening up possibilities for them to make good use of the process and begin taking control of their lives. Searching for strengths may yield little at a first meeting, but if the counsellor looks for the *absence* of difficulties in a particular area of functioning, this can begin the process. More than with any other type of client it is important to allow low-income clients to set the pace and frequency of sessions as this gives them tangible evidence of control over their lives. Their attendance at counselling can also be facilitated by scheduling appointments to fit in with public-transport timetables and ensuring that the counselling facilities are child-friendly. Refunding bus fares also makes a difference as we found out when seeing a couple for a second session. Our delight in their reporting of only one row in the intervening period was tempered when they explained that they argued about whether to spend their last two pounds on bus fares to attend counselling or on food.

Linguistics

Thompson (2003) draws our attention to the importance of oppression through the use of language. The most powerful people, those who can enter people into stories about themselves, also create the language used in the process; language is, indeed, man-made (Spender, 1985), reflecting racial, gender and class divisions as we have seen in earlier sections in this chapter. Counsellors, who are in the business of creating coherent narratives with their clients, have a particular responsibility to use their words carefully so that they do not confuse clients, such as the Essex builder talking about his experience of alcohol counselling on television: 'they use these words . . . powerlessness and unmanageability . . . two things I have to say before I can move on. But I don't understand what these things mean' (Inside Clouds, BBC2, 30 May 2001).

There is interplay between language and social structure, with language helping to reproduce social values. For example feminine is a 'marked' category in language where there are pairs of words, such as 'actor' and 'actress' (Graddol and Swann, 1989); the word 'actor' functions as a neutral term, but 'actress' is formally marked as feminine. Close examination of counselling conversations indicates other ways of 'marking' for clients who are neither white nor male, with potentially unconscious oppressive results. For example, Denney (1992) shows how the word 'space' has different meanings for black and white clients. For black people it is used to describe physical space (an emphasis on black physicality), whereas for white people it indicates ontological space in which the client can explore feelings and have space to think. There is also linguistic derogation of women with pairs of words that do not match; for example fathering and mothering carry very different connotations of role performance and responsibility-taking.

There are also linguistic gaps, such as dearth of expressions that refer to women's sexuality in a positive way. For example, women cannot be 'virile', although they are many pejorative words such as 'slag' or 'slut' which provide men with an insult vocabulary for women which they cannot easily counter (Lees, 1997). The lack of words for many activities of women and black people creates silences in which whole areas of significant client experience are ignored.

This is not to say that all white men are the sole beneficiaries of man-made language; they maintain their power as a group through language but at the expense of emotional articulacy. This potentially disadvantages male clients, although its effects are most evident when men who are violent are referred for counselling. The influence of feminist theorising about the nature of male violence has given women a previously unheard voice but has also given rise to thera-peutic interventions based on assumptions that men always minimise their behaviour, are resistant to change, and require challenging in group settings of both their actions and the language they use to describe it (see, for example, Dobash *et al.*, 2000). Where men are listened to and encouraged to articulate their understanding of their behaviour, there is little evidence of resistance, denial or collusion (see, for example, Milner and Jessop, 2003).

Adultism

The starting point of assessment, says Bond (1993), ought to be the assumption that the counsellor will respect the client's choice and autonomy. He goes on to suggest that these can be overruled where there is evidence that clients lack the capacity to make their own decisions. Although he uses the examples of suicidal clients and chil-dren at risk of abuse, because counselling theory is based on notions of healthy adulthood there is a risk that whole groups of clients may be assessed as incompetent. Adultism, combined with clientism, has the potential to underestimate competence in clients who are mentally ill, elderly, disabled and youthful.

Of these groups, elderly people are the most likely to be assessed as incompetent because, although counsellors can remember what it is like to feel the oppression of youth, we can rarely anticipate what it will be like to be old. Perhaps worrying about our own futures, influenced by experiences of caring for our own parents, we tend to homogenise older people as automatically ill, deteriorating, inflexible, miserable and dependent. Much of this stereotyping of older people arises from being focused on current problems – most usually bereavement in the counselling of older people – at the expense of biographies (Bornat, 1999). For example, the 'inflexibility' of an older person may well be a lifelong continuity of 'determination' or 'stubbornness' that an older person wishes to preserve. Older people actually find old age a better experience than they anticipated (O'Leary, 1996), and there is no reason why they should not be able to avail themselves of counselling to develop their lives rather than simply come to terms with losses. Older people are, in fact, a large heterogeneous group of people covering an age span of 50 or more years who are still living and developing, rather than people at a biological life stage or biographical end point (Thompson, 1995).

It is worth remembering that two-thirds of significantly older people are women who are likely to experience illnesses not being treated, more likely than men to be admitted to psychiatric hospitals or to end their days in residential care. Due to their position as women in a sexist society, they may also have internalised ageist attitudes – people saying 'what else can you expect at your age?', so they may not see themselves as people with strengths and entitlement. Booth (1993) reminds us that anti-discriminatory counselling practice should highlight the importance of enablement, the validation of people's coping abilities, which sits uneasily with a focus on individual dysfunction. The latter can reinforce notions about the inevitability of the dependency of older people, removing their capacity to make choices that may appear risky to their carers and counsellors.

Disabled people, too, have been educated and socialised to believe that disability is a negative state, one that will reduce their capacity to use counselling effectively unless they are encouraged to view this as an external element of power relations rather than simply an internal state. Iveson (2001) asserts that thinking, choosing and exercising choices are the fundamental characteristics of personhood, and that if we treat people as incompetent in these areas we treat them as less than human. Counselling is centrally concerned with encouraging thinking and choosing but, because it depends on two-way conversations, it frequently fails to facilitate thinking and choosing on the part of clients who are non-speaking through physical disability or unintelligible through intellectual impairment. Few counselling models accommodate potential clients such as muddled older people, those with no speech at all, and those whose thoughts are influenced by 'voices', although narrative approaches have developed to meet these clients' needs (see, for example, White, 1995; Milner and O'Byrne, 2002). Iveson (2001) suggests a simple way round the problem for the counsellor faced with a client who has difficulty communicating. He simply asks the family to select one member to speak by asking 'if [the client] could speak and I were to ask her to choose someone to speak for her at this meeting, who would she choose?' and when a person has been selected, he asks 'can you answer as if you were [the client]?' This assumes that the client without a voice is capable of thought, choice and expression, in other words, human (pp. 80–2).

The group of clients most likely to be identified as vulnerable to adultism are children and young people, but counselling has a long tradition of adapting conversations to young people's developmental progress, ensuring that power differences are minimised. Counsellors are skilled in talking with children but not always consistent in their efforts – the child who sexually abuses tends to be adultised in terms of treatment models, and child–centred models have only been developed relatively recently for these clients (see, for example, Cameron *et al.*, 2001).

The most problematic area for counselling children is when to breach confidentiality; the notion of Gillick competence is not always easy to apply in complex child-protection situations, especially where the counselling organisation has a policy requiring counsellors to report instances of abuse (Hamilton, 2001). We return to this issue in Chapter 11 where we consider risk generally. The central question for counsellors working with clients who are considerably older, young or more disabled than ourselves is to remember that the client is addressed as a specific individual with the capacity to make use of counselling if the model is adapted to the needs of that specific individual.

Sexuality

Counselling has a long history of insensitivity towards lesbian, gay and bisexual (LGB) clients, stemming from explicit and implicit homophobia. To a large extent this is due to the tendency of psychology and psychoanalytic theories' contributions towards reinforcing prejudice and polarising sexualities in the past. Although the heterosexist bias inherent in many traditional counselling theories and theories of personality development (see, for example, Crain, 1985) has been increasingly recognised as damaging (see, for example, McLeod, 1998, pp. 250–3), the effects of homophobia continue to be not dissimilar to those of disablism: 'It is practically impossible for a lesbian, gay or bisexual person who has grown up in British society *not* to have internalized negative messages about their sexuality' (Davies, 1999, p. 55)

It is all too easy for counsellors to view this as an internal state rather than an enduring feature of oppression, as recent research shows. Kitzinger and Perkins (1993) suggest that counselling has the potential to privatise pain; Malley and Tasker (1999) found that counsellors have little training or knowledge and are unsupported in their work with clients whose sexuality differed from their own; and, although Mair and Izzard's (2001) clients felt their overall experience of counselling to be helpful, they felt their experiences of their sexuality was silenced or not adequately explored. What LGB clients want is a counsellor who can discriminate when a client's sexual orientation should be the focus of counselling and when it should be left alone (Davies, 1999) and, most of all, that they have a gay-affirmative counsellor (Liddle, 1997). It is not necessary for the counsellor to have the same sexual orientation as the client (Davies, 1999); indeed, this can create difficulties in maintaining confidentiality when dealing with lesbian clients whose networks tend to be small and closely linked. This is particularly pertinent in working with lesbian victims of same-sex violence as there is evidence of their safety being compromised (Renzetti, 1992; Leventhal and Lundy, 1999; Milner and Jessop, 2003). A gay-affirmative counsellor is one who regards LGB identities as having equal value with heterosexual identities, and who has reflected on any possible heterosexist bias in her counselling model. For example, a gay-affirmative counsellor will have rethought family life models, recognising that they do not reflect real families as much as different social and political forms. Rather than talk about families, a gay-sensitive counsellor is more likely to ask questions such as 'who are the most important people in your life?' and 'if you could design the perfect social network, what would it look like?'. This would not preclude asking about children, especially where the client is childless, as LGB clients all have feelings about children, parenting and childlessness (see, for example, Hargaden and Llewellin, 1999). Therapeutic openness to these issues allows for new 'knowledge' to emerge (Simon, 1999).

The counsellor also needs to be particularly sensitive towards the way in which sexuality and age can compound oppression. For older lesbian clients, Young (1999) suggests that the primary purpose of counselling is to support them in countering the effects of a lifetime of oppression and the opportunity to define themselves. Ratigan (1999) finds that older gay men are often uncomfortable with the increased visibility of contemporary gay cultures after a lifetime of living in a mental and physical male ghetto, and can be very isolated. He considers sensitive assessment to be important with these clients as therapeutic goals may need to be modest. HIV is another signifi- cant issue is counselling gay men, few not being affected in some way through personal experience, leading to preoccupation with death, or through HIV 'burn out' and social stigma (Hanson and Maroney, 1999). Assessment of the significance of HIV in counselling gay men need not necessarily be entirely problem-based; White (2000), for example, asks 'what are people's positive experiences of HIV, what are the knowledges and skills that people bring to these experiences, and how might these knowledges and skills be elaborated?'

Summary

It will be clear from our discussion of the 'isms' above, that in the same way that our clients cannot be truly autonomous individuals because of their social connectedness, so they do not operate simply from a broader network of social, political and economic factors. They also operate within a wider context of cultural assumptions, formations and practices. Not only is it necessary for understanding to recognise and acknowledge differences in cultural frameworks between coun- sellors and clients, it is also important to realise that the ideas that are presented to us through our cultural frameworks are neither neutral nor objective. As language both constructs and reflects reality, these ideas represent the interests of dominant cultures: 'Domination is not merely power over a particular group, it is also a relationship between individuals in which recognition of legitimacy ensures the persistence of power' (Poupeau, 2000, p. 72).

Thus power and communication are closely entwined and, in a communication encounter, clients do not start with a level playing field. As counsellors have the power to influence clients in the construction of identities, and identities are frequently constructed in the counselling literature in terms of oppositions such as straight/gay, normal/deviant (Woodward, 1997), it is important to avoid overgeneralising from practice theories to the point of stereotyping. Stereotyping not only overgeneralises certain characteristics, but also ascribes those characteristics as having negative or positive value, thus limiting our understanding of human behaviour as well as providing justification for preferential or discriminatory treatment.

Where there is a difference of gender, race, class and so forth between the client and counsellor, there is often a tendency to focus unduly on deficit or risk rather than on strengths. If clients' needs are to be met, counsellors must help them make their stories visible in order to gain an awareness of where oppressions are located, how structural as well as psychological obstacles operate, and to have a sense of clients' abilities to be agents of change and locators of resources. Asking clients to share their stories of both struggle and survival in the face of structural inequality is helped by asking 'what keeps this problem alive?' rather than 'what caused this problem?' (Smith, 2000). Other questions that are useful in discerning difference include:

- What is the client's story of injustice?
- How can their experiences be validated?
- What awareness have they of the impact of oppression?
- What beliefs do they have about their capabilities and about the possibility of escape from their plight?
- Do they blame themselves or social inequality?
- How can they be empowered to take action?
- What would improve their sense of control over their lives?

And, most of all, counsellors need to be aware of the consequences of their theoretical 'maps' and to seek to move from a 'reproductive' approach to an 'abductive' one in which collaborative accounts draw more on the concepts and meanings of clients. We address the strengths and limitations of the various theoretical 'maps' in helping our understanding of the nature of people and their problems in the subsequent chapters.

3

Assessment:
What, When and How?

In this chapter we move on from the broad issues of the objectives and potentially oppressive aspects of assessment, to a more detailed consideration of purpose and process. This is not to say that it is solely the domain of the assessing counsellor or that it is a fixed entity; assessment is essentially two-way and ongoing. Assessments are made at intake or pre-assessment screening, at the start of counselling proper, throughout counselling, at the end and in evaluating the work. First, we examine the nature of assessment.

This 'sitting-by' the potential client involves, at least, empathic listening and seeking to understand what is said. In counselling it also involves remaining detached enough to form a reasonably 'objective' judgement about what help, if any, to offer and its likelihood of success. It is not a one-way street, however, for as the counsellor thinks 'is this person treatable, and how?' the client thinks 'is this the place for me – is it going to be worth investing in?' When it comes to assessment at the start of counselling, interviewing for the formulation, we shall see that this is to some extent a *negotiation* about meanings, metaphors and decisions. On the counsellor's part, the process involves collecting data, analysis and the development of a formulation that draws on a theoretical foundation to produce a statement about the nature, perhaps cause, and gravity of the problem, its treatability, how best it can be treated and by whom. Cost may be an issue; work may be allowed considerable time in psychotherapy departments, but only six sessions of counselling are allowed in many GP surgeries. Assessment may involve trying out aspects of an approach to see how the client responds or to see whether they have the ability to use such an approach. Finally it involves finding a set of metaphors, a story that will be useful to both counsellor and client in plotting the journey they are about to undertake. Even those counsellors who are uncomfortable with notions of narrative (person–centred counsellors, for example), can adapt their language so as to be more in tune with that of the client and also modify the 'story' to be more helpful to the client.

Purpose of assessment

Broadly speaking, the *purpose* of making assessments varies according to whether they are *intake* assessments to decide (screen) whether potential clients fit the counsellors' or the agencies' criteria, or *first-session* assessments, that may end in written *formulations,* by the person who is to take the case. Intake interviews are usually used in busy agencies to manage waiting lists. They enable unsuitable clients to be referred back or referred on to a more appropriate service. In one agency we visited, intake assessments also consider whether the person needs a one–off session or more; if it is one–off it is offered there and then. Intake sessions can also exclude from waiting lists (screen out) those who are considered to be unsuitable for counselling for various reasons. In the agencies we visited, this was followed by spending time with the client to deal with any feelings of rejection, anger or disappointment that may be aroused by the decision not to offer help, and discussing what else might be available to the person elsewhere. First-session interviews with the counsellor who is to take the case, however, are the beginning of therapy, listening to the client's story, gaining understanding of the situation, thinking about goals, what the clients is motivated towards, what to do next, and concluding with a written assessment. This *formulation* includes the nature of the problem or the dynamic taking place, where it is rooted and what treatment it requires. It may seek to explain the present and predict the future, examine motivation, capacity to change and how best to achieve it. There are also pragmatic issues, such as potential differences between a client's expectations and needs and what an agency might be able to offer. But there is much more than this to assessment.

Mahrer (1989) says that any coherent approach to therapy must include an understanding of how problems are caused *that fits the intervention* being designed. That statement seems eminently sound, until one considers the many differing theoretical explanations for problems, not to mention those counsellors who see the search for problem causation as a wild–goose chase. Perhaps it makes for less pressure to accept that the intervention needs to fit each counsellor's philosophy about the nature of people and their problems, their assumptions and beliefs about how the mind works and their values about how people ought to be treated. It is also reasonable to conclude that the treatment and the assessment should fit with each other; for example, we see little point in a psychoanalytic assessment followed by a behavioural intervention. Explanations of cause may well be helpful to some counsellors, particularly those who see human difficulties as deficits or disorders and who have a range of counselling approaches from which to select. Others, however, have one or two main approaches and seem able to address most problems by starting where the client is, asking them where they want to go, what obstacles are in the way and helping them to find a way forward. For Corey (2000), some person–centred workers do not see assessment as a prerequisite to counselling but see it as screening for suitability and identifying strengths and liabilities with the client as the main source of knowledge. They may draw on established tests, and may do them in collaboration with the client, but they may ignore the question of cause, at least in the strict sense.

Formulations will usually include tentative *hypotheses* about cause or about what is happening in a person's life that they are not talking about. Ruddell (1997) says hypotheses may develop even before a person is seen, based on referral data for example, and adds, drawing on Malan (1979), that the building of helpful hypotheses requires empathy and trust, patiently listening for the nature of the 'fault', how it developed, what has gone wrong and what should be done. Malan assumes a malfunctioning system at one end and an expert at the other who diagnoses disorders *in* people, but, as we saw in the previous chapter, people's problems are linked to wider systems that may *put* the problem in the person. For example advertising, or social attitudes or one's family may put unhelpful thoughts into a person's mind. Perhaps it is best to leave the term *diagnosis* to health professionals who infer aetiology from symptoms and for whom it may be helpful to classify disorders, ensuring the correct medicine and the communication of expert knowledge – that is beneficial for the profession as well as the person. Counsellors can retain the term *assessment* as descriptive of a more collaborative and ongoing process, with much emphasis on finding wider influences and then focusing on resources both within and around the person.

Assessment has at least three aspects: it describes the problem; it finds personal and systemic strengths and unique abilities that would help to create change; and decides with the client where to focus intervention, whether on skills, cognitive processes, feelings, behaviour, problem-solving or solution-building. As will become evident, we like to make a clear distinction between data and analysis, and also between intake assessment and formulations that emerge over time. First, we will concentrate on intake assessment.

Holistic intake assessment

Aids to *holistic* assessment have been developed such as questionnaires that ensure important aspects are not missed, Questionnaires can be administered at intake or at the first session, which ask, for example, 'What do you see as your main problem? How has it come about? How do you see yourself as a person? How do others see you? What seems to happen in your relationships? Who or what do you see is responsible for your problem? Are you in any way responsible for it? Why are you seeking help now? Would you like to bring anyone with you?' Leeds University counselling service has developed a Clinical Outcomes Routine Evaluation (CORE) list of 34 questions that provide a measure of four elements: well-being, problems, functioning and risk. While it is intended that it be repeated at the end of counselling to measure change, clients have found it a useful starting point too. Other agencies have checklists to assess suitability, and individual counsellors sometimes have checklists to screen out those unsuitable to their particular approach. Such screening, as we shall see later, is often linked to agency requirements and theoretical perspectives about clients. Agencies may design checklists for their own purposes, but we are more concerned with processes, such as ways of setting baselines, assessing for psychological-mindedness or assessing the client's previous experience of counselling.

Palmer (1997) says there are seven modalities of the human personality which can be used to obtain a more holistic assessment: behaviour, affect, sensation, imagery, cognition, interpersonal and drugs/biological (BASIC-ID). When clients come with a specific issue they may be ' temperamentally uncomfortable' with such a range of questioning, but Palmer suggests that these headings cover all aspects of problems and provide a full picture of the client's world, other than political realities. Many experienced counsellors simply have a list of criteria in their heads. Such lists do not always facilitate holistic assessment, but they meet the needs of those clients who do not like too many questions before a rapport is established. Because we consider it important to consider social aspects of problems alongside the psychological aspects, we put forward the grid shown in

Figure 3.1 based on Milner and O'Byrne (2002b). It is not intended for formal completion by counsellor or client, but simply to act as a reminder to counsellors to widen their assessments.

Tantam (1995), too, suggests that counsellors look to such matters as housing conditions, debt, family conflict and offending behaviour, among others. So we suggest the community column might reflect a rundown neighbourhood and the society column racism or a media campaign against a particular user group. Both are situations that may profoundly affect the client or the problem. It is always important that these 'social' columns, and not just the individual or 'psychological' parts of the grid, are considered. When we come to the 'Maps' chapters we will see that various theories are interested in different data, but the collection of general *background* data can be widened to everyone's advantage.

Among the psychological data that are collected, there are some items that appear on most writers' and counsellors' lists. These are 'psychological-mindedness', a capacity for self-reflection, motivation, and acceptance of responsibility at various levels. Counsellors may employ instruments that clients complete, such a problem scales, mini logs, the Myers–Briggs Type Indicator and other such psychological tools to open up the assessment and perhaps measure how serious the problems are. Others will check for signs of severe psychosis, organic problems, medical history, suicidal indicators, clients' hopes of counselling, realistic goals, prior use of counselling and its outcome. The level of detail is influenced by counsellors' theories about the nature of people and their problems and how best to help them. Some, for example those who think about family systems, will elicit a family tree or life-lines. Questionnaires enable the collection of much information but require interviews to discover whether liaison with other professionals is needed or who is the best person to help a particular client. Indeed most counsellors never use questionnaires; in Partington's (1997) study, 45 per cent of counselling psychologists used them as against 25 per cent of counsellors. Many counsellors believe that clients find them intimidating and offputting, or at least prefer to use them with a client after they have established some rapport and trust. One of our interviewees uses the term 'significant others' to cover people at home, at work and in the neighbourhood. Others placed more emphasis on picking up a sense of various emotions from transferences during the meeting with the prospective client.

Intake also can address practical issues such as ability to pay, willingness to spend the necessary time in counselling, ability to travel to

	Person	Partner	Family	School/ work	Home environment	Community	Society
Historic							
Physical state							
Behavioural							
Cognitive							
Affective							
Relational/interactive ? oppressive							
Risk							

Figure 3.1 A data collection grid

sessions, and whether other support may be required. It can explore whether the person may be too ill, too demanding, too troublesome or dangerous. One interviewee told us that she considers whether work over the telephone might be useful or necessary, and another has been asked to consider counselling via email.

Intake gives clients an opportunity to assess the counsellor, their level of care and sensitivity, their care over confidentiality and the quality of the environment they provide for the work. It enables them to ask questions about counselling, the approach adopted and processes used. A benefit of good intake work is the matching of client to counsellor. This means that the counsellor who does the next stage of the work (assessing for intervention – the formulation) can be the one who carries out the intervention, helping the relationship to be developed.

The intake or screening work that we have been discussing is ideally operated in a triage system, where the intake assessment is carried out by a counsellor who knows the qualities and styles of various other counsellors and is able to refer on to the counsellor who might best fit the case. In a triage system it is easy to be clear with the client about the purpose of the first meeting – that it is limited to deciding whether to offer counselling and what sort of counselling that might be. So the content can be restricted to hearing briefly the nature of the complaint or the current predicament and completing an intake document covering only the data needed to make that decision. One of its main benefits is that it avoids clients having to endlessly shop around for the right counsellor.

Selection of intervention for clients

The purpose here is to discern, having broadly understood what is needed, what will be the most efficacious intervention or type of counselling. Tantam (1995) maintains that the quality of object relations is a good indicator for all approaches, while clients with low resources may call for brief work and those with a risk of harm need someone experienced in that risk management. The match between attributional style and therapy has been shown to correlate to progress; those who use internal attribution (seeing cause in self) do well with exploratory therapies, whereas those with external attribution do better with rational therapies. Coltart (1988b) draws a distinction between clients who are psychologically minded and those with borderline personality disorder, although there is not much evidence that reliable judgements can be made about personality. However, McCallum and Piper (1990) found that while many non-psychologically-minded people drop out of counselling, those who remained did as well as those assessed as psychologically-minded. Whilst it is generally agreed that borderline personality disorder is a predictor of poor success, this is not the case in all studies (see, for example, Furman and Ahola, 1992). Such clients cause more anxiety to the counsellor and they may call for more creativity, but they can benefit. It is worth noting that they also do less well with drug treatments, so referral to specialist medical professionals is not necessarily the answer for this client population.

In deciding what type of help to offer, Ruddell and Curwen (1997) suggest that when clients are referred by others, counsellors need to consider whether they acknowledge a problem, even a little; have some motivation to address it; and show minimal acknowledgement of how they may be contributing to the problem, sometimes largely. Then, like all clients, they need to have the ability to tackle the problem by recognising their thinking/feeling and an approach that is matched to their psychological development. Finally, any repetition of a mismatch of approach from the past needs to be avoided. As regards motivation, so long as there is a willingness to engage, the motivation to change can often be developed by the counsellor. Indeed, we would say it is our responsibility to be able to do that and not blame clients for being unmotivated when we fail with them. By being responsive to clients' wants and being supportive of their goals, so long as they are legal and moral, motivation can be improved.

The research tells us that certain approaches do better with certain problems (for details, see the outcomes sections in the Maps chapters), however, Crowe and Ridley (1990) maintain that many problems can be helped by several approaches and so, in theory, the choice can be arbitrary. The general outcomes studies provided by Roth and Fonagy (1996) and Bergin and Garfield (1996) suggest that receiving counselling is better than not receiving it (a typical client is better off than 75 per cent of untreated people), but that although the different approaches have broadly similar results, there is considerable variation in the effectiveness of counsellors. As counsellors are not equally effective, intake assessment needs to consider the counsellor's effectiveness and whether the client will be best served by individual, family or couples work. Couples work is strongly indicated if the problem is linked to their relationship *and* the relationship is continuing *and* the problem is not too acute for couples work. Reibstein (1997) suggests that the indicators of an enduring relationship are the degree of protection, focus, gratitude, balance and pleasure couples are able to exhibit, and Sternberg (1992) looks at three qualities of the relationship: intimacy of true friendship, passion and commitment in assessing for suitability for couples counselling. Family counselling may be indicated after assessing for the child's developmental needs, the parents' parenting capacity and community resources (Gary, 2001), whilst Wilkinson (1998) uses six dimensions based on the Child Psychology Portfolio (NFER, 1998) in child and family assessments.

Entering into a therapeutic relationship can be rather daunting, a factor welcomed by Strupp and Binder (1984) who maintain that it requires clients to feel sufficiently discomforted, have sufficient trust and be willing to consider conflicts in interpersonal terms, examine feelings and have a capacity for mature relationships. So they exclude those who are so isolated and distrusting that a dynamic focus cannot be defined in a meaningful way. They ask, does the available counsellor have the necessary skill to treat this person and the time and the interest to take on the work? If not, who has?

In seeking to assess where a client is in life, Aveline (1997) asks 'What is your life like? Where are you going? Where would you like to get to? What obstacles are in the way? Are these self-made or not? If not made by self, by whom?' The counsellor may ask herself 'How can I interpret this story, these facts? Is what is wanted relevant to counselling (there may be a better way to get it)?' These questions are linked to the view that to lead a satisfactory life one needs two abilities; trust in others and independent action – in other words, *mature dependence*. Others say that assessment should look for factors such as willingness to face feelings and to look beneath the surface, ego strengths, a capacity to change and the ability to form a therapeutic alliance.

The counsellors we interviewed said they would exclude certain types of client. Some would exclude those who were too psychotic (we are not sure what 'a little psychotic' means); those who did not want to engage; those they felt unsafe with, those with whom they feel out of their depth and those for whom a specialist counsellor was available locally (for example, a debt counsellor). These judgements are basically concerned with the question 'am I a suitable counsellor for this client?' although they also address the client's suitability for the counsellor.

Formulations and theory

Denman (1995) says that formulations, in addition to describing the key features of a case, motivation and capacity, and bringing some coherent structure to these details, should have a clear *theoretical* foundation They should make a diagnostic statement but be sensitive, specific and have predictive implications, set some guidelines, capture the essence of the case and be human. Such formulations get the work off to a good start, help audits and help research. This work calls for thorough *data collection* about the client and the problem and an *analysis* of the data, as the counsellor's theoretical map is explicitly or implicitly applied. While a *beginning* formulation is possible at this starting stage, it will shift and develop throughout the counselling process, with a *full* formulation being possible only when the work is finished. In many counselling approaches, psychoanalytic work for example, it is clear that only at the end of the journey can the understanding be complete – that *is* the therapy. So we speak of assessment throughout counselling, rather than diagnosis at the start. Some will argue that it can be the reverse, while others (see, for example, Dryden,1997) take a middle road, maintaining that the best assessment needs several sessions of counselling first, testing what the client is able to use or take from the process.

Our question to our respondents, 'Do you need to understand the cause of a problem?', brought a wide range of replies. One respondent said she was not (looking) into cause, but for information that throws light on a situation, to gain some understanding of what is happening. Another replied that it was not cause in the medical sense – more a question of 'what ails you?' Another said that it was more about 'what's the matter?' in the sense of what has happened to them. Yet another said it was about how they got to where they are and by what decisions. One narrative counsellor would discuss cause only if the clients wanted to do so; his interest was much more on the effects that the problem creates for the client. Another narrative counsellor declared that she has to try hard to resist seeking cause – it is tempting to ask about it but it is almost invariably a waste of time, or it gets her bogged down in the past. One said she did not ask about it but she listened for it, should clients happen to express a view.

It is interesting that the approach that depends least on formal assessment, the person-centred approach, is the most commonly used if we discount those who are eclectic. Young, Feiler and Witmer (1989) studied counsellors' primary theoretical approaches and found that while 32 per cent were eclectic, 22 per cent were person-centred, with only 6 per cent cognitive-behavioural, 5 per cent psycho-analytic, 4 per cent reality therapy, and other methods 2–3 per cent ($N = 66$ counsellor educators and 69 counsellors). The majority of counsellors and counselling psychologists in Partington's (1997) sample identified themselves as integrative in orientation and it is our experience that more counsellors are describing their approach as *integrative* of at least two methods or, more often, sets of skills. This suggests they are more thoughtful or discerning in what approaches they do *not* use, so, in arriving at formulations of problems, they are combining two or more theoretical approaches that fit with each other or at least that fit with the counsellor's philosophy of people. The question of integration will be discussed in more detail in Chapter 10. Some of those we interviewed were also aware that, in selecting a theory, they were concerned much more with helpfulness rather than whether it brought then to a correct understanding. Rather than seeking the one 'true' understanding of the situation or its cause, they were trying to arrive at an insight that fitted the client's metaphors as well as their own philosophy. We see this as a move towards being more 'narrative'–orientated, looking to write a 'story' based on a set of *metaphors* that illuminate the difficulty in a way with which the client and the counsellor can live and work.

We cannot, it seems, extricate our own views from our understanding of what people tell us; we can only know by our own ways of seeing. However, bringing our ways of understanding to clients can serve to help matters; we can compare our view with that of the client and ask ourselves if what they say could be a clue to something still to be discovered. Since we cannot empty our minds of all theory we need to remind ourselves that our ideas always run the risk of foreclosing understanding rather than expanding it. Then we can use theoretical ideas as other ways of seeing the world that may sometimes illuminate a situation – with some ideas being more illuminating of some situations than of others. Theories serve their purpose better however, if we first look closely at the data with as open a mind as possible, and only when we have examined it minutely apply theory to explaining it. Reading the positions of the 12 discussants brought together by Pulver (1987), we wonder how they could argue for differing approaches to the same client without, apparently, considering the impact of their model on the client's experience. We feel that leaps of inference need to be curbed; it is preferable to shape our way of listening to the data without theoretical bias or prejudgement so that the client's ability for self-observation may be enhanced. Since 'facts', *per se*, do not exist:

> Everything new that we have inferred must nevertheless be translated back into the language of our perceptions, from which it is simply impossible for us to free ourselves . . . reality will always remain unknowable. (Freud, 1940, p. 196)

The common phrase 'seeing is believing' thus becomes 'believing is seeing'. What we think we know is often only our way of seeing things. What constitutes data and what is worth recording is determined by the theoretical bent of the worker; data collection by counsellors steeped in any theory is inevitably biased. Pulver argues that the effect of our theories 'can best be thought of in terms of the narratives we construct' (p. 293). Like Stern (1985), he sees formulations as a special sort of story-telling which is influenced by a set of (theoretical) metaphors that help to make sense of the plot; a variety of narratives may be valid, depending on the mutually interacting viewpoints of the teller and the listener, the client and the counsellor working out the version together.

Perhaps the *subjective* meanings of the individual experiencing a difficulty should be seen as central, and their 'story' seen as mattering as much as any theory. Their attributions and explanations are part of the 'reality' and even serve to create that reality. What matters is the currently created 'truth' of the person and, secondarily, considerations of how a theoretical map might help us to co-construct with the person a more helpful and empowering account. Lives are 'authored' by clients as well as others, and if they are unsatisfactory we can help clients to re-author them. People can have more confidence in one story rather than another, so we can draw on the metaphors of various theories to articulate understandings and meanings that are useful in facilitating change in a particular situation. For this to happen we need to begin with open minds, holding on to uncertainty rather than the security of a pet theory, developing several hypotheses perhaps, and comparing various understandings for fit with the client's meanings. Thus the process becomes one of mutually building and negotiating meanings that empower clients and restore their control over their lives. Assessment, done in this narrative way, can be the start of the process. This, however, is not to argue that counsellors should not study theory because, as Mcleod (1998) comments, 'being able to use a theoretical model to make sense of what is happening is highly desirable' (p. 201). We would stress the word *use* – use collaboratively – as distinct from *impose* or *prejudge*.

Comparing assessment with qualitative research, Everitt *et al.* (1992) stress the value of the spirit of enquiry, making assumptions explicit, thinking through theoretical perspectives, clarifying hypotheses and testing them while engaging and listening to people's worlds and remaining conscious 'of the pervasiveness of ideology in the way we see the world' (p. 4). If assessments are undertaken with the same methodological rigour as sound qualitative research, they will necessarily include: a clear statement of intent; the development of more than one hypothesis about the nature of the problems and solutions; and a clear statement on how the final judgement can be tested in terms of demonstrable outcomes. The acid test of the assessment is satisfaction with subsequent decisions and actions taken by both counsellor and client.

Ongoing assessment

Assessment during treatment is concerned with both progress and outcomes. The questions asked at this stage include: 'Are we on track? Is the problem lessening? What is this transference? How is the therapeutic relationship? Do we need to change approach? Is there enough change?' Progress can also be assessed by the use of scaled questions such as scales for feelings, thoughts, behaviours, sensations, relationships and specific goals. In person–centred work, however, it is the process and the therapeutic relation that is focused on. Again, it is the theoretical maps that mainly influence thinking during treatment, as we will see in subsequent chapters. One respondent commented that assessment during treatment was the most difficult for her because she wonders whether she is being drawn in to the client's mind and whether she can be fully objective.

Assessment for ending

There is an important ethical principle in counselling to the effect that to counsel for even one session more than is necessary is unprofessional and potentially harmful to clients. It is important to do no more than is necessary; that is, do what works and not what is interesting for the counsellor as these are unnecessary and possibly unethical excursions. Assessing when to end is therefore an important and not altogether straightforward matter. As we listen to clients' views about whether they will benefit from more involvement with us, we may feel honoured that they want to see more of us, or wonder whether they simply have become attached to us and enjoy seeing us when sufficient change has already been achieved. Sometimes the decision to end is made by default or for financial reasons. In our interviews with counsellors we found that most counsellors frequently review progress with clients with a view to facilitating ending. Many also set up contracts for a set number of sessions, so that a discussion of ending is almost built-in to the plan. One counsellor who sometimes has a two-year contract begins to review this after the first year, starting conversations about what change will be good enough. Those with six-session contracts sometimes do such a review after three sessions

The attainment of client *goals* is seen by many as a key indicator of when to end. This requires that goals be considered at the beginning of counselling or at intake. Goals may shift in the course of counselling or there may be new goals, with counsellors needing to be vigilant that goals do not become endless. Many counsellors we interviewed stated that when things are 'good enough' they end; others end when the client's 'observable' goal is attained, that is when inner change is evidenced in outer behaviour. One counsellor ends when she feels tired of the client – perhaps that feeling results from coming to a natural conclusion. Another ends when the client is managing to cope with problems satisfactorily.

Ending can be the start of the process of evaluation or research into effectiveness. Some counsellors seem to spend much time discussing cases that have not gone well, perhaps in the hope of learning from mistakes or learning how to work better next time. We feel, however, that we can learn more from our successes, however modest. Perhaps time could be well-spent in exploring how we have helped people to make progress, and considering how to build on that success.

Risk assessment

In public services such as the National Health Service counsellors are required to carry out risk assessments on all cases and to write a care plan. In such agencies a risk-assessment form is usually provided for completion by the counsellor and discussion with the client. In smaller services, usually in the voluntary sector and in private counselling, risk assessment is rather *ad hoc*. Several of the counsellors we interviewed consider risk in cases of suicidal, severely depressed, anorexic and self-harming clients, and they also consider risk to themselves in cases of violent and mentally-ill clients and those who

make the counsellor feel uncomfortable for some unknown reason
that 'makes the hair stand on the back of one's neck'. This assessment
of risk to self usually leads to refusal to take the case where the counsellor works from home, or putting precautions in place such as have
other staff nearby for those working in an agency. One counsellor
rejects cases that cause her to have a sense, or gut feeling, that she is
not in control. Another asks herself 'what am I hearing from the
client?' Both the psychoanalytic counsellors we met consider the risk
to the client of counselling where the client may lack the necessary
ego strength to undergo counselling or where counselling might risk
dismantling fragile defences or supports. One narrative counsellor
assesses strengths and signs of change to determine the level of safety.
Another felt that unmet need went hand in hand with riskiness. We
tend to agree with the counsellor who felt that risk–assessment forms
do not necessarily assess risk; while they ask many questions, the
answers to which are mini assessments, they provide a general score
that may not tell us what is needed to reduce risk to an acceptable
level.

Here we wish to mention the 'Signs of Safety' approach to risk
developed by Turnell and Edwards (1999). They are concerned that
signs of danger can give an unbalanced picture and that engaging
with clients over risk only can be difficult because they become so
defensive. Therefore they show equal interest in the signs of safety and
engage people in examining how these can be strengthened. More
progress/change can often be made by increasing safety that is
measurable rather than by trying to reduce risk that often defies
quantification. This is not to say that dangerousness is ignored, but the
main effort goes into looking for, developing and expanding signs that
contribute to a sense of safety and creating new safety signs. Safety
approaches avoid some of the dilemmas and difficulties of making a
risk assessment by inviting clients who are abusive towards other
people to take responsibility for their own behaviour. Effective safety
plans resulting from this approach have been obtained in the fields of
domestic violence (Jenkins, 1990, 1996; Sebold and Uken, 2000;
Milner and Jessop, 2003), child abuse (Berg, 1992; Turnell and
Edwards, 1999), and cases where suspected sexual abuse is strongly
denied (Essex *et al.*, 1996).

The Signs of Safety approach can also be used to assess clients who
self-harm, such as those who feel suicidal (Hendon, 2002), those who
suffer from severe eating distress (Jacob, 2001), and those who cut themselves (Selekman, 2002). Curwen (1995) defines suicide as self-inflicted,

with intent to kill. Many suicidal people have a psychiatric disorder or a severe addiction problem, or suffer from social isolation or from a sense of profound loss, or have a life-threatening disease, chronic illness or chronic unemployment. Assessment of such clients begins with questions that determine whether the client is entertaining suicidal thoughts *at the present time.* The counsellor can ask 'how do you feel about the future?' and listen, and watch, for verbal or non-verbal signs such as planning to give away possessions or not buying food. Expressions of hopelessness are also important, as are previous attempts, substance abuse and a family history of suicide. Where the client is open about suicidal thoughts, the counsellor can ask about the plan or method being contemplated and consider whether it is potentially lethal.

Where there is a precise plan, with a lethal method, arranged for the next 24 hours, Curwen suggests the risk is *high* and hospital admission should be promptly arranged in consultation with a psychiatrist and one's supervisor. Similarly, counsellors will monitor the weight of a client who is experiencing severe eating distress. Jacob (2001) works with other professionals where the client is seriously unwell and makes an agreement with the client that if she has cause for concern, she has the right to stop work at least until weight is regained: 'if the BMI drops to a dangerously low level . . . the brain is not well enough to engage in the work we do. Carrying on would waste money and time, which I think would be unethical' (Jacob, 2001, p. 141).

Beck's Depression Inventory is usually recommended as a useful tool for gauging the severity of depression. Burns (1992) distinguishes between a *passive* death wish and an *active* one. As an example he describes a young man who said 'Every night when I go to bed I pray to God to let me wake up with cancer'. Similarly, one of us has met a client who wanted to die in her sleep as soon as possible. An active death wish is much more dangerous. Burns says that, as a rule, the more concrete and well-formulated the plans are the more likely that an attempt will be made. Rather than interpreting suicidal thoughts or acts as cries for help, it is important to take them seriously. Many suicidal people want help least of all because they are certain that they are beyond help – what they want is to die. Because of the importance of the belief that things are hopeless, a useful question may be 'do you believe you have any chance of getting better?' A high degree of hopelessness indicates the need for in-patient treatment at once. Burns puts forward any one of the following three states, coupled with a lack of deterrents capable of holding the person back, as requiring immediate intervention: severe depression with feeling hopeless; feeling suicidal with a past history of attempts; and concrete plans and preparations made.

In Chapter 11 we discuss in more detail the process of decision making in risky situations, and the question of disclosing information to others.

An assessment framework

We consider it to be useful to distinguish not only between data and analysis, but also between intake and formulation. We realise, however, that there may be some overlap between the thinking at intake work and at formulation writing, especially in private practice. In our meetings with counsellors we could see that they all made judgements about suitability, but many counsellors in private practice wrote no formulation as such, only notes of their thoughts, feelings/transferences, as they went along. So we hope that the following comprehensive overarching framework may be useful and may fill some gaps. It is based on various ideas from the literature, on the practice of respected counsellors and our own experience, although it may not all be relevant to all situations.

A. Intake (To screen for *suitability* for counselling, what sort of counselling, what length – it may be called a pre-assessment interview, screening or initial assessment)

1 *Data collection* (by asking the client):
   Name, address, telephone, date of birth, work, family/household.
   Doctor's name and telephone number.
   Clients reason for coming – the problem – or why referred. Their main concerns.
   Their understanding of the problem; what it means to them.
   Who or what is responsible for it?
   How long has it been a problem?
   Previous interventions, approaches taken and their outcome.
   Why now?
   Do they want to be here? Are they interested in counselling?
   Is there something they want to change?
   Hopes of counselling. Goals.
   Health, physical and mental. Use of medication.

Eating.

Substance abuse.

Where there is an element of risk, what is it? Will the client give permission to liaise with others? What are the signs of safety in the situation?

Relationships.

Emotional state.

Behaviour problems.

Supports.

Strengths – what is the person good at? Successes. Times when things were better.

Are they prepared to work hard at trying to make changes?

What do they need to know about the counselling available? Do they have some idea what it will be like?

Are they interested in the counselling that is available; do they wish to contract for a number of sessions?

Can they afford it, if it is private?

Will they be able to attend regularly?

(The assessor may wish to refer to an agency protocol, or other check-list or grid, to ensure nothing important is overlooked. As the list grows ever longer, it is unlikely to be completed in one session, unless there is a pre-session questionnaire.)

2 *Judgements for the counsellor to consider.*

If in an agency, are the agency criteria met?

Am I clear about what the client wants?

Are the goals realistic?

Does the person desire change enough?

Is there sufficient motive to make change?

Do they hold themselves accountable for making changes?

Do they have a sense of personal agency?

How have they responded to a mini intervention?

Is there a minimum of psychological mindedness?

What metaphors do they use in telling their story?

Are there signs of psychosis or severe depression? What is the general affect?

How does the person make me feel?

Can this person cope with the demands of counselling? If so, what sort would be best?

Will this person need individual, couple, family or group interventions?

Risks? Self harm, harm to others, threat to the counsellor?
If so, what precautions are needed? Is collaboration with another
professional needed?
Is treatment by another person or agency required? If so, who is the
best person to whom to refer?

Finally, what to offer them, if anything? – do they understand what
might be offered? Can a contract be considered? If not suitable for
counselling, how will I deal with them?

B. Formulation (This is the *theoretical* analysis – the understandings, insights, interpretation and intervention plan. It may be called
the first treatment session, the assessment proper or the comprehensive assessment; it may be written after the first session or after several
sessions.)

1 *Data collection*
   Like analysis, the data required by various counsellors will vary
   with their theoretical map/s and personal philosophy of people and
   of counselling. Some will seek a detailed history of the problem or
   the meaning of significant events; some will be interested in early
   experiences; some a detailed discussion of thoughts associated with
   the difficulty; some will be more interested in previous solutions or
   part-solutions and strengths. (The main alternative approaches are
   provided in the next six chapters.)

2 *Weighing the data*
   This involves considering such things as the seriousness of the
   problem, persistent themes in the story or how the client makes the
   counsellor feel, identifying gaps in the data, and any priority actions
   to be taken. Are there enough data to show that the client is sufficiently psychologically-minded? How attached to the problem are
   they – will they be able to let go of being destructive? Is counselling necessary?

3 *Analysis*
   Applying one or more theoretical perspective to gain depth of
   understanding. (How this is done will be addressed in each of the
   'map' chapters.) Developing tentative hypotheses, possible explana-
   tions and influences.
   What understanding makes sense to the client?
   What change may be required so as to have a satisfactory outcome?
   Are the goals realistic? If not, what would be realistic?

4 *Utilising the Analysis* – decision-making and planning

How can intervention best start? Any priorities or issues needing to be addressed at the beginning?

What will the rest of the therapy entail?

How long is the process expected to take?

What will indicate progress? What changes to expect?

How will change be measured? What will be good enough?

How will any risks be addressed (including possible risks from the type of counselling being offered)?

Any issues for supervision?

We have noticed that counsellors who are provided with an agency protocol are sensitive to the possibility of putting clients off if they are too formal or rigid about getting all the answers in the first meeting. One counsellor told us that she meets the client in an informal way and has a conversation with questions casually dropped in to see what she discovers. Later she checks her findings against the protocol to see what needs to be covered in the next meeting when some rapport and trust has started to build up. A key skill is having a conversational style, combined with empathic listening, that makes it easy for the client to tell their story.

Summary

There are many kinds of assessment and many approaches to managing the process. The importance or otherwise of cause-finding is disputed or at least understood and employed differently by everyone with whom we have discussed it. The very need for assessment is sometimes doubted, but the vast majority of counsellors engage in it, at least in deciding whether counselling is suitable for their prospective clients. Lastly, we have offered what we consider to be a useful framework for approaching the task.

4

Psychodynamic Approaches: A Map of the Ocean

In this and the following five chapters we will present a selection of established theoretical 'maps' or models commonly taught to and used by counsellors. These maps sum up the philosophy, beliefs about people and about problem causation as well as the approach to and method of helping. We set them out in a logical order that is based on their underlying view of problems and, along with O'Hanlon (1993), suggest that they have come in 'waves'. As we said earlier, the first wave saw difficulties as pathology; the second was problem-focused, seeking to understand problems and their maintenance before attempting to solve them; the third was solution-focused, seeking to understand solutions, with little need to analyse problems.

In this chapter we present the first of the 'wave-one' (pathology-based) models of counselling, one that continues to be influential in that it has remained popular despite numerous critiques and revisions. Psychodynamic theory's main figure is Sigmund Freud, but it has been developed and reinterpreted by many; Elliott (2002), for example, clearly sets out the influences of Klein, Erikson, Winnicott, Lacan, Fromm, Marcuse and several others, including Kovel's work on narcissism. Here we will focus on the predominant versions by first briefly outlining the central Freudian theory, and then addressing Kleinian theory which is also widely used in counselling.

Freudian theory

This approach can have a feel of descending into the unconscious as if exploring in a submarine – as one of our respondents commented, it enables us to address our dark and hidden depths. Our chapter title comes from a comment by Hall (1954, p. 2) that the id is 'oceanic', in that it contains everything and recognises nothing outside of itself; if there is too much rough weather, it can turn nasty. We begin with a simplified explanatory diagrammatic presentation of the core ideas (see Figure 4.1), but, as Jacobs (1988) reminds us, Freud's diagrams and structural division of the psyche serve 'more as crude pictures of the relationship between conscious and unconscious functions within the psyche' and can be 'more fully understood and appreciated if they can be seen as much as metaphors as literal statements' (p. 9).

Nelson-Jones (1995) describes the superego, ego and id as three agencies of our mental apparatus. Although the id might not be capable of recognising anything outside itself, Freud certainly did recognise the outside world and its impact on the ego, so we have shown the world of reality on our version of this map, and, as we shall show later, a large part of the 'map' will deal with the interaction of the ego with reality.

Freud's earliest distinction was that between the conscious and unconscious mind, considering the latter as the greater part with consciousness being only the tip of the iceberg above the surface. In the 1920s, Freud developed the notions of ego, superego and id. While a large part of the ego, although by no means all of it, can be conscious, the vast majority of the superego and probably all of the id are unconscious. Freud also identified the 'pre-conscious' that we can readily recall, since it is just under the surface.

The *superego* develops through a process of *internalisation*. The child internalises the values, rules, prohibitions and wishes of the parent and of authority figures, but the process is one that magnifies these rules

The Mind		The World
Unconscious	*Conscious*	*(Other people and the environment)*
The superego ('parent')		
	The ego ('adult')	Reality
The id ('child')		

Figure 4.1 Mind and world

and records them in the raw, without editing, and laden with amplified feelings. So it is not just what a parent says to a child, but all the emotion, perhaps terror, that was felt at being blamed, abandoned or hurt in various ways: the small child who breaks a cup can feel that s/he has destroyed everything. Admonitions and rules go straight into memory, carrying the weight of total truth, never to be erased from the tape. The research of Penfield (1952) has helped to shape this view of the superego, the part that tells and teaches. Even though the telling is long lost from consciousness, the recording remains active in the unconscious, shouting loudly.

The superego may be restrictive or permissive (Caplan, 1961). People riddled with guilt can be said to have an overrestrictive superego, and people with too little guilt an overpermissive or weak superego. Those with no internal rules, no conscience about hurting others, are labelled sociopaths (commonly called psychopaths). Caplan (1961) talks of the superego as the condemning and prohibiting part of the mind that says 'Do not . . .', or 'I must not . . .', distinguishing this from the *ego-ideal*, which says (of a desirable act), 'So as not to let myself down, I ought to do it because that would fit my ideal me'. So, some people's conscience tells them they have to strive for great heights of achievement and set themselves high standards, be thrifty, and so on. On the other hand, too rigid and dominating a superego could create difficulties by way of excessive guilt, leading to neurotic effects such as depression, phobias, obsessions, compulsions, neurotic anxiety and moral anxiety or shame. Reality anxiety (Hall, 1954), however, is seen as an ego reaction to the threat of loss.

The *id* is that aspect of the person which is primitive, the animal drive, full of feelings, capable of rage, operating on instinctual drives and urges, hungry to fill any voids that are felt. Nelson-Jones (1995) says that the libido is the energy for the two instincts, one for life and the other for destruction/death. Berne (1978), however, distinguishes between two main id drives – *libido,* which is sexual impulse, desire and attraction, and *mortido,* which is the killing instinct, hating, attacking and hitting out violently. This thinking is based on Freud's work; Freud first developed 'seduction theory', namely that female neurosis was due to sexual abuse by fathers. Later, while not disbelieving the accounts of his clients, he privileged fantasy over the reality and, rather than emphasising the victimhood of abused children, stressed their sexual fantasies, desires, identifications and repressions. He has been heavily criticised for this (see, for example, Masson 1984; Wolff, 1995).

Concerning libido and mortido, Berne suggests some people are more prone to one rather than the other, although these are close relatives born of the need to propagate and survive. They explain something of what some people are looking for, so the id is described as being governed by the *pleasure principle* (which is seen as our motivating force); the lack of sufficient pleasure leaves the id hurting, demanding and wanting irrationally, sometimes leading to a chaotic life of acting out, living for 'kicks' or sending out cries for help, such as the abused person who shoplifts to attract attention to his/her plight, behaving in a way that could be interpreted as asking to be caught.

The third area is the *ego*, the I and Me, the self that thinks, decides, plans and relates to the world of *reality*. It is governed by the *reality principle*, which is exploring and testing, born of curiosity. The ego is placed between the superego and the id in Figure 4.1 because it acts as a referee between them, struggling to keep a balance between the gratification of needs and impulses and the sacrifice of this gratification to the demands of reality. This is what *psychodynamic* means – an interaction and tension between the id drives, the superego, with its possibly guilt-ridden prohibitions, and a tension between inner needs and outer realities, in an attempt to keep a balanced ego. Freud saw ambivalence at the heart of self-and-the-world relationships. Society imposes severe demands; culture leads to neurosis as we struggle to balance sexual drives with moral imperatives. Fromm (1985), for example, says society seeks to produce individuals *who want to act as they have to*. Freud also saw the ego as a man on horseback, striving to control a superior force (the id), whereas later ego psychologists saw the ego as masterful, at least potentially. This giving of primacy to the ego goes hand in hand with Western, male individualism.

Defences

The ego lives under great pressure from three sides: the id, the superego and real threats in the world. Anna Freud (1936, 1968) itemised various mechanisms of defence used by the ego to help it cope with unconscious anxiety, with the demands of the instinctual drives of the id and, to a lesser extent, with the condemnations of the superego and the demands of reality: 'the infantile ego experiences the onslaught of instinctual and external stimuli at the same time; if it wishes to preserve its existence it must defend itself on both sides simultaneously' (Anna Freud, 1936, p. 191). She identified *denial, repression, reaction formation, intellectualisation, displacement* and *sublimation* as the main defences. Repression gets rid of instinctual derivatives, just as external stimuli are abolished by denial. Reaction formation secures the ego against the return of the repressed impulses, while by fantasies, in which reality is reversed, denial is sustained against attack from outside. The ego uses sublimation to direct instinctual impulses from their sexual goals to higher aims, and reaction formation is the ego further draining itself of the capacity for reversal (p. 190). The existence of neurotic symptoms itself indicates that the ego has been overpowered and some plan of defence has miscarried (p. 193). Getting to the *truth* is seen as important, as is the overcoming of *denial*, even if it is at the cost of considerable pain. 'Bad' earlier experiences need to be replaced by good nurturing experience so that autonomy and maturity can develop. This, however, is a long and slow process.

Post-Freudians have added to Anna Freud's defences, up to 44 such defences being mentioned in the literature. Some, for example, suggest that there are dual aspects of defences: first, warding off anxiety in relation to unconscious conflict and, second, actively supporting adaptive functions of maturation, growth and mastery of the drives. Among the more commonly discussed defences are asceticism, clowning, compliance, depersonalisation, eating or drinking, falling ill, identification, ritualisation, whistling in the dark and humour. Most people use several of these, at least from time to time, and they can be helpful or not depending on the degree of usage and the particular circumstances. It is important, however, to remember that defences can be helpful or unhelpful, particularly in a crisis when the ego is under great stress. For example, intellectualisation might helpfully involve making lists of tasks or thinking through the traumatic event. On the other hand, defences can be unhelpful when they lead to ongoing denial of loss or projection of cause on to others. We sometimes think that projection is the curse of contemporary life in which no-one accepts responsibility for anything. Part of the task of assessment in psychodynamic counselling is to decide which defences are being used and whether they are a help or a hindrance, and, if the latter, to consider how they can best be confronted.

Defences serve a purpose, so the psychodynamic approach respects defences in two ways (Jacobs, 1998. p. 81). In assessing clients, we need to see whether the ego can tolerate self-scrutiny without becoming too anxious. In cases in which such scrutiny does not promise change, we need to ask ourselves what level of support is needed to help the person cope with external pressures. Laying bare repressed feelings, or offering interpretations to that end, is to be avoided if the ego thereby risks being overwhelmed. An immature, weak ego needs defences to be strengthened, rather than torn down; ego-supporting is to be preferred to ego-modifying in such cases. However, Nelson-Jones (1995) describes as neurotics those who have significant repressions that may have supported a weak child ego but that now weaken the ego, whereas self-knowledge strengthens it. The aim is to reeducate the ego so that expression is allowed and the ego is effectively used in acts of judgement, free of impulse, able to appropriate more of the id and moderate the superego so that it is more 'human' and less punitive.

Wasserman (1974), an ego psychologist, points out that it takes a strong ego to be able to mourn, suffer, verbalise anger and even be depressed. So the absence of depression in some situations, while it might appear to be adaptive, might in fact be due to an overdefended ego and thus be maladaptive. In psychodynamic assessments, therefore, counsellors need to look not only at behaviour but also at the situation, and consider the stresses that may be operating, the degree to which the ego is pressed upon and the stresses with which the ego can or cannot cope. Ego functioning is not only influenced by internal pressures from the superego and the id, but very much also by external stimuli. Social, cultural and economic factors, injustice and oppression, do not remain outside the person; they become internalised. Since counselling is often concerned with efforts to influence adaptive capacities, assessments are more likely to be useful if they focus on the interface of the ego with the world: how the ego is learning, controlling and balancing with self-reliance and pride. This will mean that a counsellor may not be concerned with intensive psychoanalytic techniques of free association, the recovery of the repressed, or the interpretation of dreams and breaking through resistance. Rather than a blank-screen approach, he or she will offer a relationship, listening and reflecting with the client, joining the resistance (Strean, 1968), so that they can get going with the problem-solving that needs to be done. This does not in every case require the reliving of past traumas.

Ego functions

We would now like to consider the *functions of ego*, an area that can offer useful possibilities for assessment, particularly of the strength of the ego. It is the function of the ego to provide stability, equilibrium and predictability in such a way that, once we get to know someone, we can say that in certain circumstances s/he is liable to react in a certain way that is 'true to character'. This makes for sound relationships. Bowlby (1982) explains this in terms of the child making stable internal representations that will depend upon attachment styles developed in infancy but persisting into adult ways of relating. The prediction of others' behaviour that makes people feel in control of social situations is explained in different ways in the psychological literature, for example attribution theory.

The ego also manages cognitions, perceptions, planning and problem-solving. It makes judgments and decisions, adapts to reality and controls impulses, for example not hitting out at someone being offensive who is much bigger than oneself! The ego is responsible for personal growth, coping with stress, using skills and tolerating frustration, loss, pain and sadness. It is the ego that neutralises pressures from the superego and urges from the id. It produces self-assertion, the ability to verbalise feelings rather than act them out, and finally directs our striving, our attempts to achieve and to care. To do all this the ego needs to be flexible, adaptable, resilient, reality-based, stable in the face of pressure and tolerant of anxiety and loss.

The ego, therefore, has a massive task to perform, which can make it feel overwhelmed and in need of defences. We all need some defences at times but many clients may particularly need us to strengthen or support their egos, not by breaking through defences with interpretations but by respecting and working with defences; acknowledging the threats they face and discussing the implications and confusion of their ambivalent feelings; considering their unfinished emotional business; and providing support perhaps through a corrective relationship that provides an emotional reeducation so that the client can move on to be an independent coping person.

Kleinian psychotherapy

The work of Melanie Klein (1976, 1988) can be taken as representative of the post-Freudian group that is known as the *object-relations school*. Klein is less interested in aspects such as mortido and libido, and more interested in how emotions are triggered by early experiences and how they shape or affect identity. Early experiences lead to fantasies concerning other people, parts of people, even animals or symbolic objects of various sorts. She stressed that individuals need relationships with others – they are seen more as object-seekers than as pleasure-seekers. Problems stem from early relationships with care-givers and from early emotional deprivations that result in *splitting* in the unconscious. Klein emphasised fantasy, by which we shuttle our inner and outer worlds, while we are caught up in a mass of 'part objects'. Our tendency to destruction is directed at the earliest part object (the breast), but as anxieties become too terrifying the infant 'splits' the mother into good and bad objects and fantasises about attacking the mother – which is called the 'paranoid-schizoid' position (in counselling we meet those who split life and people into the idealised good or the loathed bad). To move past this position, split objects need to be integrated and the mother accepted as a separate integrated person with some good and some bad aspects. However, the child fears that its violent fantasies have injured that separate person and so it has to make 'reparation' – as it enters the 'depressive position', with feelings of guilt and ambivalence. Self involves an interplay of destruction and reparation as we deal with aggression, envy and grief on the road to maturity. Elliott (2002) claims that this theory is a reflection of Klein's own unhappy childhood.

Like Freud, Klein is interested in interpretations of unconscious processes, in understanding the past to understand the present, and in understanding resistance and the defences used to cope with the discomfort of inner conflict, but she is more willing to leave defences intact if it is assessed that the person is too fragile to let go of them. A key element in her work is the understanding of identity; like Erikson, there is concern over identity confusion and the lack of clear boundaries of the self; like Bowlby, attachments are also seen as important. Self-formation is enhanced by the 'emotional provisions' of others. The use of the therapeutic relationship is central, as is the interpretation of current feelings in terms of past events. In this way, and also by constantly checking 'how that feels', the counsellor gets in touch with feelings that lie below the surface. There is a belief, too, in the value of catharsis.

Trust, too, is a key issue. As the child comes to trust responsive and consistent parents, a secure self can go on to develop meaningful relationships later. Erikson said that reliance on others is necessary so that an adaptive self could comfortably link self and society. In modern life, trust is needed to cope with the ambivalence, contingency and uncertainty of being, mixed with great possibilities and high risks, as we pursue autonomy. In modern risk cultures can we ever be secure? There is a constant interplay of trust and risk, of security and danger. Such a life requires the ability to trust, bolstered by helpful habits and *routines,* to screen against unconscious anxiety. Routine helps to bind fears and anxieties.

Klein's work was frequently with children, with an emphasis on the relationship with the mother. Early child relations with their mothers were seen as relations with 'objects' that may be part of the mother, for example the breast, which may have been experienced as 'good' or 'bad' (splitting). If the mother or breast was experienced as 'bad', destructive rage is a possible response. As a child matures, however, splitting reduces and it is possible to recognise both good and bad in everyone. Where splitting is not well outgrown, a person may revert to it in stressful situations; thus some people have either friends or enemies. The early mother relationship sets the pattern for later relationships – the mind is said to evolve out of these interactions and motivation is based on the need to establish and maintain relationships and human contact, whereas for Freud it is based on the need to relieve tension. For Freud, we are driven by biological needs, whereas for Klein we are essentially social beings. Josephine Klein (1987) continues the work of Melanie Klein and has interesting points to make about assessment, which we will address shortly.

Transference and counter-transference

In all psychodynamic therapy transference is a key concept, describing a process of transferring unresolved feelings or emotional attitudes from a person or object in the past on to the counsellor/therapist. The client is thus able to reexperience and work through those feelings, be they love, hate, anger and so on, with the counsellor who is able to accept and discuss them. The relationship with the counsellor enables some regression to childhood to discover ways of overcoming blocks to development, so there is a kind of reparenting or a 'corrective emotional experience' (Alexander and French, 1946). Counter-transference is the term used to describe the experience whereby the counsellor picks up the transference and experiences positive or negative feelings in return. These feelings aroused in the counsellor are valued as 'unconscious understandings' (Heimann, 1950), although there is much debate over the nature and role of counter-transference. A skilled counsellor is said to be able to use the transference/counter-transference to bring the client to therapeutic insight and resolution. The process enables a gaining of awareness of how one avoids one's true feelings, and the client is encouraged to accept what is hard to accept. The client is also encouraged to avoid 'projective identification', whereby she behaves in such a way as to get the other to behave as though they really had the feelings that are projected on to them. In this there is a blurring of the self–other boundary that comes from an early child sense of grandiose omnipotence. An example of this is the (unrealistic) need some people have to be dependent on a more 'capable' person; they promote this by frequently and unnecessarily asking for help/advice. For others, it may be the other way round, making the other person dependant by offering unnecessary help/advice.

Psychodynamic explanations of personality development

Psychodynamic theory sees people as developing in a sequence of stages, each one dependent upon the successful negotiation of the earlier stage for its own success. Freud was interested in the early stages of child development, particularly sexual development, while Bowlby (1982) focused more on the social and emotional interactions of this period. Erikson (1948) extended Freud's developmental outline across the lifespan, including social as well as sexual and emotional influences. Table 4.1 attempts to set out the main concepts.

The psychodynamic approach differs from all other models of counselling in that the counsellor remains aware of these developmental issues (Jacobs, 1998, p.11), exploring whether, and how well, these stages have been negotiated or whether aspects of some stages are still presenting difficulties in the present. It is also important to bear in mind, however, that maturational crises can be compounded by situational crises.

Silverman (1987) writes that there are two key aspects to psychodynamic practice. First, clients attempt to use the therapist to help them 'explore and resolve the unconscious sources of their overt symptomatology and of the restrictions, inhibitions and self-defeating tendencies' (p. 285) that block them from realising a satisfactory life. Second, without realising it, they try to 're-establish [with the counsellor] the same wishfully passionate but disappointing, dissatisfying, insufficiently fulfilling, and even painful relationships with key persons in their past.' They do this in the hope of gaining some control over what has been 'experienced passively and helplessly' (p. 286). The counselling task then is two-fold – to allow self to be utilised in two ways, and to be aware of this – as the client is helped with verbal interventions to render conscious

Table 4.1 Freud/Erikson, stages of human development

Age	Stage	
	Freudian	Eriksonian
Birth to 1	Oral (hunger)	Trust vs mistrust Level of confidence in reality in being able to form attachment, and have needs met
2 to 3	Anal (excretion, muscular control, retention/letting go)	Autonomy vs shame and doubt Who is in control of holding and letting go. If parent is over-controlling, child learns shame and doubt
4 to 6	Phallic/oedipal Male child loves mother; has castration fears Female child loves father; has penis envy; jealous of mother Stage passes as desires are seen to be impossible and child identifies with same-sex parent	Initiative vs guilt Planning to act independently, avoiding if possible guilt about relationships
5 to c.12	Latency period	Industry vs inferiority Focus on conscious memory and learning skills, testing others, finding identity
c.12	Genital – beginning with puberty	Identity vs role confusion
12+	Young adult	Intimacy vs isolation Seeking satisfactory sexual relationships
	Adult	Generativity vs stagnation
	Maturity to old age	Integrity vs despair Seeking to accept the past and one's achievements, the mix of good and bad times, and valuing the resulting self

what has been unconscious 'so that mature (and maturing), rational, reflective thought' can be mobilised for the resolution of inner conflicts. To do this effectively, according to Silverman, requires being able to monitor shifts and movements in one's self and make corrections in responses so as to 'read' the client without lapsing into 'permanent identification–counteridentification and transference-countertransference enactments' that lead to stalemate. It is said that training for this work requires training analysis, although this is never complete or perfect, and the counsellor has therefore to struggle to read not only the client but his or herself.

In this approach there are probably two therapeutic agents, insight (both cognitive and affective) and the therapeutic relationship. The particular insights offered will vary with the counsellor's theoretical sub-group, be it structural, developmental, Kleinian or interpersonal, for example. Some will offer insight into oedipal conflicts, others pre-oedipal, others the dynamics of transference, others childhood neurosis. The therapeutic relationship may provide the client with a new experience and an opportunity to internalise aspects of the therapist, such as a less severe superego. Nowadays, the insight seems to be less important than the relationship and the process of *seeking* understanding; process taking precedence over content. However, some theories seem to produce better understandings for certain clients; Silverman (1987), for example, suggests that theories applicable to narcissistic clients are more helpful with cases where the significant dynamic is of a narcissistic nature.

Feminism and psychodynamic counselling

While Freudian personality theory has as many feminist adherents as it has critics (see, for example, Baker Miller, 1973; Barr, 1987; Pearson, 1988), Erikson's lifespan developmental outline has proved more resistive to feminist revision. However, the criticisms remain acute whether they are specific, such as Gilligan's (1982) analysis of moral development, which suggests that while boys may develop from identity to intimacy, the process is reversed for girls, or more general (Rorbaugh, 1981; O'Hagan and Dillenburger, 1995). This is probably because Erikson's entire text is riddled with sexist and racist terms; for example, he refers to 'the non male form of the female genitalia' and he describes black identity as three different forms of 'nigger' identity (1948).

The term 'coping' has particular connotations for feminist writers, who read it to mean putting on a front of coping by splitting off unwanted feelings, getting on with life without a fuss. Women often have no other choice; they dread failing to cope and are likely to suffer serious consequences if they do. For example, women tolerate much domestic violence rather than risk losing their children and put up with accusations that they have failed as mothers to protect their children (Kelly, 1994). Worse still, a black woman is stereotyped as being expected to cope with 'all kinds of hardship and material and emotional deprivation, as though she had no feelings or needs at all' (Lawrence, 1992). Thus, we need to consider how reality is structurally more difficult for some people due to the oppressions of society, sexism and racism and other forms of discrimination.

The terms 'independence' and 'separation', so central in psychodynamic explanations of 'healthy' personality development, have difficult connotations in that, because society is fundamentally patriarchal, women are more likely to have feelings of vulnerability, weakness, helplessness and dependency (Miller, 1973) or, on the other hand, to have learned from their mothers that they must orientate themselves towards meeting the needs of others and to be a carer and not to expect to be cared for (Lawrence, 1992). Thus a feminist model of psychodynamic counselling, such as the Stone Centre, would focus on the relational bonds of mutuality between mother and daughter, with empathy taking into account the empathic sensitivity of the client as well as the counsellor (Jordan, 1997). Dependency is seen as being able to count on the help of others, an empowering rather than a pathological state (Stiver, 1991).

Bocock (1983) provides a useful discussion on the links between Freudian psychology and the sociology of areas such as deviance, the family, gender and sexuality. As social systems are made up of personality systems, sociologists such as Talcott Parsons have been interested in how one influences the other.

Central philosophy

The psychoanalytic approach (see, for example Freud, 1937) has been labelled 'psychic determinism': viewing our actions as determined by inner forces that develop in early childhood. It places great store on a person's early childhood and on early parental relationships, the past influencing the present. Some Freudians go so far as to say the post can even be tyrannical in its influence. The approach can be said to be pathology-based and its formulations can be close to being diagnoses. Faults have developed in early life and they need to be corrected but, since the roots of these faults are buried deep, the therapeutic task is long and arduous, requiring much training and self-analysis. There is a belief that insight can bring about change. The process can be expected to be intrusive and painful; making the client comfortable is not seen as related to effectiveness. There is a solid belief in catharsis, in stages of development, in resistance, in transference and in counter-transference – valuing feelings aroused in the counsellor during therapy.

Undertaking an assessment

Suitability of client/problem

Psychodynamic counselling can be brief (see for example, Malan, 1975), and Jacobs draws a useful distinction between psychodynamic counselling and psychodynamic psychotherapy, the former dealing more with current issues, the latter being longer, slower and deeper. He suggests that *counselling* is indicated if the following client conditions are met: recent onset, clear reason for problem, ability to verbalise thoughts and feelings, relates to at least one person, trusts counsellor, can see their own contribution to the problem, wishes to understand and to change, does not act out, normally functions well, copes with difficult thoughts and feelings. *Psychotherapy* is indicated if: the problems are long-standing, there is no clear reason for the problem, the client is unable to form sound relationships or to trust, is overconcerned about self (narcissistic), wants insight and change, is able to cope with the work with the therapist's support, has bizarre thoughts but recognises this, and can manage daily life.

He would rule out people who cannot express themselves in words, who have no wish to relate to the counsellor, who cannot allow dependency on others, who can only blame others, who want a quick cure, who severely act out, who do not desire change, who are highly dependent on drugs or whose bizarre thoughts dominate or prevent normal functioning. Fundamentally he asks himself: can this person and I work together, will insight be useful to them to make behavioural change, are they presenting an impossible scenario, and are their expectations realistic?

Burton and Suss (2000) write that the Freudian psychodynamic approach works best if the client can discuss the relationship between thought and action (think psychologically). They say it is not so effective if the client cannot relate to the counsellor, or has a fixed view of the world or of themselves; that is, if their own fantasy is primary, the

approach working best when the client can be reflective. They add
that the approach's main benefit may be helping counsellors to have
a framework that is supportive and that allows them more flexibility
of action and more interpretation of their own behaviour.

Segal (2000) maintains the Kleinian psychotherapeutic counselling works best when clients are aware that there is nothing basically wrong with them but they have a difficult situation such as
being a student, being ill, suffering a loss or a marital problem.
Nevertheless they need to acknowledge that there is something in
themselves that needs attention in the situation, for example if they
have tried a new relationship and they are still unhappy perhaps there
is something wrong in their approach to life. It may be indicated
where quick fixes have failed and the client wants some insight or
self-understanding.

Kleinian assessment can include the attitude of the client towards
a treatment contract; motivation; psychological-mindedness; capacity
to sustain relationships; ability to relate to the counsellor in treatment;
and the clarity with which the problem is definable. Clients may be
asked to complete a life-history questionnaire; trial interpretations of
current feelings in terms of past events may be used; and it is necessary to ask what current event has triggered the request for help.

Following Kernberg (1993), Klein (1999) offers the following
criteria:

1 Is there identity confusion – how clear are the boundaries?
2 To what extent is the client in touch with reality? (This could
  apply to any approach.)
3 How much ego strength has the client? (a) to control impulses, (b)
  to tolerate anxiety, (c) to react constructively to frustration.

If the client is good at all three, they are suitable for psychoanalysis; if
the third is low they need 'expressive' counselling; if all three are low
they need supportive counselling.

Based on Fonagy's Adult Attachment Interview (Fonagy, 2001),
Klein also adds:

1 Awareness of own and others' mental states.
2 Capacity to reflect on these.
3 A sense that mental states underlie what people do.
4 Awareness that mental states are affected by early experiences.
5 Aware that counsellors too have feelings.

Others add the possibilities/potential a client presents; difficulties s/he may present; will s/he be too difficult for a particular counsellor?

There is a certain integrity in the psychodynamic search for psychological-mindedness – if the client can't make use of what the counsellor has to offer, they are not 'reeducated'. However, it does mean that many clients whose world views differ from those of psychodynamically-oriented counsellors and, perhaps, those who have internalised this worldview through the dominance of the model, do not have the opportunity to challenge what is essentially a male view of the world – there is not much evidence of psychotherapists referring their clients to feminist psychotherapists. Josephine Klein remarks that when we know what works best for whom, and who is best to provide it, we could avoid taking on all-comers or just guessing who to refer to. This would avoid the waste of energy of suppressing our doubts when we take on whoever comes.

The psychodynamically-orientated counsellors we interviewed would take on most clients but not those who were unstable psychotics, or who were considered to be addicted to drugs or alcohol, or (in publicly funded work at any rate) those for whom there was a more cost-effective alternative. They would work with those who were suicidal or anorexic, but only in collaboration with another professional who would monitor safety. They would also try to assess the possibility of forming a good therapeutic relationship and, finally, try to calculate how long the case would take – the range being between 16 weeks and four years.

The formulation

This is based on a summary of the early history and on what the counsellor hears/learns concerning the developmental stage the client has reached, what defences are operating and what the ego strengths are. There may be a diagnosis of neurosis or psychosis in various degrees. Jacobs (1993) says that he observes and listens for *words* – can the words being used have more than one interpretation? – as well as *moods* and *feelings*, *threads* that run through the story. He listens also to his *own feelings* about the client and their story (as this leads to empathy), and he listens for *reflexive responses* and for *exploratory responses*. He may interpret defences that he encounters, partly to test the client's ability to cope with this kind of work, and he may make observations on possible links between the here and now counselling event/relationship and either the past or other events out there.

Jacobs says this involves keeping an eye on three dimensions and the connections between them: the here and now; the past; and other relationships out there. This process will lead to an assessment (perhaps a written report) on the state of the client and what work may be required. In her work Josephine Klein makes 'one explicit guess' (trial interpretation, perhaps) about an unconscious process that may be operating to give a client an idea of what to expect were she to do the counselling. Others might present the client with a benign welcome and leave defences intact; others avoid being too benign, believing the client should be aware that work will be intrusive and that painful issues may be exposed. These counsellors want to test if the client can cope with 'deep' therapy.

The psychodynamically-oriented counsellors that we interviewed explored carefully any previous treatment or reports; they explored family history, looking for scapegoating, rebellion, expectations, pressures and links between the past and the present. They did not, however, see this as a search for the truth, but rather the beginning of a journey during which they use interpretations to gain, and the client to gain, understanding. We asked if they were looking for an understanding of a cause of the problems, but they put it as looking at 'reasons why', as the 'underpinnings' of the problem, looking for what happened and how that affected the client. They would ask a client for one or two childhood memories that might be significant; use trial interpretations; and try to establish whether the client was strong enough, and sufficiently psychologically-minded, to endure the journey of insight. One said she was seeking to explore how capable the client was of letting go of being destructive to self or others.

Holmes (1995) writes that, for Kleinians, there are two tasks: the taming of aggression and the achievement of emotional object constancy through the construction of whole object relations from part objects. To this end one can classify people as follows:

1 Severe narcissistic – schizoid people who cannot tame aggressive or genital drives, nor escape from splitting. These are the most difficult and are unsuitable for counselling.
2 Moderate narcissistic – people who are promiscuously dominated by part-object relations, treating others as if they were breasts, penises or lavatories. In borderline conditions the object is whole but unstable, and alternatively idealised and denigrated.
3 Neurotic – people who have stable relationships but are genitally inhibited.

4 Mature – people who integrate genitality in a loving relationship and harness aggression while relating to others as whole beings.

Holmes begins an assessment by asking 'what have you been thinking about on the way here?' Then there is an enquiry about the presenting problem 'why have you come here?', also 'why now?' (at this point in time) and a discussion on 'who really wants change?' These 'moves' provide the 'three legs' of the assessment. The conversation covers early memories, dreams and ambitions, and trial interpretations. Then options for treatment are discussed. Holmes listens for ego states, object relations, is the problem based in the self or in a drive, is it oedipal or pre-oedipal, what defences operate – are they primitive (splitting) or immature (acting out), neurotic (obsessionality) or mature (capable of humour)? In Holmes' view, people need to be ill enough to need therapy and healthy enough (not too sick) to cope with it. By 'healthy enough' is meant at least one good relationship, basic trust, one achievement, able to make a working relationship, motivated, able to see self from the outside and to be psychologically accessible. By '*too* sick' is meant: addicted, seriously destructive or self-destructive (poor frustration tolerance), prolonged psychotic breakdown under stress, entrenched somatisation or organic brain disease. Holmes is strong on counter-transference – how the client makes one feel, for example my face hurting could be their grief, my irritation could be their rage, my boredom could be their neglect, but these hunches need to be checked out with the client.

Concerning assessment, Josephine Klein (1999) says that while we counsellors may use 'diagnostic-sounding' terms such as depression or anxiety, in our world we have no sound etiology or reliable treatment: 'The well-analysed and sane assessor identifies something in the transference . . . that guides the treatment' (p. 334). She accepts that we tend to rely on intuition, 'using our unorganised unconscious knowledge in an intuitive rather than systematic kind of way'. While she supports the use of counter-transference, she does not think it should be left at that and she calls for commonly agreed categories of problems and conditions.

She asks whether assessment is about uncovering fantasies (object relations) that work against the person or about finding out if the client can understand a particular approach or cope with it? More fundamental still, is it a diagnostic sort of activity or is it gatekeeping, testing for suitability? We feel it is both of these. Klein adds that each school of thought or approach needs to be clear about how they assess, about how they treat, who they treat best, and about *making recommendations* for the most suitable and effective approach and what clients may expect to gain from a particular approach or counsellor (see outcome research in the previous chapter, that outcomes vary between counsellors even *within* a particular approach).

Advantages and disadvantages

The psychoanalytic approach is rigorous and thorough, standing firm against superficiality and believing in the need for indepth work for those who need it. Its appeal is said to be based on the way it combines mythical themes with scientific metaphors. Some practitioners extemporise by using novel methods that are professionally shared, so that there is lively ongoing debate. The approach offers ways of understanding seemingly irrational behaviour, and insight can empower clients. Sometimes its use can be brief. It helps to create a healthy suspicion of surface behaviour. It has influenced our understanding of the importance of good listening and the avoidance of overdirectiveness.

However, it can be argued that all attempts to theorise the psyche or the subject are themselves 'imaginary fictions' (Elliott, 2002). The postmodern view is that modernity needs to come to terms with its own impossibility and accept that it is debating words rather than worlds. In Colledge's (2002) view, no objective way of studying basic problems of technique exist, so new ways of looking at psychoanalytic interaction are still being developed. The therapy is lengthy and uncertain and has limited application, and is therefore not cost–effective. Freud seemed to want to give his ideas a certain hegemony (he once described himself as a conquistador). Klein likewise does not provide the scientific evidence needed to support her hypotheses and she struggled to address the society in which people live. Interpretations can drive goals and also find what they expect to find.

Outcomes

Outcome studies of the psychodynamic model suggest it is no better than others and no worse overall. Some problems do better with other approaches. McLeod (1998) cites early studies that showed that two-thirds of clients improved and one-third remained the same or deteriorated. Later Eysenck (1952) found that two-thirds of neurotic clients who were *not* treated also improved, demonstrating a need for control groups. Slone *et al.* (1975) compared psychoanalytic work with behavioural work at a psychiatric outpatient clinic ($N = 94$).

Treatment was selected randomly and progress was measured at the end, at one-year follow-up and at two years. Eighty per cent improved and maintained their progress, the key factor being the relationship with the workers. Clients rated the behavioural work as more congruent, empathic and accepting. Both groups beat the control waiting list. Smith *et al.* (1980), in a meta-analysis of outcomes, found no sound evidence that any approach is better than any other.

A recent study by Hilsenroth *et al.* (2001) showed that after nine sessions, while 59 per cent of clients felt some improvement in subjective well-being, only 25 per cent showed reliable improvement in symptomatic distress as measured on the Global Assessment of Relational Functioning (GARF) scale. They report that some rapid improvement happens early in the process and is followed by a 'negatively accelerating positive growth curve' – improvement diminishing as the number of sessions increase. It took six months to a year to get 75 per cent improvement. In the early phase, the subjective experience of well-being precipitated reduction of symptoms.

Summary

This chapter has raised many possible questions that may be in the minds of psychodynamic counsellors during assessment. By way of a summary, we offer the following selective list; it is divided into suitability and formulation headings, but the distinction between these two types is not always clear in practice.

- *Suitability.* These might be the key judgements being made by a psychodynamic counsellor concerning whether to proceed with counselling:

  o Is the client sick enough to need counselling and healthy enough to cope with it?
  o How strong is the client's ego? Is s/he motivated enough?
  o Is s/he sufficiently in touch with reality?
  o Is there addiction to a substance?

- *Formulation.* The counsellor will probably wish to consider these questions:

  o At what stage of personality development is the client?
  o How well is the ego functioning? How rigid is the superego?

- ○ What is the level of narcissism? How does the client respond to interpretations?
- ○ What is the nature of the counter-transference?
- ○ Is the client able to reflect? Is s/he sufficiently psychologically-minded?
- ○ Is s/he able to attend?
- ○ Are the risks manageable?
- ○ Is the client able to pay (if private client)?

5

Transactional Analysis: A 'Games' Map

This chapter forms the second of the theoretical maps belonging to the first wave of counselling practice in that its origins lie in the psychopathology-orientated theory of psychoanalysis. As the term Transactional Analysis (TA) indicates, it is primarily interested in the communication patterns both within and between people. The Freudian structures of id–ego–superego are replaced with the not quite analogous three ego states of parent–adult–child. Concepts of transference, counter-transference and resistance are retained. It provides a comprehensive theoretical framework for counselling that encompasses not only processes between two or more people, but also the relationship between an individual and society over the lifespan. The use of everyday language demystifies Freudian ideas, making TA particularly user-friendly. It is often combined with Gestalt therapy in longer-term counselling but can also be used briefly, Berne (see below) promoting the short-term ideal. The underlying philosophy of TA requires an equal relationship between therapist and client. As clients are considered to have the resources to think about change themselves, they are responsible for the way they live their lives. Thus the counsellor's role is to educate the client to use the therapeutic process profitably and confront the client when their share of therapeutic responsibility is not taken up (Cox, 2000).

Transactional analysis was developed by Berne (see, for example, 1964, 1978) and others such as Harris (1973, 1986). While it was theoretically founded in psychoanalytic thinking, it developed a more humanistic philosophy. It can be seen as part of the human-potential movement that grew out of critiques of the two main previous approaches to psychopathology; namely psychoanalysis and behaviourism. The former began to be seen as overly structuralist, with too much emphasis on the determining power of early experiences;

whilst the latter came to be seen by many as overly concerned with scientific (often laboratory-based) study, to the neglect of real people's thoughts and feelings. Like other humanistic approaches (see particularly Chapter 7), TA sees people as responsible and capable of growth to maturity as caring loving people with fulfilled lives and a system of values. To some extent, psychoanalysis and behaviourism viewed people as machines (see McLeod, 1998), whereas this approach begins to see them as social beings who interact, playing a range of *games* with each other, hence the title of Berne's 1964 book, *Games People Play*. It pays great attention therefore to the relationships between family members and the client and between significant others, especially the counsellor, and the client, seeking to bring about not only behavioural change but also more basic relational change. Reflecting Freud's ideas of superego, ego and id, TA describes *interactions* between people as taking place between the Parent (superego), or the Adult (ego) or the Child (id) of one person and the Parent, or the Adult or the Child of another. Harris (1973), and later Berne (1978), developed the idea of transactional analysis to look at relationships and habitual patterns of interaction between people.

Hayes (2000) states that the main concept in TA is that of *ego-states*. Jacobs (1999) says that the model describes the related behaviours, thoughts and feelings that are manifested in one's personality and that have both internal and external functions, while Steward and Joines (1999) stress how the interacting states are constantly overriding each other in positive and negative ways. To help counsellors and their clients address this, Berne and others have developed the *language of TA* to enable counsellors to feed back to clients what they do and say. As various sports have words that enable communication about behaviours, skills and emotional aspects of the play, TA has a language for the successful and less successful elements of living and for talking about the behaviours and emotions involved. This originated with a successful lawyer who was being treated by Berne saying that sometimes he felt like a little boy, asking 'Are you talking to the lawyer or the little boy?'

If appropriate, the client is taught the use of TA language, and thus TA can sometimes feel more like a teaching and learning event rather than the confessional or the deep explorations of the psychoanalytic approach. It provides clients with a tool from which they can benefit. For Berne, the language required to discuss the psychic conflicts uncovered by Freud appeared to be beyond the grasp of most clients, and, secondly, he wanted to discuss what was happening when one person did something to another and the other did something back. TA provides a fairly simple language for doing this, and in the remainder of this chapter we will look at the concepts and terms used in this language. We will return to transactions later in this chapter, but first we explore the ego states more fully.

Structural analysis

We now consider in turn the three ego states, followed by some points concerning how they can be contaminated.

Parent

This is the file in the 'computer' (the brain) of 'unquestioned and imposed' internal and external events and pronouncements by parental figures perceived during a child's first five years or so (Harris, 1973, p. 18). The data are raw and unedited since the child was unable to modify or correct the content. Events and the *feelings* they produced are inextricably linked to each other in the memory; fights are recorded along with the terror they produced; rules and admonitions, dos and don'ts, are stored in the Parent file, as well as praise and delight. These rules are recorded as 'truths' and this recording can never be erased; therefore it is available for replay at any time. We can, however, decide to turn off the recording when it is oppressing us. The recordings in the Parent include inconsistencies – for example, 'do as I say, not as I do' – and these inconsistencies can have the effect of blocking out the Parent or of weakening the Parent so that its positive aspects are lost or reduced.

Child

While external events are being recorded in the Parent file, the Child file is recording internal events, experiences, responses and feelings – mainly feelings. When a three-year-old sees a sour look, it produces feelings, not interpretation; feelings such as 'it's my fault, it always is'. 'Civilising' demands cause frustration and feelings of being not OK. This is part of the life of any child, even those with the most kindly of parents. The Child file also records positive data, such as rewarding experiences and positive *strokes*, but TA maintains that negative feelings often predominate in the Child and therefore we all have a 'not-OK Child' in need of more strokes. The Child is a get-love creature, but so long as their parents are good enough, children can grow and stay afloat.

Adult

Until about the age of 10 months, life is full of unthinking responses to the demands of being, but then a person begins to make choices and to manipulate the surroundings, rather than just taking what comes. This is the start of self-feeding actions, deliberate movements and a hint of self-determination. As a baby starts to find out things for him/herself, the first fragile bits of Adult are acquired, although this is easily 'knocked for six' when someone shouts 'No'. Yet as more and more pieces of information are assimilated, the Adult gradually strengthens. Gradually the little person can distinguish between life as taught (Parent), life as felt and wished (Child) and life as figured out by self (Adult). Importantly, the data in all three files are never erased and so all three live together, interacting at various times with the Parent, Adult and Child of other people. As the Adult matures, however, it will be able to *switch off* the playing of the other two recordings, at least sometimes. The Adult can be a give-love creature; an enabler in that the Adult can be seen as the lawyer, often defending the Child from the accusations of the Parent in the courtroom of life. Most commonly, the Parent says 'you ought to', the Child says 'I want to', the Adult thinks 'how to'. Put another way, the Parent asks 'can I', the Child asks 'do I want to', the Adult asks 'will I'.

Harris, (1973, p. 18) claims that 'These states are not roles but 'psychological realities'; dependent on situations, we can be more in one state than another. Changes from one ego state to another are seen not only in what people say, but also in behaviour and appearance and in changes of voice and attitude. In the TA approach, problems can also be rooted in the inner structure of one's ego states that are subject to *contamination*.

Contaminations

Not all our Parent, Adult, Child (PAC) ego states are equal. In some people there is Parent contamination (of the Adult) when the Adult is holding to unreasonable, taught ideas, such as a strong prejudice against a certain group. This may be accompanied by a *blocked-off* Child, making it difficult for the person to play, have fun or 'let their hair down'. Others have a weak or blocked Parent, and perhaps an

Adult that is contaminated by their Child. Child contamination of the Adult is when feelings from the Child are being inappropriately externalised/exhibited in the Adult, for example as delusions. This may be accompanied by a blocked-off Parent, leaving a risk of a weakened conscience, a low sense of guilt or responsibility, and a lack of social control, remorse or embarrassment, plus a tendency to manipulate others for their own ends. Harris describes a psychotic person as one with a blocked-out Adult, at the mercy of Parent and Child who appear in 'a jumbled replay of early experiences that do not make sense now because they did not make sense when they were recorded' (Harris,1973, p. 101). The Parent can have A and C elements; the Child can have P and A elements, for example the 'little professor' A in a Child. The boundaries of P, A and C are fragile and trauma can throw them into confusion. Figure 5.1 may help to clarify the types of Parent or Child that can develop.

Harris (1973) further expands the Parent–Adult–Child metaphor to describe a manic person as one who's Parent is applauding the Child, and a depressed person as one whose Parent is 'beating on the Child' (p. 105). In both of these, there is Parent–Child contamination, and Harris suggests that such people are probably brought up 'under the shadow of great inconsistency' (p. 105).

It may help at this point to recap and show an ego-gram of a particular service-user, Miss O, aged 70, based on the work of Berne (1978) (Figure 5.2). This can be seen as a graph of the family 'within' Miss O, who had become quite depressed when relatives were 'nasty' towards her because she would not give them a loan. It is based on conversations with her, listening to her memories of her responsibilities as the eldest child, her impressions of her parents as strict and stern, and her assessment of herself as being afraid to have fun but planning little deceptions to help her cope.

Her Parent is therefore represented as highly critical and not very nurturing. What nurturing there is to more rescuing than encouraging. Her Child, on the other hand, is not very free, being fearful of the critical Parent. It is, however, fairly well-adapted, meaning that it has found a good deal of (possibly 'naughty') ways of making do. Meanwhile, her Adult (ego) is reasonably strong, but she still has some growing to do. The critical Parent and the adapted Child are both difficult to manage. Much depends on what level of stress is caused by the world, especially the world of relationships. If this proves to be too bleak and stormy a place, this ego will need quite a lot of support and luck. This example illustrates the power of TA to view relationship

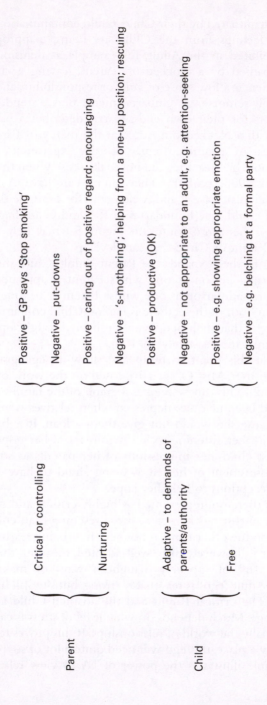

Figure 5.1 Parent and child types

Parent
(superego)
{ Critical – positive: negative

  Nurturing – encouraging: rescuing

+	–

E	R

Adult
(ego)   ....

Child
(id)
{ Free – positive: negative ......

  Adapted – positive: negative

+	–

+	–

Figure 5.2 An ego-gram

patterns across the lifespan and the limitless potential of people to change and develop.

Transactional analysis

Social interaction is seen as made up of units called *interactions* between the ego states of two or more people, and these are probably best set out in the traditional diagrammatic manner as in Figure 5.3.

If a person A is being irresponsible, sulky or childish, this behaviour is likely to *hook* the Parent of person B. This transaction is shown by the line *x*, and *y* is a complementary reaction from B; it is expected and appropriate. So, too, Parental behaviour by person A can hook the Child in person B, causing a sulk, for example. Other obviously complementary interactions are Parent–Parent, Adult–Adult and Child–Child. However, if the transactions are *crossed*, there can be trouble, for example if A's Adult addresses B's Adult, but B's response is from B's Parent (telling A off, perhaps), as shown by lines *p* and *q*.

For Berne (1978), the transaction, 'the unit of social intercourse', is the key unit of study. Transactions will vary depending, for example, on whether the client is relating to her counsellor, to a partner, to a friend or to her own children. In some situations, she may find that she may need to be helped to practise using her reasonable, reasoning, grown-up Adult more. If practice makes no difference, she may need to be encouraged to get in touch with feelings from the past that, because they are presently out of consciousness, are dominant in

Person A   **Person B**

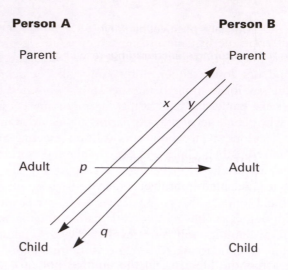

Figure 5.3 Transactions

certain circumstances. Events and people in our lives can hook our Parent or our Child, which can appear to 'take over' for a while. Berne further developed notions of 'life scripts', laid down in childhood and often followed later.

Scripts

Penfield (1952) demonstrated that all past experiences are stored in the brain's computer-like memory, along with their associated feelings, even if the person is unable to recall either. The term *script* refers to how life patterns are recorded (written into the mind) in childhood, and is probably the second most important concept in TA. The plan for life is laid down by the child – it is specific to the person, not just a general world view. When we act out the plan we are unaware that we are making choices that bring us to the conclusion in the script. Scripts are pushed underground, influencing present behaviour and relationships. They lead to automatic unhelpful behaviours; not realising that the feelings and behaviours are coming from the P or the C creates an illusion of autonomy, whereas a person needs to break out of them to be able to act autonomously. The aim of TA counselling is to help the Adult to resume the executive role, without being script-bound – that is, capable of autonomous, spontaneous and intimate functioning.

A person can have a winning script, a losing script or a non-winning script; the first means one achieves one's goals, the second means one does not, while the third person plods along, not winning much and not losing either, not taking risks, or achieving in an unhelpful way, for example being successful in business but having a heart attack. Understanding scripts is important because it helps explain why people act as they do. Scripts are recorded in infancy and include decisions made about survival and meeting needs. When people grow up, their Child seeks to arrange the world so that their decisions are justified; furthering and supporting the script. 'We attempt to meet adult problems by re-playing infant strategies' (Stewart and Joines, 1987, p. 113). Parent scripts will usually include injunctions such as 'be good', 'work hard', 'don't make mistakes'. Successful parenting will also involve giving *permissions,* that is permissions to exist, to ask, to be close. Both injunctions and permissions may be 'heard', not only via the ears but also via feelings, behaviours and non-verbal communications. Breaking injunctions leads to physical discomfort/sensations such as sweating. Scripts have characteristic processes, particularly drivers and injunctions.

Drivers, injunctions and permissions

Drivers are a part of scripts that particularly push people to do even better – be perfect, please, try hard, be strong, hurry up. While we all have these, individuals usually have one dominant driver, called the *primary driver*, which fulfils the function of making a person feel 'I'm OK if I do this . . .'.

Injunctions are the reverse of drivers in that they are mainly negative. Stewart and Joines (1987) list 12 injunctions: don't be (don't exist); don't be you; don't be a child; don't grow up; don't make it; don't be important; don't belong; don't be close; don't be well; don't think; don't feel; don't (don't do anything). Injunctions can lead to decisions; for example, 'don't exist' can lead to suicide or a fatal accident.

Script processes have been grouped into six patterns: Until (I can't relax until I finish this book); After (if I have fun today I'll have to pay afterwards); Never (I will never get it right); Always (It always happens to us); Almost (I did it except for . . .); and Open-ended (I've got the job I wanted, so now what?). In TA therapy, clients' attention is drawn to script patterns, with a sense of proportion and rationality. This is achieved not by replacing injunctions with drivers, but by providing permissions. *Drivers* and *injunctions* could be said to ignore the agency of the recipient and the co-creative nature of parent–child relationships; whereas the notion of *permissions* acknowledges personal responsibility and competencies. Its power is reflected in the frequency with which permissions are found in children's stories such as Harry Potter: I can do it; we can rely on friends; I don't need to be able to do it all myself; do what you believe in; we need to take risks; I will be recognised; the underdog can triumph; we have hidden strengths; you can find what you need; be a real person; it's OK to change; have faith in the process.

Stamps

When we store away feelings, we are said in TA to be saving *stamps* that can be cashed in later. If someone upsets us we can show no emotion at the time, but store up anger for more satisfying use later because this may help to move us towards our script pay-off.

Strokes and discounting

Strokes is the TA term for rewards or reinforcers, mainly verbal, which may be included in everyday interactions. A smile is a common non-verbal stroke. Strokes may be positive (pleasant) or negative (painful), conditional or unconditional. Conditional strokes relate to what one does; unconditional strokes relate to what one is; for example a positive conditional stroke is 'Good job done'; a negative conditional stroke is 'You wear awful shirts'. A positive unconditional stroke is 'You are good to have around'; a negative unconditional stroke is 'I hate you'. Steiner (1971) says children learn unhelpful stroking rules, such as; don't give strokes when you have them; don't give strokes to yourself; don't ask for strokes when you need them. The idea of strokes has been explained in terms children can understand by using terms like 'warm fuzzies' and 'cold pricklies'. People's stroke patterns influence how they think positively or negatively about themselves and others, the life positions they have developed. Counsellors, of course, are expected to have positive stroke patterns, to be straight A–A.

Discounting refers to exchanges where a person is ignored or devalued in some way by self and others. Children feel discounted when their parents do not reply to their questions or calls for attention, but this happens between adults too. For example, A asks B how his holiday went. B gives a long boring account during which A is distracted by his own inner dialogue such as: 'I wish I had not asked', and his Parent says 'You should listen to your neighbour', and his Child responds 'I want to get away from this'. Meanwhile B has said something that expects a sympathetic response and A has not heard it. B feels discounted. Discounting leads to low self-esteem and feelings such as 'I have no right to ask'. Discounts differ from negative strokes in that they usually start with 'you': 'You are hateful'. A negative unconditional stroke, however, starts with 'I': 'I hate you'. Both are aggressive but the discount more so. Because discounting involves some distortion of reality, it can be expressed as grandiosity – put-downs and exaggerations, or as passive behaviours, doing nothing, overadapting, agitation and incapacitation (violence directed inwards, being ill, for example) or violence (kicking walls). Discounts can indicate script themes such as: 'That's life' (one gets nowhere); 'No good crying over spilt milk' (a 'Be Strong' driver, or 'Don't feel' injunction); 'can't win 'em all' (Try hard – don't succeed).

Life positions

Four possible life positions are described (Harris, 1973):

1 I'm not OK; You're OK. This is the basic position of early childhood, at the mercy of others and needing strokes from them.
2 I'm not OK; You're not OK. This is the position of the child who did not get strokes, feels abandoned and gives up trying, and stops using the Adult in relationships.
3 I'm OK; You're not OK. This can be the position, for example, of the abused child, I'm OK if you leave me alone. This person may feel all others are not OK and deserve no respect. This position is taken to protect self from others, but it can lead to criminal attitudes towards others, particularly where the person feels they have been 'dissed' (jargon for discounted/disrespected).
4 I'm OK: You're OK. The Adult position, consciously taken, based on thought and not expecting instant joy. The other positions are not consciously taken; they are based on feelings.

However, the experience of strong feelings warns us (our Adult) that the Child has been hooked, enabling the Adult to use restraint, take a breath and count to 10, rather than automatically responding out of the emotion.

For Stewart and Joines (1987) the aim of TA is to expose the childhood predicament that underlies the first three positions and show
how current behaviours perpetuate these positions. It promotes freedom of choice and especially the freedom to change, which is often
lost in childhood leading to neuroses. It seeks to help people to 'sort
themselves out' by asking 'who is reacting?', separating P and C from
A, in an internal dialogue. It is A (the Adult) who works out one's
system of values, how to conduct relationships, estimate consequences
and defer gratification. The OK person can commit to being loving,
caring, responsible, whereas the not OK person reproduces archaic
behaviours expressed in TA terms as Games and Rackets.

Games and rackets

The most common way of dealing with life in the first three positions
is by *playing games*. According to Berne (1964, p. 48) a game is a series
of ongoing complementary ulterior transactions designed to achieve
a predictable outcome; whilst superficially plausible, they have a
concealed motivation and conceal a snare for others. Games may be
played to justify a life position. Nelson-Jones (1995) says that TA is a
way of removing obstacles to emotional and mental development,
and therefore, because games are often employed to justify a life position and win strokes or pay-offs, one needs to find more satisfying
ways to get strokes. Harris describes these processes as being 'a misery-
producing solution which compounds the original misery and
confirms the NOT OK' (1973, p. 50). Games may have a pay-off and
win strokes, but these strokes need to be acquired in more satisfactory
ways because 'games always entail an exchange of discounts, at a
psychological level' (Stewart and Joines, 1987, p. 92), and 'a discount
always entails some distortion of reality' (*ibid.*, p. 85).

As a psychological game is played by a set of rules and has a
predictable structure, games are repetitive and played without awareness. They involve ulterior transactions and frequently a moment of
confusion or surprise. The Drama Triangle is a common way of thinking about games – it suggests that people take a 'persecutor', 'victim'
or 'rescuer' position. These are not authentic roles, in that they consist
of responses to the past rather than the present. Thus they involve
using outdated strategies to get what we want; that is, strokes and the
resulting survival. In TA counselling, games need to be named,
brought to consciousness so that the person can find alternatives or
learn to play them better.

Games are distinguished from pastimes. Pastimes are ways of passing time in which transactions are straightforward and often organised in some way. They can be used to ward off emotions such as guilt or fear or they can simply be for enjoyment. In TA, however, games are another matter. Most games cause trouble, wreck relationships. The essence of most games is 'I am better than you', or 'mine is bigger than yours'. Although they do have a pay-off, they are better than no relationship at all. Therefore they are often played by those whose not–OK position makes a close relationship impossible. Berne describes about three dozen games, among them: 'Why don't you?'; 'Yes but'; 'Ain't it awful'; 'If it weren't for you I could'; 'It's all them'; 'Kick me'; 'Let's you and him fight'; 'Nobody knows the trouble I've seen'; 'Poor me'; 'Try and catch me'; 'Uproar' (a shouting match over something as trivial as a lost can-opener). Game-calling can be aggressive and offensive – 'You are playing a game here' can cause anger, but in the context of PAC analysis, games analysis or discussion can help insight into relationships and how our behaviour impedes them. Games leave people feeling bad as they are re-runs of strategies from childhood that are no longer appropriate/useful to adults.

Stewart and Joines (1987) define a racket as a set of script behaviours employed outside of awareness as a means of manipulating the environment; it usually leads to a required feeling, known as a racket feeling. Expression of racket feelings does not aid problem-solving, whereas expression of authentic feelings such as sadness, anger or fear can do so.

When is TA counselling needed?

Harris makes a distinction between a sprain and a broken leg. The former impairs us and treatment may make recovery easier; the latter cripples us and we need at least supports for a while. We may be impaired by old programmes but we can manage, although some counselling may make it easier; however, if our Adult cannot function, for example because of overwhelming guilt, we need help because we may be unable to do our work, cope with children or we may behave inappropriately. TA can be effective in 'sorting out' the data that we experience and finding the data we need to make decisions. This involves being able to avoid the transfer of feelings from childhood. Success is shown when the client no longer fears the counsellor's Parent and is able to talk without selecting what is safe to reveal (resistance), that is, they can relate on equal terms with the counsellor as two adults. Goldberg (1992) maintains that it is the TA counsellor's role to confront the client, even where they appear fragile, as it is important for clients to learn to take charge of the cathexis of their ego states at will (Adult social control). When the client is hindered by feelings, these are discussed directly, using the PAC metaphors, such as *hooks*; Adult to Adult interpretations of the interaction are made.

How much counselling is needed? Harris suggests that the length of treatment is determined as much by client expectations as anything else, and we can affect these expectations by keeping contracts brief and by speaking of the time restriction as a challenge during which 'we will see how far we can get'. Our understanding is that most TA counsellors work in an open-ended way, unless there is some external limit to the number of sessions.

What about motivation?

In TA this is seen as beginning with wanting. Others may want the client to change, but motivation has to come from the client and Harris and Harris (1986) maintain that three things make people want to change: pain, boredom and enlightenment. Pain can be the agony of beating one's head against a brick wall, hitting bottom or feeling this has to stop. Boredom may say, 'is this life – there has to be more to it – I want to do something about it'. Enlightenment comes to those who discover they *can* change. It may come from reading or discussions that open up new possibilities and get them thinking. It is important to note that since realising that they can change is part of motivation, those who first seem to not be enlightened in this way may have their motivation improved by the work of the counsellor in the opening sessions.

Motivation may be positive or negative. It is positive when it wants to *do* something; it is negative when it wants to *stop* doing something. Positive motivation is seen as stronger than negative; those who want to *quit* a habit do less well than those who want to *start* a new behaviour. Likewise, those who are tuned into Parent and trying to rebel against its expectations often struggle because their goal is dominated by the old programme. Freedom and maturity comes when our Adult does what is good for us, even if our Parent also wants us to do so. This does not say the Adult cannot be helped by the Child; motivation can be strengthened by listening to the Child and asking 'how will it feel when I do that?' Change is more likely if there is something in it for the Child in us.

The best change usually happens a little at a time, and slowly. Therefore it can help to consider not only 'what difference do I want?', but also 'how far do I want to go, what are the gains and losses and what will I be *doing* differently'. It may be useful to ask 'who wants the want?' – it may be Parent, Adult or Child. If the Child wants it, it may not be good for us; if the Parent wants it, it may cause fear in the Child and that is not the best of motivations, even though it can preserve life in certain situations. Ideally, the Adult needs to want the goal, since it is the Adult who works out the 'how to'. Wants can have contradictory consequences, for example children want security and novelty/excitement. For those who may say 'I can't afford it' or 'I have no friends to do it with', four types of wants have been set out by Harris and Harris (1986): things we can do alone and cost nothing; things we can do alone that cost something; things we can do with others that cost nothing, and things we can do with others that cost something. 'Possibility lies in specifics' (Harris and Harris, 1986, p.159).

Application to assessment

Suitability

Our view is that since TA is essentially an *educational* process (for a therapeutic effect), perhaps the main criteria for suitability is the ability of the client to learn the PAC theory, or ways of looking at self and at one's relationships with others. The more common view is that it is a therapeutic process during which the TA language is taught only if it is appropriate to the client. Questions at this stage include:

• Does the prospective client want to be different?
• What is the goal? Is it measurable?
• Which 'part' (or ego state) wants the goal?
• How far do they want to go?
• Are they able to consider the losses as well as the gains?

Other questions considered at the assessment stage include:

• Do they have a sufficiently strong Adult who can be helped to withstand their Parent and/or Child ?
• Can I provide what they want?

- What do I want? Can I have an OK–OK position with them?
- Can they commit to a contract – Adult to Adult?
- Do they have sufficient integration to accept and cope with challenges?
- Do they have the ability and willingness to reflect on their own inner process?
- Is the goal positive and legal?

Stewart (1989) asks all the usual questions at intake – address, GP, and so on, with much emphasis on health matters, physical and mental. In addition he considers what he calls 'the three Ps':

- Protection – any risk of harm to anyone concerned?
- Permission – in the TA sense of inner permissions to change or proceed with the work, in the case of both client and counsellor.
- Potency – the ability of the counsellor to work with a particular prospective client and their type of problem.

There were three counsellors among our respondents who saw themselves as predominantly TA in orientation, and this is reflected in how they would make decisions about which clients to accept. One would not continue to work with those who would not take safety measures when necessary, and those who are unable to grasp the idea of counselling. Another would not take those who are not willing to share responsibility for the process or those who, due to the degree of risk, need a greater level of support and structure. Another looked for sufficient ego strengths and psychological-mindedness, and the client to be not heading for a psychotic breakdown, not violent, nor failing to respect boundaries, nor playing games over the fees, although some felt that this issue can be dealt with in the therapeutic process. They would all collect basic background data and health data. One would listen for how clients identify their problems; another would consider 'why now?' and 'is this due to an earlier decision?'

A typical assessment would start with transactions, stroking patterns, rackets, games and drivers, and discounting:

- Identify the client's preferred frame of reference (thinking, feeling behaviours);
- Ask how they might sabotage therapy;
- Look at decontamination;
- Help the client find alternatives to rackets and games;

- Confront the client to move them on;
- Creatively devise relevant activities outside the treatment session. The counsellor would look at strengths, scripts and so on later, on the grounds that it is obvious early on when a client is playing a game.

Formulation

Formulations will develop as the work proceeds, and further discussion and insights about the interplay of P, A and C move on: does the Adult want the goal, what is in it for the Child, and so on?

- Client pathology can be seen as their best attempt to get wholeness – so what is lacking?
- What are the precipitating factors? What is the PAC structure? Are transactions crossed?
- What is the predominant life position?
- What are their stroking patterns?
- What scripts or overall preferred modes of action are evident?
- What drivers do I notice? What discounting is being revealed?
- Strengthening the Adult – can the client work on separating the past from the present?
- Can they cope with challenges?
- Deconfusing the Child – what does helping their Child get in touch with unmet needs require?
- Can they examine their original decision?
- Can they question their current course in life? What are its advantages/disadvantages?
- What do they need in order to make a new decision?
- What support will they need when they 'redecide'?

Ego-grams may be constructed and discussed. Centrally, the relationship with the counsellor will be analysed in PAC-to-PAC terms, and progress will we measured by how much of the interaction is A to A:

- What stroke economy is reflected in their presentation?
- What is their main ego-state, P, A or C?
- How much A is available?
- What are the most common games being used?
- What are their favourite rackets?

- What are the main script injunctions?
- What are their main passive behaviours?

Of our interviewees, one would write a formulation addressing the client's past decisions, ego states and their contamination, as well as the client's view about how things went wrong. Another would formulate a joint understanding of the situation and why now, what is in the client's script, and any indicators of risk, while yet another would maintain ongoing reflection about what is happening with the client.

Stewart and Joines (1987) say that since the basis of TA is ego-states – Critical Parent/Nurturing Parent/Adult/Free Child/Adapted Child – a behavioural assessment involves observing and listening for words, gestures, postures and facial expressions and *grouping the clues under those five ego states* CP, NP, A, FC and A. Historical clues can be collected via questions about how the client was as a child. In addition, structural information about contamination of the Parent or the Child needs to be noticed, and transactions, whether complementary, crossed or ulterior, need to be noted. The giving and receiving of strokes need to be assessed as positive or negative, conditional or unconditional. They suggest a stroking profile, listing the *frequency* of giving, receiving, asking for and refusing to give both positive and negative strokes.

Ongoing assessment

- Reevaluate in the light of the original goals.
- Re-contract if appropriate.
- Continually challenge games; resist invitations to play games or join rackets.
- Reflect and question in support of the decontamination process.
- Consider homework tasks.
- Reevaluate the therapeutic relationship.

Among our respondents, one would be reflecting on how the client is coping with counselling, their ego strengths and their motivation, their supports and risks. Another would refine hypotheses in an ongoing way, and another would be continually assessing and tweaking her ideas when necessary.

Advantages and disadvantages

While its underlying theory is Freudian, transactional analysis has a more cognitive feel in that it seeks to educate adult-to-adult and, in a sense, it engages people in working with a teacher rather than a healer, although it can be and is used therapeutically. Many clients like its user-friendly style and are able to distinguish between the three states of PAC. TA does not require a training analysis of counsellors and it can be taught, and indeed is taught, on many counselling courses.

Hutnik (2001) shows that TA can be usefully employed to examine issues of difference between client and counsellor, particularly race and culture. She writes that 'TA has the technology and the language available to cater for the needs of minority group members who present as clients . . . TA is acceptable to even the most poor rural situations' (p. 17). She believes it can help to avoid pathologising what is normal in a particular culture. Stewart and Joines (1987) also comment that TA has a wide application from single problems to deeper relationship problems, and even some kinds of psychoses.

McLeod (1998), however, suggests that although TA is conceptually rich, this can be a weakness as some counsellors and clients allow themselves to get wrapped up in talking about problems rather than resolving them. He also adds that TA has not been associated with any major innovations in therapeutic technique, and this may be why so many TA counsellors borrow techniques from other models of counselling. The potential pitfalls of this practice are discussed further in the chapter on integrated approaches. Also, the cognitive nature of TA is a handicap to some counsellors; one of our respondents had abandoned TA as a preferred model of counselling on the grounds that:

> there's more to me than the head [indicates his heart], this thing pumps the blood round . . . and gut instinct. So I moved away from TA, did some Gestalt training that's pulled me back into thinking about those other parts, emotions, instincts. That's given me a more rounded approach.

TA's research base is also poor.

Outcomes

Because we were unable to find any studies of the effectiveness of TA, we contacted the Institute of Transactional Analysis (ITA). They are not aware of any substantial outcome study of TA, which is unfortunate and surprising considering its fairly wide use over the past 30 years. However, the ITA is currently supporting a research project to explore the efficacy of TA, although the project is not expected to report for several years. It has been found that there is great difficulty in finding cases that have been treated with only a single model of counselling, such is the growth of eclectic versions.

Summary

The focus of TA is on here-and-now behaviour and processes within the therapeutic situation and outside it. It is cognitive in nature, seeking to establish the predominance of reality through testing ego-states and to help clients take control of their symptoms and their social life as they recognise their interactions and change their behaviour. Berne claimed that the five key words of its specialised vocabulary are Parent, Adult, Child, Script and Games. It has more of an emphasis on actions and behavioural outcomes. It is accessible to most people and can be used in brief therapy. Its philosophy is humanistic despite being rooted in Freud's medicalised model. Some current teachers of the approach stress its cognitive components, seeing unhelpful behaviours and thinking habits as learned.

6

Cognitive Approaches: Handy Road Maps

This chapter will discuss some of the cognitive approaches to counselling and assessment, principally the cognitive behavioural therapy (CBT) of Beck (1967, 1989 and 1997), and the rational emotive therapy (RET) of Ellis (1962, 1998, 2001). The lifeskills approach of Nelson-Jones (1993) will also be briefly discussed. We describe these approaches as handy road maps because they are interested in clear goals towards which the therapist hopes to travel with the client, and also because of their accessibility and transparency and their potential for use in self-help. The core theory is clear and capable of being understood and used by clients. Users of such approaches say they need to understand the problem; it can therefore be said to be problem-oriented, taking an information-processing approach to the client on the principle that the way in which people *interpret* their experiences determines how they feel and act, how they become disturbed. Although startling to the world of psychoanalysis in the 1950s, this is not a particularly new idea; Dryden (1990) quotes the Roman philosopher Epictetus as saying that men are disturbed not by things but by their *views* of things. The move away from emotion and into cognition places this approach in the second wave of theory.

The main goal of the counsellor involves helping the client develop new and more helpful ways of thinking and behaving with a view to feeling better. There is no analysis of unconscious processes in the cognitive therapies, only an analysis of what people say to themselves about their situations and the reasoning/perceptions/beliefs, implicit or explicit, involved in such self-talk or thinking/cognitions. The work is 'cognitive' in that is focuses on the person's ability to think, rather than on their underlying feelings. Clients identify their own goals, then engage in a learning process aimed first at symptom relief and then the removal of systematic biases in their thought patterns. The key learning processes are:

- monitoring negative automatic thoughts;
- recognising the connections between cognition, affect and behaviour;
- examining and reality-testing evidence for and against distorted automatic thoughts;
- substituting more realistic interpretations for biased cognitions;
- identifying and changing any beliefs that cause clients to distort their experiences (Colledge, 2002, pp. 180–2).

Cognitive-behavioural therapy (CBT)

Cognitive-behavioural work is based on both behavioural psychology and cognitive psychology. Behavioural psychology regards problematic behaviour as *learned*, or acquired, and therefore capable of being unlearned or replaced by learning non-problematic behaviour. There are several types of 'learning', principally classical conditioning, operant conditioning, and social or vicarious learning (copying other people's behaviour). In *classical conditioning* we learn by association; for example, we learn to fear objects or events associated with unpleasant past experiences – these phobias are treated mainly by gradually exposing the person to the feared object until they learn there is no need to be afraid. In *operant conditioning*, behaviour is learned because it is reinforced in some way by the consequence of the behaviour – by the 'pay-off'. Behaviours are said to have antecedents (A), followed by the behaviour (B), followed by the consequence (C). When the consequence is rewarding, the behaviour is strengthened; that is, it is more likely to be repeated. When this approach is used, the antecedent may be addressed, for example by removing sweets from checkouts so that children will not pester for them. Or, more commonly the consequences may be addressed, perhaps by putting rewards in place immediately after new desirable behaviour until the new behaviour replaces the unwanted behaviour. McLeod (1998) reminds us that behavioural work studies observable processes rather than the unconscious – it is concerned with stimuli and responses.

For many years, however, psychologists have been exploring the role of *thinking patterns* in causing or influencing behaviours, especially moods such as feeling depressed or anxious. A history of this movement is to be found in Ellis (1962). Gradually, *thinking* came to be seen as a form of behaviour, a habit, that could be learned, reinforced or unlearned. Hence the name cognitive behaviour – it involves learning to change the way a person interprets or views life and its events. Early research by Ellis (1962), Beck (1967) and Beck and Tomlin (1989) showed that depressed people saw themselves as 'losers', as doomed to frustration, deprivation, failure and inadequacy. Experiments also showed that there was a marked difference between depressed people's self-evaluations and their actual achievements, showing that depressed people's thinking about themselves, their environment and their future was not only negative and pessimistic, but also inaccurate. Tests were done to see whether changes would occur in their moods, motivation and relationships when this sort of thinking was changed, and it was found that mood changed considerably; people learned how to control mood when they changed self-defeating thinking for more helpful thoughts. Burns (1992) worked with Beck and others at the University of Pennsylvania, exploring how the brain controls the levels of chemicals associated with depression. This work strengthened Beck's thesis that when a person is depressed their thoughts are less logical, more negative, more maladaptive and more self-defeating, *but* this can be corrected by straightening out 'twisted thought patterns' (Burns, 1992, p. 4), and can be done fairly quickly by simple straightforward means. In controlled experiments, these means were found to be more effective than the best drug treatments then available (Rush, Beck, Kovacs and Hollon, 1977): 'Cognitive therapy showed itself to be substantially superior to antidepressant drug therapy in all respects' (Burns, 1992, p. 14). The treatments lasted 12 weeks. A minority of clients (one in 19) did not improve, and the greatest efficacy was found when cognitive therapy was combined with drugs. In a one-year follow-up, while some clients had had occasional mood swings, on the whole both groups continued to maintain earlier gains. In follow-up, the relapse rate in the cognitive-behaviour group was less than half that in the group treated by drugs only.

The first principle of this approach is that moods are not only accompanied by unhelpful thoughts but are caused by them, that we feel as we do because of cognitions, that is the thoughts, beliefs, perceptions, mental attitudes and interpretations we have about things and one's self. Thoughts create emotions in the following ways:

- Sadness is felt when individuals fail to reach a positive goal, experience loss of status or someone close, or fail to realise their expectations. It

is common for people in such situations to withdraw their energy
and commitment from the cause of their disappointment.

• Joy is felt when we experience a gain, such as achieving a cherished
  aim. It can also result from expressions of affection.
• Anxiety can be caused by a threat or a perceived threat. It can lead
  to withdrawal or appeasement as it focuses attention on physical
  danger and emotional vulnerability.
• Anger can be caused by the offensive qualities of a threat and may
  lead to counterattack and/or aggressive self-defensive behaviour
  (Colledge, 2002, pp. 173–4).

   Secondly, when we are depressed our thoughts are dominated by
pervasive negativity. We believe that things are as bad as we imagine
them to be and that they always will be so – the future is bleak and
hopeless. The third principle is that these negative thoughts always
contain gross distortions in that they are not based on accurate
perceptions of reality. Cognitive distortions include: devaluation of
the self for falling short of personal standards; emphasis on negative
aspects of life; generalising specific deficiencies into pervasive ones;
self-attribution of responsibility for problems in all situations; and a
belief that problems cannot be removed. On the other hand, as we
begin to think more objectively we begin to feel better.

   Beck argued that people have individual 'schema' (cognitive structures) that organise experience and behaviour, and these influence
how we process data through our beliefs. Problems arise when inappropriate schema are activated that push out appropriate schemas:
'Information processing is shaped by the fundamental beliefs embedded in our schemas' (Colledge, 2002, p. 172). Automatic thoughts
become part of the inner 'self-talk', taking the form of images and
words that lead to self-defeating emotions and actions. In a nutshell,
problems are not caused by events, but by the ways in which events
are interpreted – what is made of them by the person – and therefore
we need to pay attention to self-talk and how it constructs life.
Depending on whether that talk is distorted or not, a person's
response to an event will be helpful or unhelpful. Thought can control
emotion, whereas Freud held that emotion controlled 'primary
process thinking'; he also held that there was 'secondary process
thinking' which was rational.

   Beck developed the popular Beck Depression Inventory (BDI)
with 21 headings/questions and a four-point scale: 'not a problem,
partially a problem, very much a problem and a severe problem' (see

Burns, 1992, pp. 20–2). This is commonly used in cognitive-behavioural assessments of depression. The questions relate to levels of sadness, discouragement, failure, guilt, blame, suicidal thoughts, crying, irritation, ability to work, ability to sleep, tiredness, appetite, weight, interest in sex and general health. In this approach, depression is not seen as an emotional disorder: 'bad' feelings are the result of distorted and negative thinking, thus the problem is a cognitive one, of which the feelings are symptoms. When thoughts are restructured, mood changes. When a person has been depressed for some time, the negative thoughts become *automatic*, but by identifying these automatic thoughts and ways of looking at the world the counsellor can quickly get to the underlying cognitive problem. Experiencing life or an event involves *giving it meaning*, and it is this *understanding* that enables us to *feel* it. When the understanding is accurate the feeling will be normal. Most depressed people seem to be convinced, without any logical reason, that they are a special sort of person beyond hope.

Not all CBT counsellors see people's thinking as 'distorted' (or, in Ellis's term, 'irrational'), but rather, as one our respondents described it: 'as people having their own *idiosyncratic unhelpful* beliefs'. Similarly, McLeod asks why we do not consider the thoughts of non-depressed people, who often see the world overoptimistically, as irrational. Viewing some thoughts as unhelpful is more respectful as it is specific to each person, none the less Beck's list of maladaptive cognitions provides a useful assessment guide:

- *Arbitrary inference* – lacking sound evidence;
- *Selective abstraction* – focusing on irrelevant aspects;
- *Absolutist thinking* –black and white thinking;
- *Over-generalisation* – my whole life is ruined, or what happened once will happen always;
- *Tunnel vision* – for example seeing one narrow perspective only;
- *Magnification/minimization* – exaggerating one's own faults and lessening other's faults – the binocular trick;
- *Biased thinking* – attributing bad intentions;
- *Mind reading* – for example ascribing thoughts to others or expecting them to read your thoughts or needs;
- *Subjective reasoning* – I feel it and so it must be correct. (We say feelings are not facts – they are only reflections of our thoughts, although they *seem* to be as valid as the feelings we have following undistorted thoughts);

- *Labelling/mislabelling* – 'I am a loser' or 'he is a rat';
- *Personalisation* – seeing self as the cause of negative events – 'It's me'.

The distorted thoughts associated with (causing) *depression* are said to be self-devaluation, an emphasis on negative aspects of life; generalisation of deficiencies (seeing them as pervasive and lasting); self-attribution of responsibility for problems; and a belief that the problems cannot be changed. These thought patterns need to be dealt with by addressing the key learning processes listed above.

CBT counselling is essentially collaborative, involving Socratic dialogue and 'guided discovery' (Colledge, 2002), and its success is assessed by the relief of symptoms and changes in thinking and in observed behaviour. In assessment work, therefore, one is listening for thoughts that are unhelpful and for more balanced thoughts to put in their place. It can be difficult to find the words that fit a time and culture so that no disrespect or offence is caused, and that the imposition of one's own values is avoided.

In most traditional psychotherapies the awareness and expression of feelings is seen as important for maturity, but in CBT, since negative feelings are seen as based on distorted thinking, attending to them is not viewed as desirable. Freud on the other hand seemed to accept feelings as true:

> [When] the patient represents his ego as worthless, incapable of any achievement and morally despicable . . . he must surely be right in some way and be describing what is as it seems to him to be. We must confirm some of his statements . . . he really is as lacking in interest and incapable of love and achievement as he says . . . We only wonder that he has to be ill before he can be accessible to truth of this kind. (Freud, S., 1952, pp.155–6)

Burns maintains that the great majority of depressed people are very much loved but that a sense of self-worth is missing. Cognitive therapy therefore 'stubbornly refuses to buy into [their] sense of worthlessness' (1992, p. 57) and leads people, through a reevaluation of themselves, to question whether they are right to see themselves as essentially losers. It is accepted that in depression people will lose some of their ability for clear thinking and will allow negative events to dominate their entire 'reality'. Patterns like all-or-nothing thinking make self-evaluation highly unreliable, frequently creating disappoint-ment and anxiety. Cognitive counselling, however, seeks to rapidly transform the way a person thinks, acts and feels, in that order. The CBT counsellor can accept that a person *does feel* depressed, but does not accept their negative evaluation as the *truth*.

The assessment can be aided by the use of the Dysfunctional Attitude Scale (DAS) which includes 100 self-defeating attitudes or silent assumptions that predispose people to emotional difficulties. For example: 'it is best that I give up my interests to please other people'; 'I need other people so as to be happy'; 'my self-worth depends on what others think of me'; 'I cannot be happy without being loved by another person'; 'my happiness depends on what happens to me'. These various statements can be reduced to seven *addictions*: dependency on approval; love; achievement; perfection-ism; entitlement; omnipotence; and non-autonomy. The first four are self-explanatory. Entitlement means automatically expecting that one's wants will be met by other people. Omnipotence means blaming one's self for the behaviour of others, putting self at the centre of the universe, needing to feel in control. Autonomy refers to finding happiness within one's own thinking and attitudes – seeing feelings as the children of one's inner thoughts – but the non-autonomous person needs happiness to come from outside, and this leads to problems since the external is beyond one's control.

Rational-emotive therapy (RET)

This is a variation on the above theme, based on the language of Ellis (1962, 1993; see also Dryden, 1990), which emphasises how the interlinked nature of thinking and emotion affect rational living: defined by Ellis as survival, being relatively free from pain and reasonably content. The fundamental hypotheses are that thinking, emotion and behaviour are closely related; thinking can become emotion and vice versa; and they take the form of self-talk that becomes the person's thoughts and emotions, generating and modifying emotions. These emotions are appropriate when they are accompanied by rational beliefs that aid the achievement of goals. They are not appropriate when they affect the balance between short and long-term hedonistic goals. Unlike Rogers (see Chapter 7), who believed that people will always choose to grow rather than regress once they clearly perceive which actions lead to growth and which are regressive – the actualising tendency – Ellis (1993) sees people as having an inherent tendency to be destructive of themselves and others. In his view, they tend to be irrational, in the sense that they behave in ways that prevent the attainment of their goals, make the same mistakes time and again, and are natural resisters who find it easy to block change but difficult to resist their resistance. In this he is more pessimistic than Beck who saw people more as Rogers did. For Beck, people, in their environment, simply learn bad thinking habits that lead to erroneous interpretations or maladaptive thinking. Dryden (1980) sums this up as people having two biological tendencies, one towards irrationality and one towards the ability to be rational.

Ellis, however, claimed that people also have the potential to be creative and, because they can think about how they think, they can choose to go along with the inherent negative tendency or strive to develop their creativity; they can acquire the cognitive skills necessary to counter their irrational thoughts. In Ellis's view, happiness consists of working towards one's life goals, while sharing 'social interest'; that is, supporting (not blocking) the goals of others. 'Rational' thoughts and behaviours are those that are helpful in attaining goals. This includes putting one's self first in life, while seeing the happiness of others as important too, especially significant others. Dryden (1990) clarifies this, adding that self-sacrifice is supported only if it brings meaning and happiness to the self (p. 3).

This approach provides an ABC of behaviour, but one that is not to be confused with that of Beck's operant conditioning (although Beck also wrote of the ABC of cognitive work). In RET, the A is the activating event, for example a death in a family; B is the beliefs held about that event, for example 'it has ended all our happiness'; and C is the consequent emotion, perhaps depression. The client will often see A as causing C, but events are mediated by beliefs/cognitions, so it is B that causes C. The work of counselling therefore entails breaking the link between A and C. A cannot be changed, but B can. When B is accepted as the cause of C, the consequent emotion can be helped by changing B. The client can be helped to choose between different ways of viewing A. The *more helpful view* of what happens in life enables people to be less self-defeating in subsequent feelings and actions.

Ellis (1989) classified four types of 'irrational' thinking:

1 Demanding beliefs, which he named *musterbation*. Examples include, 'I *must* do well; I *must* win approval; others *must* treat me well; life must be arranged to make me comfortable, so I can get what I want quickly'.
2 Derivative demanding beliefs. Examples include, 'It's awful *(awfulising); it's* terrible; it's horrendous; I can't stand it; and it's always going to be bad.'
3 Secondary demanding beliefs, making consequences worse. Examples include being sad about being sad ('this is dreadful, I must not be like this'), resulting in depression.
4 Derivatives of secondary demanding beliefs. This involves dwelling on awfulising or 'I can't stand it', increasing the ABC of their misery still further. (*Source*: Colledge, 2002, pp. 231–2)

Types three and four could be seen as perpetuating what might otherwise pass. Burns (1992) refers to these processes as 'defeating yourself by killing yourself to get moving' (p. 116). Ellis (1987) held that irrational beliefs were *maintained* by many influences, including looking at the past, rigidity, defensiveness, fleeing a situation rather than addressing the problem, inherited habits, illogical thinking patterns, powerful evaluative feelings, use of palliatives such as substance abuse, yoga or involvement in causes or in religion.

If a person says they *should* be happy every day, they can be helped to say instead 'it would be wonderful to be happy every day, but I can get by with less'. This lessens the likelihood of anxiety or depression when some days are less happy. When the heavy drinker says 'I can't stand not having a drink', the counsellor can help him to replace this with the idea that 'it is hard to cut down, it is not easy, it is unpleasant even, but I can stand it'. When a client says 'it is awful that the bus is often late', the counsellor can help them to replace this with the idea that 'it is inconvenient or unpleasant to wait in the rain, but it is not awful' – "awful" is more than 100 per cent bad'. When a person who has lost a family member in an accident says 'our whole family is now ruined for ever', they can be helped to see that it is very sad and painful, but life will go on and people can and do come to terms with great losses. The goal of RET is *self-actualisation,* characterised by self-direction, self and social interest, flexibility, tolerance of uncertainty and frustration, self-acceptance, self-responsibility, ability to risk and non-utopian thinking. This is achieved by attacking the illogical; first uncovering the target beliefs, then disputing them with more scientific, logical, thinking. The A–C link is exposed; the B–C link is introduced; B is vigorously disputed by logical thinking; and as B is changed, C diminishes. There is a dual goal, the removal of symptoms in the short term (inelegant change) usually happens first, and the reduction of the client's disturbability and the development of an effective philosophy of life in the longer term (elegant change) follows. Some clients settle for the former goal.

As irrational beliefs need to be continually challenged by clients, disputing techniques need practice so clients are given homework, such as completing the Disputing Irrational Beliefs form (DIBs). There are also emotive and behavioural techniques. The former include rational emotive imagery to help the client get in touch with negative emotions, unconditional acceptance of the clients as people, carefully applied humour, and rational role-playing. The latter includes assignments that challenge demandingness; exercises that attack shame; skills training; and rewards. Negative cognitions are not challenged *per se*, only irrational negative beliefs. So anxiety is replaced with concern; depression is replaced with sadness; guilt with remorse; hurt with disappointment; and shame with regret. Blocks to progress may need to be addressed, for example low tolerance of frustration (LTF). This tends to impede people, but making themselves a little uncomfortable in the short term enables them to gain greater comfort in the longer term. Dryden suggests that LTF is a predictor of poor outcomes in counselling (1990, p. 13). Blaming others is also a difficulty because, in RET, we accept that we make ourselves disturbed; it is *our* responsibility.

Modern RET accepts the ideas of Carl Rogers about the therapeutic relationship, therefore the person is accepted and it is clear that only their thinking is challenged, not their values or motives. This is done in a respectful and accepting way. Furthermore, rather than the counsellor directly disputing irrational ideas, she helps *the client* to challenge them, and to see for themselves the flaws, and what logical ideas could replace them.

RET has proved most effective with clients who are mildly disturbed; psychotic people may well hold irrational ideas but they do not seem to respond to the challenges to their thinking that make up RET. This is because RET aims to help people, via more helpful interpretations of events, to overcome emotional blocks in order to become more fully functioning, self-actualised and happier; but they also need to gain profound philosophical change to replace rigid primary thinking with preferential thinking. Counsellors may prefer the ideas of either Beck or Ellis, but it can be difficult to tell them apart in practice. It is not clear how well they are distinguished in the research as they are both cognitive-emotive-behavioural in orientation.

The lifeskills model

While both the CBT and RET approaches have an educational dimension, in that they share the theory with the client to some extent at least, this third 'handy map' is more educational still. Lifeskills counsellors are seen as personal-responsibility educators (Nelson-Jones, 1993). The aim is for clients to acquire better skills for living, so that they will be able to help themselves to take more responsibility for their own lives. The goal therefore is not to just solve a problem or to help a person to feel better; the goal is to bring *greater responsibility for making the most of their lives* into their whole future. This means also helping people to stop *avoiding* responsibility in various ways. Clients are to be empowered with self-helping skills for the *future*, not just in the present. It not only helps people to cope with difficulties in living, lifeskills helping also aims to free up their full potential. It believes that everyone has the right to maximise their competence. The problems for which this approach can be used vary from basic thinking and behaviour skills and competencies, specific to different life stages, to developmental competencies such as intimacy skills for young adults or coping with ageing and dying skills for older people. It can address partner relations, parenting problems, depression, anxiety, substance abuse and violence.

Problems are redefined in skills terms; goals are set with the client; interventions are chosen; and progress is reviewed. In all of this there is maximum client participation in decision making. The counsellor may confront or expand client perceptions rather than merely staying close to clients' views of themselves or of their futures. The client is seen as a trainee, but an active learner who contributes to his/her own learning.

Skills

Essential to any skill is being able to make and carry out a series of effective choices that enable objectives to be achieved. In this approach,

the counsellor needs to assess *lifeskills strengths and weaknesses* and rede-
fine problems in skills terms, so skills are not seen as either possessed or
not; people all possess skills strengths and weaknesses in various
measures. The aim is to help clients to move more towards skills
strengths than towards weaknesses. Choice is central: good choices are
skills strengths; the test of good client choices is whether they help the
person to *assume personal responsibility* for their own happiness. The
counsellor seeks to help the client become a better chooser:

> Lifeskills are the component skills through which people assume rather than
> avoid personal responsibility for their lives. Lifeskills are *self-help skills* [origi-
> nal emphasis] or competencies that enable people to help themselves.
> (Nelson-Jones, 1993)

Deficiencies in lifeskills can result in psychological problems. While
any skill, for example a sporting skill, can enhance life, the lifeskill
approach is more concerned with psychological skills, involving
thinking processes. The development and use of these skills is a life's
work – we can never escape choosing between possibilities while we
live.

The Lifeskills *assessment* process begins by getting a description of
a problem in the client's own language. The counsellor then explores
possible explanations of how the client's thinking and behaviour
maintains the problem, looking for ways to break down the problem
into skills weaknesses (thinking or acting weaknesses), thus getting a
redefinition of the problem in skills terms. This provides *handles* with
which to work on the problem. This redefinition, which is essentially
a hypothesis, is the core of the analysis and the formulation. Attention
is also paid to skills strengths such as skills in coping with the problem and in bringing it to counselling. This keeps a balance and avoids
too much negativity. With support, clients are helped to acknowledge
that they have some responsibility for the skills weaknesses that lead
to the continuation of problems and they are encouraged to have the
motivation to change.

Thinking skills may include what clients say to themselves and to
others about the problem. It may include various unhelpful aspects
such as anger-engendering, provocation, lack of assertiveness, poor
listening, or poor negotiating. As the counsellor contributes some skill
talk, clients often revise their accounts and their hypotheses as their
original conceptualisations are loosened up, until a jointly developed
skills redefinition is reached.

During this process the counsellor notes the strength of a client's feelings and pain, in case they may consider harming themselves. In listening to feelings, the counsellor also listens for responsiveness to themselves as well as to others, their denials and distortions and the extent to which they are in touch with their own needs and wishes. The counsellor seeks to clarify the client's 'real' agenda, rather than the 'calling-card' problem first presented. This clarity, and a clear look at feelings, helps in the selection of the problem to be first worked with in skills terms. This approach is not as commonly used as CBT and RET, but we present it in brief outline to show the breadth of cognitive approaches to assessment and counselling.

★   ★   ★

In all the three varieties of cognitive practice included in this chapter, even though the approach is problem-focused in that problems are examined for the thinking behind them, clients are not pathologised or seen as ill; they are regarded as rational beings with the ability to join in the project of attaining their goals in life and of understanding that process. Their meanings are sought; as one of our respondents said 'I want a clear understanding of the problem, not the complainer. If they say they are depressed, lots of people say this, I want to know what they mean by depression'. The counsellor is cast more as a coach than as a healer; tackling unhelpful ways of being and empowering clients to continue to improve themselves when counselling has ended. The assessment process is a collaborative one, although there are different emphases on the counsellor qualities necessary.

The CBT counsellor explains the rationale for the overall approach and the techniques used. Responsibility is shared by discussing hypotheses; for example, one of our respondents said he aimed for a shared understanding 'through checking it out, getting feedback: "tell me if I've got it wrong", ideas are up for scrutiny'. Guided discovery is used at all times and counsellors do not engage in indoctrination or cajoling. The RET counsellor style has many similarities with the CBT approach, and to some extent with the person-centred approach, in that the therapeutic rationale is explained and empathic listening techniques are employed, but clients are not shown undue warmth; they are encouraged to face their problems and find warmth and happiness for themselves. Unlike CBT counsellors, illogical thinking on the part of clients is forcefully disputed and debated in RET, but with the aim of teaching the client how to do this for themselves.

Implications of CBT and RET for assessment

Suitability

Counsellors who use this approach often give people a pre-meeting questionnaire that may include various questions from the Depression Inventory or the Dysfunctional Attitude Scale (DAS). At the assessment meeting/s, the replies may be discussed, mainly with a view to establishing whether the person can identify emotions and consider that there is a psychological component to their problem. As most cognitively-oriented counsellors seem to be in the NHS, risk assessments are done routinely. Goals are discussed and agreed, and the person has to be capable of seeing that they will have to do the hard work of personal change. The counsellor asks him/herself 'Can they see that the problem is linked to beliefs and thought processes and not something that can be more easily removed by pain-killers, for example?' Clients need to accept the model and be motivated enough to carry out the homework tasks and not have too low a tolerance of frustration, or too low a sense of personal responsibility for their problems. Many CBT counsellors would not accept severely psychotic people. One respondent put it as 'can the person psychologically construe?'

Formulation

In this approach, gaining understanding of the client's emotional responses and cognitive behaviours is essential. This understanding is best gained in a flexible collaborative way, seeking the client's own understanding of their problem and the implications of their views. Often the counsellor will explore in considerable detail specific situations where the problem presents itself. The client is asked what was going through their mind, what they were saying to themselves before and during the incident, what thoughts feelings and behaviours are maintaining the problem. They can be invited to try out less self-defeating beliefs or assumptions (to talk them out seems to be more effective than writing them) and see what difference this can make until they find what best promotes the desired change. This is like testing a new cognitive map of life. Some counsellors use the term *blocks* to refer to the thoughts and behaviours that keep the problem from being solved. Tests such as the DAS may be employed as an additional guide and baseline. The counsellor listens for distorted or unhelpful thoughts, like those listed above, and for the *addictions* mentioned earlier. They may discuss where these ideas came from – perhaps early experiences. As one of our respondents said, 'Early experience. I look at this. Cognitive behaviour therapists need to understand how the person got into the predicament . . . what we don't do is interpret that for them'. The counsellor would explore the impact of their way of thinking on their life. Finally, a baseline is established concerning the severity and frequency of the problem so that progress can be easily noticed and used to reinforce the work.

Ongoing assessment

Reviews are usually built in to the plan to check on progress and whether the most useful ideas are being used in the work. Ending is mainly planned by discussion with the client.

Advantages and disadvantages

Burns (1992) lists the advantages of CBT as providing rapid relief from symptoms. It provides clear understanding of how habitual automatic thinking can cause moods and unhelpful behaviours; leaves the client with increased self-control; and, lastly, helps to prevent future mood swings and allows personal growth founded on modified values, attitudes and basic assumptions about life.

However, cognitive approaches to counselling tend not to address social factors sufficiently; they could be said to help people to accommodate to their lot rather than change it. Much of the approach can be said to be based on unquestioned assumptions about the value of white masculine assertiveness. Challenging women's 'irrational' beliefs is difficult when they may be embedded in the 'rational' context of patriarchal relations. Although the literature emphasises that effective practice requires a good working relationship, no theory is offered for this in any way similar to how person-centred work offers congruence theory. Mcleod (1998, p. 84) adds that the approach problematises individuals, the model being easier to use when difficulties are defined as personal problems. Behaviourists can be judgemental about which goals are appropriate and more rigid in determining what dysfunctional behavioural patterns exist. It is most useful for clients who can share the basic assumptions, mostly those who endorse ideas about self-control and, as we noted earlier, is has not been shown to be effective with people who are seriously disturbed or who have clusters of symptoms. Motivation can be a difficult issue in assessment as, in some cases it may not be assessable until later in the process. One respondent expected to be able to see signs of motivation at intake, some indication that the client is prepared to collaborate, but the respondent felt he could not measure motivation except in how the person presents. This could be open to cultural bias.

Outcomes

Reading the Department of Health's *Evidence-Based Clinical Practice Guidelines* (2001) it would appear that CBT has considerable standing in the NHS. The report considers CBT to be well-supported by Cochrane-registered reviews (The Cochrane Library, Oxford) and other high-quality reviews from 1990 to 1998. CBT is reported as having the best evidence of effectiveness in the treatment of depressive disorders when compared with 'other therapies' (not listed). For agoraphobia, it 'has shown efficacy' (p. 24), but less so for panics. It is 'effective' for anxiety (p. 24) and 'may have an impact' on post-traumatic stress disorder. It 'appears to be efficacious' in the treatment of obsessive compulsive disorder (p. 24) and its efficacy 'has been established' for eating disorders (p. 25). For deliberate self-harm, a Cochrane review found 'some evidence of efficacy' (p. 26). McLeod (1998) comments that 'the effectiveness of cognitive-behavioural therapy for a wide range of conditions is amply confirmed in the research literature' (p. 80).

However, the large Sheffield study of 1994 (cited in Roth and Fonagy, 1996) compared the effectiveness of CBT with psychodynamic/exploratory approaches and found they were equally effective in treating depression. Interpersonal approaches were also as effective as CBT. On the other hand, Roth and Fonagy report that while there is no significant difference between the models in treating young people with depression or anxiety, with older people, cognitive behavioural work does make significant improvement. For those who abuse alcohol, all the approaches studied were equally ineffective. The social constructionist approaches were not included in the comparisons.

Summary

Cognitive behavioural counselling is one of the most respected methods, especially in the NHS where it is the method of choice for dealing with depression, anxiety, panic and many other emotional problems. The theory is clear and easily grasped and shared with clients; the practice, which is well-based in scientific method, can be rigorous. The use of tests to measure progress is virtually built-in to the process.

The assessment process is quite specific, examining the beliefs associated with *specific* situations. It begins with assessing consequence (C) – is the consequent emotion inappropriate? Does the client want to work at changing it? Can goals be agreed? How does the client feel about antecedents or the activating events (A)? Are there any secondary emotional problems? Having taught the beliefs– consequence (B–C) connection, B is assessed for rationality/ unhelpfulness.

7

The Person-Centred Approach: A Growth Map

This chapter will discuss the other main second-wave approach, the person-centred approach to counselling and assessment, an approach that is basically problem-orientated but with a strong focus on the person. This is a humanistic approach with links to phenomenology and existentialism. The person-centred approach has its origins in the work of Carl Rogers, whose basic belief was that clients know best what is the problem and how to make progress in dealing with it, *provided* that they have a relationship that offers the *climate* in which they can *grow* towards fulfilment. The theory is therefore much taken up with the conditions for growth, first the conditions for getting the work started, and second the conditions for a successful process, for progressing towards a successful change outcome.

Philosophical links

In this chapter, theory moves away from the 'science' of the earlier chapters to include a greater emphasis on *philosophy*. Rogers' ideas are mainly philosophical, although he was greatly interested in researching their effectiveness. He made a radical departure from his psychoanalytical colleagues who focused on pathology and had a negative view of human nature. He commented on how people are mistrusted, watched over, examined and given goals, usually given by referrers. This approach believes that people have a 'constructive directional flow', also described as 'the actualising tendency' (Kirschenbaum and Henderson, 1989, p.137) or, in Rogers (1980, p. 121), a 'constructive tendency'. People are *trusted* to make progress without being guided or influenced; all people are in a process of *becoming*. This optimistic view of people is also evident in Chapters 8 and 9.

120

Person-centred counselling claims to have the capacity to release the directional flow. In this process, the client's phenomenological world is central. This means that the way in which the client knows and *experiences* their world is respected. Objective knowledge is seen as a myth because in knowing the world we can see only with our own biased eyes and interpretations. If there is truth 'out there' we can only perceive it dimly and in a limited way, not receive it directly. Experiencing is a combination of imperfect selective perceptions along with some interpretations. However, in the right climate we can explore what makes sense to us, explore connections and meanings, check out feelings, reflect and thus gradually make our own changes in how we put our worlds together. This means that counsellors need to be aware of their own preconceptions about situations and set them aside; they ought never to explain or interpret the client. Rather they reflect or describe back; give equal weight to all aspects of what is described; and realise that they cannot 'see what is going on' — they can only know their own perceptions.

The second philosophical link is with existentalism. This philosophy says that we Exist (upper case E, to denote 'fully exist') as humans when we are conscious of others. Our identity is assembled in a social context, thus being is relational, as is self. As humanity is constituted in relationship with others, without their positive regard and empathy we cannot come to Exist. We start with nothing and cannot be anything until we make something of ourselves, and we make ourselves fully human by caring and taking responsibility, first for ourselves and then for others. This is authentic living. Relationships are said to precede individuals (in the logical order, they are not subsequent to individuals existing) because we do not begin to Exist until we have related. It is not surprising therefore to find the *therapeutic relationship* and its qualities and components central to Rogers' work.

Philosophers have long debated what it is to be truly human, and if counsellors are involved in the process of facilitating people to do this they need to have some ideas of what it means for themselves. Theologians may say it is being in relationship with God; Descartes said it lay in thinking; Sartre said it was self-constructed by one's actions. Perhaps authentic living can be in various modes: thinking, believing, feeling, behaving, imagining, hoping, writing? According to Worsley, (2002, p. 167), Rogers held that existential living means:

- Living every moment, letting go of defences, experiencing each moment as new.

- Seeing experience as growing out of the present moment, not from the conditional past or the conditioning other.
- Feeling the self and personality as emerging from experience (not the other way around).
- A loss of rigidity and of the imposition of self-structure on experience.

Existentialist ideas are far from new. The twelfth-century mystic, Hildegard Bingen, wrote that we cannot live in a world that is not our own – in a world that is interpreted for us by others. An interpreted world is not a home. Part of the terror is to take back our own listening, to use our own voice, to see our own light. Therefore, existentialism is not euphoric about the prospect of having to create one's self. Finding an identity in a confusing world is anxiety provoking, and not without difficulty, but humans have the *potential* to do this and to find meaning. The language is one of *if . . . then*, rather than debating causation. Rogers said that *if* there is a constructive relationship, *then* a person will grow; the therapeutic task is to provide the growing conditions. Person–centred counselling is a shared journey of possibilities for choices, free of preconceived diagnostic categories, in a moment-by-moment engagement, providing respect and care, so that defences and rigidities are loosened. A well-adjusted person in Rogerian terms has a self-concept consistent with thought, experience and behaviour, whose self is not rigid but flexible. Rogers uses the terms self-concept and self interchangeably as the person evaluates every experience in relation to the self-concept. Mearns and Thorne (1998) refer to this as the person's 'conceptual construction' of self.

Problems are seen as arising from *conditions of worth* and from *incongruence*. Conditions of worth arise when an outside person sets out conditions to be fulfilled for a person to feel valued. We cannot be sure where these come from, probably mostly from upbringing where a child may be valued only for something they do, or for some talent they have, for example. To have a true sense of worth, a person needs to feel valued for being one's self, or for just being. This is unconditional worth. Without it one may deny one's self in order to get acceptance, learning ways of coping with the conflict caused by the imposed conditions of worth. This can lead to a state of *incongruence*, conflict between the self and the conditions of worth, and a loss of self-esteem when the person gets out of touch with important parts of self. Self-expression is restricted so as to cope; unacceptable feelings

are denied. Then people give over to others that evaluation of themselves, resulting in a further loss of self. In the present world, many are
said to be not only lonely, cut off from people, but also out of touch
with their real selves, which is the worst hell of isolation. In this state,
problem-solving abilities are restricted, if not annihilated. This can
include trying to please everyone while being unsure of one's own
wants or needs because there is a fear that one's inner experience will
be criticised or defined by others.

As regards children's problems, contrary to his expectations,
research supervised by Rogers and replicated later showed that:

> the degree of self-understanding, the degree of self-acceptance, the degree to
> which the child could accept the reality of his or her situation, the degree to
> which the child was taking responsibility for self – that these factors predicted
> future behaviour [more than the family environment]. (Kirschenbaum and
> Henderson, 1989, p. 208)

In other words, it was what the children made of their situations, how
they were left feeling about themselves, that mattered.

Therefore, there is an emphasis in person-centred counselling on
the person as subject, not object, coupled with a refusal to let the
client hand responsibility to the counsellor. People's experiences are
valued and they are challenged to be responsible and to value and
trust their own inner resources. Clients' self-concepts may be so low
that it can be difficult to get them to start to view themselves as
acceptable, let alone as trustworthy or competent, so self-rejection
needs to be countered by persistent acceptance on the part of the
counsellor. Poor self-concepts usually result from criticism, rejection,
put-downs, insults, name-calling, belittling, demeanings – nothing
they did was right or good enough – so they come to feel they have
no right even to exist. Sometimes, when a low self-concept is internalised, the person concerned adds to it, not only in thought but in
action, demonstrating as it were that the negative assessment is
correct, thereby lowering themselves further. Most people seem to
have a shred of self-worth remaining, even though they may feel they
dare not put one more foot wrong, and whatever worth they have is
dependent on the approval of others who impose conditions of worth
like a straitjacket (Mearns and Thorne, 1988). Such persons become
cut off from what Rogers called the *organismic self* (real self) upon
which we rely to achieve a sense of worth through growth and the
realisation of potential. But Rogers believed that people know what

they need to achieve this – *if* left to get on with it, free from oppression and from being walked on, *then* they can progress.

To put this another way, when following our own inclinations incurs the wrath of significant others, when the organismic self repeatedly comes into conflict with the need for approval, the person can develop a distrust of the organismic self and bow to the oppression, eventually losing all confidence and coming to feel that self-expression is wrong and one has no right to feelings such as anger. A person wants to behave in ways that are consistent with their self-image, therefore experiences and feelings that are not consistent are threatening and may be denied admittance to consciousness, which notion is not unlike the Freudian concept of repression. Person-centred counselling aims to restore trust in the real self and in its actualising tendency and abilities and ideas. This includes taking back to self one's self-evaluation and decision-making, being in touch with one's own feelings and becoming *fully functioning*. Rogers set out seven aspects of the fully functioning person:

1 Open to experience, not defensive, having all experiences available to consciousness.
2 Symbolisation is accurate.
3 Self-structure is congruent with experience and will change flexibly with new experiences.
4 Self is experienced as the locus of evaluation.
5 There is freedom from conditions of worth and an experience of unconditional positive regard.
6 Each situation is met with adaptive behaviour because all available data is available to awareness and is used; no experience is distorted or denied; and failure to achieve satisfaction is corrected by effective reality testing.
7 The ability to live with others in harmony because of the rewarding nature of reciprocal positive regard.

This is not to say that these are the goals of each client. Goals are not set for people; these aspects are used only to work out how the counsellor needs *to be with* the client. This brings us to the *core conditions* for inaugurating an effective counselling process. According to Kirschenbaum and Henderson (1989), Rogers, after many years of rethinking and rewriting, listed the core conditions as follows:

- Two persons are in psychological contact.
- The first, whom we shall term the client, is in a state of incongruence, being vulnerable and anxious.
- The second person, whom we shall term the therapist, is congruent and integrated in the relationship.
- The therapist experiences unconditional positive regard for the client.
- The therapist experiences an empathic understanding of the client's internal frame of reference and endeavours to communicate this experience to the client.
- The communication to the client of the therapist's empathic understanding and unconditional positive regard is to a minimal degree achieved.

These conditions set out the therapeutic relationship in a way that was ground-breaking at the time. No other method has made such a contribution to the client–worker relationship in counselling practice, and indeed most counsellors now accept that to be effective they need to have similar values. The conditions are ways of being rather than techniques or instructions.

By way of clarification, the counsellor's *congruence* involves being one's self, open about feelings and attitudes, genuine in one's respect and caring. There is no façade or professional front, knowingly or unknowingly. Even when there are negative feelings, such as fear, they are not to be denied – there is no pretence. Congruence promotes trust (Mearns and Thorne, 1988). *Unconditional positive regard* includes acceptance of the client as he or she is, valuing the client in a total way. The philosophy is that people need positive regard if they are to grow and move forward towards fulfilment. It helps people to feel safe enough to face sadness, able to be honest without fear of rejection, and to accept self. This regard also applies to the client's choices and self-determination. The counsellor does not take charge; authority remains with the client, thus the counsellor abdicates power so as to empower and be responsible to the client, not for the client. Mearns and Thorne (1988) say that this approach 'puts the loving into helping' (p. 19), but it is free of imposition, entrapment or manipulation, 'desiring the client's freedom to be himself' (p. 34).

Empathy includes accurately sensing the feelings and meanings a person is experiencing, sensing the client's world *as if* it were the counsellor's own, being clear about what the client means, making remarks that fit with the client's mood, using a tone that shows you can share their feelings, but not losing the *as if* or taking on the feelings concerned. Rogers did not see empathic reflecting back as a technique to be used in a wooden fashion, but as a way of *checking perceptions* to get the exact meaning of the client and be a reliable mirror. Accurate empathy paves the way for valuing the person as they are in a way that lessens the alienation of the person. The *communication* to the client needs to result in the client *perceiving* that the counsellor has unconditional positive regard and is coming to an understanding of their internal experiences. This is difficult work, and it is not always clear what the distinctions between positive regard and empathy are. It is not just an intellectual grasp of these conditions that is needed, but what Rogers called *qualities of experience* gained through experiential training.

We have said that these conditions launch the process of growth. Their effects, according to Rogers, are that:

- Clients feel free to express themselves and to distinguish perceptions.
- Clients become aware of incongruence between experiences and the concept of self, and aware of the threat of this incongruence.
- Clients become aware of previous denied feelings.
- Clients' concepts of self gradually become congruent with experience and they are then able to include feelings that were previously too threatening.
- Clients' distortions and denials are reduced.
- Clients become able to experience the counsellor's unconditional positive regard.
- Clients experience self as the locus of evaluation.

To sustain a helping relationship and see the process through to a satisfactory end, in Rogers' view, a counsellor also needs to be able to:

- Be trustworthy, reliable, consistent, *dependably real*, open – to be what she deeply is.
- Communicate unambiguously, be aware of feelings and able to accept and express them, listen to what is going on inside of one, be transparently real; no feeling relevant to the relationship is hidden.
- Experience positive caring, warmth, liking, respectful feelings and attitudes towards the client. Not staying aloof – it is safe to care and have a relationship between two *persons*, not a person and an object (which happens if we become diagnostic).

- Be strong enough to be a separate person from the other, respect one's own needs as well as the client's, so as not to become downcast when the client is depressed.
- Permit the client separateness, not induce conformity to the counsellor, but interact with the client without interfering with client freedom to develop a personality different from that of the counsellor.
- Enter fully into the world of the client's feelings and meanings without evaluating or judging it, or trampling on any part of it, extending empathic understanding without limit.
- Accepting each facet of clients as they are, receiving them unconditionally.
- Being sensitive enough to be not threatening to the client, freeing her as completely as possible to be herself.
- Free the client from the threat of external evaluation or judgement, good or bad (even a good judgement conveys the power to judge).
- Meet people as persons in the process of becoming (not bound in the past) and not label diagnostically, but confirm their potentiality. People behave as they are perceived, so if we are to have any hypothesis it needs to be positive.

As Mearns and Thorne put it, the theory believes in the ability of all people to become 'a unique and beautiful creation' (1988, p. 13) with the help of counsellors who provide 'nourishment for growth', rather than the poison that kills self-esteem.

Worsley (2002) describes the process as client-led, with the counsellor sharing her grasp of the client without behaving as an expert. Client and counsellor together, observing the core conditions, puzzle out what is happening. Choices about the process are shared with the client who is seen as an equal partner. Worsley is concerned with the big debate in person–centred counselling practice over the nature of the process. At one level the process can be said to be the cognitive, emotional and behavioural activities of the session, yet Rogers stressed that his descriptions of the process were not sets of instructions and were not meant to lead to goals. Moreover, they were not just about the counselling process but about the whole client. Rice (1974) spoke of *evocation* – the counsellor facilitating the client in a reprocessing of experience, as if going back to experience with the suspension of earlier automatic constructions (which the counselling relation enables the client to leave behind). Worsley, on the other hand, sees the process as exploring new experiences; working through issues is a function of the client's actualising tendency. Accepting Saunders' (2000) premises, he sets out the primary and secondary principles for person-centred counselling:

- *Primary principles*
  - The primacy of the actualising tendency in motivating the change process.
  - The necessity of *actively* including all the core conditions and the therapeutic behaviour that is based on them, never assuming their presence.
  - The primacy of a non-directive attitude at least at the level of content, not necessarily at the level of process (expert process directing is accepted).

- *Secondary principles*

  - The client's right to self-determination and autonomy – not to violate their internal locus of control.
  - The counsellor as non-expert.
  - The counsellor as non-directive, even as regards process.
  - That the core conditions are sufficient – using other techniques or methods is a mistake.
  - Holism – it is an error to respond to only one part of the client.

Worsley's position is that counsellors should and can be 'process orientated' (p. 29) and still remain within the core conditions, for the following reasons:

- The client's process is an aspect of their frame of reference, their way of being, and addressing it resembles empathy.
- Clients are always in process and counsellors have a choice whether to address content or process – 'they have no choice but to choose' (p. 30) – process and content exist simultaneously.
- Clients can be trusted to know their own need and where to focus.
- When counsellors use evocative empathy (defined as the reflection of feelings with the intention of facilitating the client in repro-cessing experience), they can still trust the client's actualising tendency.
- Evocative empathy can be a tool, a technique or an attempt to understand, while trusting the client's actualising tendency to use the response for her own good.

- The quality of process work is not solely based on verbal interactions – it is also attitudinal.
- Because there is an existential base to person-centred thinking, it will 'stand against' the thinking of the client.
- To minimise process is to move away from the holistic principle
- The client is expert on both her content and her process. (Others claim the counsellor is the expert on her process and the client is expert on her content; see, for example, Rennie, 1998, p. 2.)
- The client's process is trustworthy – in engaging with it we can let it be our guide.

He sums up the, at times bitter, debate as one between classical and experiential therapists. The former want to rely on the original core conditions for the therapeutic relationship; the latter want to grow and develop by learning from other approaches. It is worth noting that Rogers' ideas developed over a period of many years (see, for example, Rogers, 1951, 1980).

Implications for assessment

This approach is sceptical of diagnostic thinking and says it could be harmful. Therefore most person-centred counsellors do not make formulations, and we found no-one who did this formally in our small study. However, some assessment of suitability is made, especially if there is a system of intake sessions in the agency. (We understand that in parts of America, at least, insurance companies will not pay for counselling if there is no diagnosis of a recognised problem, so counsellors there probably need to find a way of dealing with that issue.) In this approach, Rogers has said that even if the counsellor knew exactly the cause of the maladjustment of the client, she would not be able to make effective use of such knowledge – telling the client would certainly not be helpful. He goes on to say:

> One cannot take responsibility for evaluating a person's abilities, motives, conflicts, needs; for evaluating the adjustment he is capable of achieving, the degree of reorganisation he should undergo, the conflicts he should resolve, the degree of independence which he should develop, without a significant degree of control over the individual being an inevitable accompaniment . . .
> If however, as we think, the locus of responsible evaluation may be left with the individual then we would have a psychology of personality and of therapy which leads in the direction of democracy. We would have a place for the professional worker in human relations, not as an evaluator of the self,

behaviour, needs and goals, but an expert in providing the conditions under which the self-direction of both the individual and the group can take place. (Rogers, 1951, p. 224)

What mattered to Rogers was not how a counsellor assesses a client but how a client assesses herself. He approached people without any need to categorise them, believing that they had sole potential for knowing themselves and the constructive force needed to bring about change. He did accept, however, that tests could have a place later in therapy when the client wishes to measure some aspect. He urged caution in using tests and in taking case histories. One of our respondents said she did not diagnose in a medical way but she did ask 'What ails you?', as she sought to understand *what was happening to* the person rather than seek a cause for the problem.

Selection/intake

Rennie (1998, p. 35) maintains that assessment is a problem because it shifts the locus of evaluation to the counsellor and further away from the client, but some information may be important at intake, such as: is the person on medication; do they sleep well; have they been in counselling before? Hawtin (2000) places no restriction on who can benefit from this approach so long as the core conditions can be present for the counsellor. The counsellor needs to feel reasonably comfortable and *not have blocks* in respect of either the person or the problem. One of our respondents reported that she asks more questions of herself, questions such as, 'am I prepared emotionally to take this case?' Halgin and Caron (1991) ask, 'am I emotionally capable; what is my personal reaction to this client?'

The approach has been helpful with a wide range of issues. Some say it is not suitable for those with severe mental illness, but this is disputed. It works best if a client can be *actively involved* in an issue and *can engage in exploring it*. Rogers originally gave the following criteria for selection (1951), but later said they had proved less than helpful (1980):

- The degree of stress caused by the problem needs to be greater than the stress of dealing with it.
- The client needs to have some capacity to cope with life.
- The client is able to express his tensions and conflicts and has a conscious desire for help (the latter being useful, not essential).

- The client is reasonably independent, emotionally and spatially, of close family control.
- The client is free of excessive instabilities, particularly of an organic nature.
- The client has adequate intelligence and is of a suitable age.

He adds that experience did not lead him to say that client-centred counselling is applicable to certain groups and not to others: 'This does not mean that it will cure every psychological condition, and indeed the concept of cure is foreign to the approach' (1951, p. 230).

Mearns and Thorne (1988) say there are five elements that indicate a 'low state of readiness'. These are: indecision about wanting to change; a general lack of trust in others; unwillingness to take responsibility for self; or unwillingness to recognise or explore feelings in counselling. On the other hand, such difficulties may be seen as only affecting the *speed* at which trust can be developed; assessment involves considering 'have we (the client and I) got the *time* to achieve what the client wants in the way I like to work?' In an agency that restricts the number of sessions, the counsellor can still say to the client 'in the time we have available, where would you like to start?', and take it from there. Clients retain the role of determining their own counselling needs and in the last resort they are the main assessors.

Most of our respondents would check for issues of safety, suicidal ideas, people's expectations, a history of psychosis, the precipitating event that brought the client to counselling, and their main issue or concern. This questioning usually goes alongside the self-questioning of the counsellor: 'am I the best person to help?, how do I feel with this client?'

Ongoing assessment

There is ample scope in this model for ongoing assessment or evaluation by the counsellor, but it mainly refers to the counsellor's maintenance of the core conditions. This applies particularly to what are seen as the three central conditions: congruence/genuineness; unconditional positive regard; and empathy. To this end, Mearns and Thorne (1988) offer several examples of useful questions for the counsellor to ask him/herself:

- *Assessing the state of congruence*

  - Am I able to admit my feelings to this person?
  - To be spontaneous?

- To acknowledge sexual attraction?
- To be open about my weaknesses?
- To trust the client?
- To model openness?
- Are my words and actions in line with my experience of the client and my feelings?

• *Assessing positive regard*

- Is the acceptance such that the client feels valued throughout the process?
- Is the client respected?
- Is there a sense of warmth in the relationship?
- Is the client prized?
- Does the client feel affirmed?
- Is the person able to cope with acceptance?
- Does he or she trust me?
- How does the client interpret my acceptance and warmth?
- Is the way I show warmth effective?
- What is it about the person that makes unconditional acceptance difficult?

• *Assessing empathy*

- Is my empathy communicated to the client?
- Does the client feel understood?
- Am I staying with the client in his or her sadness?
- Am I clearly mirroring how the client is?
- Overall, am I providing the necessary climate for this client to grow?

Given the nature of this self-questioning, counsellors will understand the importance of the element of self-questioning at the intake assessment stage.

Endings

Here again, it is the clients who usually decide since they are seen as the best judges of their needs. However, if the counsellor feels a client wants to continue because of an attachment or dependence, congruence would require that this be addressed so that it can be jointly examined. In Rogers' view, it does not matter whether dependency feelings are caused by transference or by the therapist's behaviour;

what matters is that 'if the therapist is sensitively understanding and genuinely acceptant and non-judgemental, therapy will move forward *through* these feelings' (Kirschenbaum and Henderson, 1990, p. 130, original emphasis); there is no need to make a special issue of it. Rogers wrote that making transference feelings the core of therapy serves to foster dependency and lengthen therapy. He added that a counsellor can 'accept dependent feelings without permitting the client to change the therapist's role' (ibid.). Accepting a person's wish to be dependent does not mean that the counsellor will behave in such a way as to meet that wish, for example by being an authority figure. One of our respondents ends when the clients feel that their goal is reached. Another had no formal measure and was not looking for a once-and-for-all cure. Yet another hoped for a happier client.

Advantages and disadvantages

Person-centred counselling provides more guidance on the client–counsellor relationship than any other approach. It emphasises being non-directive and can therefore be expected to be empowering of clients who are in need of a more positive self-image. It is totally humanitarian and strongly promotes the respect for, and acceptance of, clients. It plays down the expertness of the counsellor, claiming that expertness can worsen people's desperate need for external authority and validation. It rejects any control over clients, rather they are to share power – exercise equal power – as authority lies with the client, not the counsellor. As Palmer and McMahon put it, 'it is anathema to think that an 'expert' knows another person better than she knows herself' (1997, p. 15). One respondent felt the approach made for a high degree of comfort between client and counsellor, for example when the work is not going well she can be open about that and discuss it. If she felt discomfort at any point she could share it.

However, one respondent felt the approach was so gentle it risked not challenging when necessary, and another felt the method needed a high level of self-awareness. As the person-centred counsellors in our sample tended to also use other approaches when stuck (rational-emotive counselling, for example, was mentioned by two of them), one must query how anti-diagnostic it is possible to be in eclectic person-centred counselling. The notion that there is an essential, 'real', authentic self is a modernist concept of desirable normality, thus person-centred counselling does have an idea about deficits that need remedying.

A further possible disadvantage is that the emphasis on personal transformation can focus so much on personal choices and personal responsibility that individuals' social and political realities can be ignored. Kearney (1996) suggests that it is important to focus on the self-actualising tendency of the *socially-positioned* individual.

Outcomes

In a comparison of person-centred counselling, psychoanalytic counselling and a learning-theory approach in work with hospitalised alcoholics, contrary to expectations, behavioural counselling made no improvement, psychoanalytic counselling some improvement and person-centred counselling showed the greatest positive change, which was confirmed by follow-up data over 18 months (Kirschenbaum and Henderson, 1989, p. 115). However, Greenberg, Elliott and Lietaer (1994) found no research to support the greater effectiveness of person-centred counselling as compared to other methods, although it seemed to work best with those interested in their inner experiences and who had good social skills and a high need for intimacy. Such people with relationship problems, anxiety and depression had good outcomes with person-centred counselling.

Summary

Rogers' person-centred approach has made a significant contribution to counselling, and most forms of counselling accept his views on the necessity of establishing the core conditions for effective work. Principles like empathy and acceptance are almost universally used. Outcome research is not as strong as one would expect for an approach that is so widely used, at least in Britain. Perhaps this is due to a falling-off in the use of this approach in the USA. Also, the integration of ideas from other models makes research difficult. The heavy reliance on the core conditions is often abandoned by the integration of other approaches like cognitive-behavioural therapy or solution-focused ideas. This latter approach is addressed in Chapter 9.

The assessment process does not focus on clients very much, assuming that their actualising tendency is intact. Instead the focus is on providing the conditions necessary for the client's growth; that is, the core conditions of congruence, positive regard and empathy, and on how well these are achieved by *the counsellor*.

8

The Narrative Approach:
A Forecast Map

This chapter presents the first of the theoretical maps belonging to the third wave of counselling; unlike approaches described in previous chapters, it is more interested in clients' futures than their pasts, in potential rather than pathology. The term narrative refers to the differences that can be made through particular tellings and retellings of clients' stories of their lives (developing alternative stories), but the term has been developed further than the story-telling involved in psychodynamic or cognitive behavioural approaches. Narrative therapy shares the solution-focused notion (addressed fully in Chapter 9) that there are no fixed truths but, additionally, emphasises that some 'truths' are more powerful than others. Narrative therapy involves ways of understanding the stories of people's lives, and ways of re-authoring these stories in collaboration between the counsellor and the clients whose lives are being discussed. It is a way of working that is interested in history, the broader context that is affecting people's lives and the ethics or politics of therapy (Morgan, 2000).

Hence the need for narrative assessments to take into consideration the 'climate' of counselling, addressing power issues explicitly through the deconstructions of dominant cultural stories that have the capacity to marginalise and oppress clients. There is always a context in which the stories of our lives are formed and the contexts of gender, class, race, culture and sexual preferences are powerful contributors to the plot of the stories by which we live; the beliefs, ideas and practices of the culture in which we live play a large part in the meanings we make of our lives. Narrative assessments build on clients' own metaphors, developing a 'forecast' that adds in all those 'sunny spells' that are often edited out when problem stories are told or written, without ignoring the 'highs' and 'lows' of oppression by powerful narratives.

Narrative therapy challenges people's beliefs that a problem speaks their identity – a totalising effect which conflates the person with the problem – seeking to separate the person and the problem and develop a sense of incongruity between the two that opens up new possibilities for responsibility-taking and accountability. Traditional psychotherapeutic concepts are reconstructed in narrative therapy: interpretation is how clients can make meaning of their lives rather than be entered into stories by others; and resistance is the way in which they can resist the influence of the problem on their lives.

Narrative theory

Narrative therapy was developed mainly in Australasia by White and Epston (White,1984, 1993, 1995; White and Epston, 1990; and Epston, 1998). It is more political and social than other therapies; the thinking being located in poststructuralism (Foucault, 1972, 1973, 1980, 1988), it represents a radical departure from the structuralist thinking that characterises most contemporary Western thought on counselling. Narrative therapy is also located in the work of the sociolinguist Halliday (1978) concerning the oppressive effects of dominant narratives on people's understanding of the validity of their ways of living, and the postmodern and social constructionist ideas of Gergen (1985); in particular, alternative understandings of what a person is and how change occurs are offered by narrative ways of thinking. Zimmerman and Beaudoin (2002) suggest that these points of view represent a challenge to the 'truthfulness' of certain ideas and practices that more traditional counselling models take for granted: 'The effects of these alternative understandings is to create *a very different clinical process* than is created by traditional psychologies' and that these ideas are difficult to describe in a didactic manner because 'the reading will be influenced by the structuralist understandings already present and reacted to accordingly' (p. 31, our emphasis).

Poststructuralist thinking suggests there is no essential person to be discovered, instead there are countless versions or identities which are socially or culturally produced and maintained. It is not possible to separate identities or problems from the contexts that produce or maintain them, thus problem stories create rather than reflect reality for clients. White (1995) argues that there isn't a single story of life which is free of ambiguity and contradiction and that can handle all the contingencies of life. These ambiguities, contradictions and contingencies stretch our meaning-making resources, especially when there are dominant cultural stories about particular sorts of behaviour. These stories tend to concentrate on identifying the behaviours seen as desirable by the most powerful groups of people, and thus people whose behaviour does not conform to this become storied as deficient in some way. White refers to this as being entered into a story, a story which people come to believe about themselves:

> these stories or narratives form the matrix of concepts and beliefs by which we understand our lives, and the world in which our lives take place; and there is a continuing interaction between the stories we tell ourselves about our lives, the ways we live our lives, and the future stories we then tell. (Payne, 2000, p. 20)

Thus narrative assessments involve collaborative conversations with clients where their experience is privileged in deciding what the problem is. Questions are asked to help the client separate from the influence of the problem story, experiences that contradict the problem story are noticed, and questions asked about the meaning of these experiences. The goal is to co-author an alternative story with clients and make it more influential than the problem story. The central principles of narrative assessments are: always maintain a stance of curiosity, and always ask questions to which you genuinely do not know the answers.

In narrative assessments the problem is deconstructed. This takes the form of searching for *unique outcomes* – times when the client actively resisted the influence of the problem, a contradiction to the dominant story, or plot in Epston's terms (1998, p. 11). Deconstructing the problem is done by reflecting with clients how they came to be recruited into a *problem-saturated story*. This includes discussing that story in a way that separates the problem from the person, developing a sense of alienation between the person and the problem. This *externalising* conversation is helped by giving the problem a name of its own and by asking questions that establish the influence of the problem on the person, and their influence on it. This can be seen as discussing the client's *relationship with the problem*. The client, having been invited to explore the effects of the problem, is then asked if that is something they want in their lives or not (an evaluation of the problem or their relationship with it). If they do not want it, they are asked to justify that evaluation by explaining, for example, reasons for not wanting it, and what that says about them as people. In this way they make a decision to start reclaiming their life

from the influence of the problem. The narrative counsellor's expertise lies in creating a context for change rather than solving problems,
and this means that assessment is continuous and fluid; as one of our
respondents commented: 'there is no clear pattern after the first assessment session; what happens next depends so much on what happened
in the previous session, and it is so individual, no clear template, only
principles'.

White (1995) states very clearly that while the alternative narrative
offered may be seen as part of radical constructionism he does not
accept that 'anything goes' simply by giving it a new name. Because
narrative is constitutive of people's lives, shaping and structuring
them, we must be accountable to those we seek to assess or help. Not
all stories are equally good in their effects. And not only do clients
enter themselves into stories but so do counsellors. Payne (2000)
discusses the implications for counsellors of deconstructing their own
stories. While he acknowledges that racism and patriarchy are cultural
beliefs rejected by most counsellors, he reminds us of the need for
constant vigilance against the more subtle manifestations of these
stories, for example the way sexism may be demonstrated through
verbal tone and the dominance of conversations. This is particularly
difficult for male counsellors as they live in a culture in which such
attitudes are embedded.

Jenkins (1996), too, cautions against the danger of acting from a
position of self-righteousness and moral superiority. In narrative
assessments, therefore, critical self-monitoring and regular checking
out with other people is essential (as we discussed more fully in
Chapter 2). There is only a fine line between responsible assessment
and intervention and therapeutic abuse says Jenkins:

> I work hard at establishing a context for a client to own his own 'discoveries'
> and do not see myself as the architect of his new thinking and behaviour. Yet,
> all the same time, I am acting strategically and intervening towards this end.
> Is this really self-enhancement? (1996, p. 129)

He advises being mindful at all times of the risk of insensitively pursu-
ing our own agendas at the expense of client experience, and this is
probably complicated where counsellors are impelled by agency-led
assessment requirements. Much of narrative therapy originated from
work with people who had no choice but to attend therapy; not only
mandated clients but also people who were living in situations in
which they had little choice over aspects of their lives or who were

initially reluctant to join a conversation with a counsellor – people who were locked in psychiatric wards, were not speaking to anyone, or who were living reclusive lifestyles. Narrative therapy derived from a desire to find ethical and effective ways of working in such situations (Morgan, 2000). Payne (2000) also addresses the ethics of externalisation, concluding that the process is transparent so the client can hear exactly what the worker is saying. Nevertheless, in deconstructing and reconstructing stories, counsellors need to be aware that the choice of questions asked is influential on the way the assessment is focused, and differences in values, beliefs and meanings between the client and counsellor require explicit attention (Milner and O'Byrne, 2002a). It is the counsellor's role to engage with the experience and meaning of the client who is consulting them in whichever way or shape the expressions of this meaning occur.

Strand (1997) suggests that externalising the problem and its internalised narrative in an attempt to unmask the relationship between self and hidden political realities requires advanced conceptual understanding, whereas a solution-focused approach (see Chapter 9) only demands a rethink of the definition of one concept – the problem – without concern for its effects on self-definition. This, he thinks, makes narrative approaches unsuitable for people of limited intellectual ability. We have not found this to be the case. Indeed, the similarities between narrative and solution-focused approaches in terms of their theoretical base, particularly the relevance of social constructionism, means that the approaches can be combined in assessments.

For a helpful account of this approach we recommend Gilligan and Price (1993) which presents the (American) de Shazer's solution-focused approach and White's narrative approach as different and opposing in some ways, giving a particularly clear analysis of White's approach. O'Hanlon (see, for example, O'Hanlon and Beadle, 1994) has also combined the American and Australasian approaches in a creative fashion which stresses the importance of language. In his view language can easily make difficulties sound, and become, fixed. His aim is to reconnect clients' sense of possibility and hope when things seem unchangeable. He is concerned about the danger of 'iatrogenic inquiry' whereby problems are caused or worsened by an assessment or attempted intervention; stressing the importance of avoiding negative assessments 'that discourage, invalidate, show disrespect or close down possibilities for change' (O'Hanlon and Beadle, 1994, p. 10). He maintains that, since clients are experts in their own lives, we need to check our work with them as we might with another professional. Included in this approach is Milton Erickson's principle of *utilisation,* considering carefully how a counsellor can identify and fully use the strengths, exceptions or unique outcomes that the client brings to the assessment. Like White, O'Hanlon holds clients accountable for behaviour that impacts on others, but this is about accepting responsibility for future behaviour, not blaming, looking for bad intention or suggesting that clients are bad people. People are presumed to be resourceful enough to deal with changing, the task being to connect them with their often unrecognised resources and join with them in locating these and any other resources they may need, be they external, personal, interpersonal or spiritual – in a word, possibilities.

The techniques

Narrative approaches to assessment tend to be fluid and wider-ranging. The client's alternative stories are developed via the techniques of *externalising the problem*; *externalising internalised narratives*, which support dominant stories or plots about the problem; *thickening the counterplot*, to strengthen the alternative story; and the provision of *narrative feedback*. As all these techniques reveal and increase unique outcomes, they are not necessarily used sequentially, there being considerable overlap.

Externalising

Central to externalising is how people have come to believe that *they* are the problem, separating the people from problems via externalising conversations being an effective way of identifying unique outcomes. These unique outcomes include not only when the client actively resisted the influence of the problem, but also ways in which they subverted it, endured it or delayed its effects. In order to encourage a client to have a different relationship with both the problem and the narrative that supports it, early on in the assessment the problem is spoken of as an external enemy oppressing the person. This aids the non-pathologising of the client; it is the problem that is the problem. Externalising conversations help the client to stand back from the problem and recover a sense of self-agency as they separate themselves from their own subjugation and begin to resist the influences that recruited them or that invited the problem into their lives.

To aid separation of person and problem it helps to give the problem a name as soon as possible, using the client's own narrative metaphors. Often the client can suggest a richly descriptive name for the problem; for example, we have experienced 'temper' named as Total Upset, Fiery Red Bomb, Black Cloud, and Raging Bull. Equally common is a more anonymous naming, such as It, particularly for clients who have been abused or suffer from eating distress. In naming the problem, clients then find it easier to describe the influence of the problem on their lives, using their own language and metaphors. As one of our respondents says about the advantages of narrative counselling for her:

> it's a refreshing change for them to be listened to and respected as stake holders. Before they've not been active participants. If they're able to tell their story, it's helpful. It's completely different from the pathological model they've experienced.

Zimmerman and Beaudoin (2002) say there are two practice points that make the difference: having the client describe the problem from their own experience keeps the counsellor 'right on the mark', and ensures that they are clear about being *against* the problem.

Externalising conversations are particularly useful in the assessment of clients who hear voices. Instead of assessing for the possible presence of auditory hallucinations or delusions, the counsellor interrogates 'voices' as unhelpful beliefs that can be resisted or subverted. For example, Jacob (2001, p. 70) provides a set of cartoons depicting 'Monster Bashing Methods' for thoughts and beliefs underpinning eating difficulties. White (1995) suggests that it is helpful to question the purposes and motives of the 'voices':

- Are these voices *for* you having an opinion or are they *against* you?
- These voices throw you into confusion. Whose interests are best served by this confusion?
- What is it like for the voices to have to listen to your thoughts for a change? and, later,
- What is like for them to know that you are developing a disrespect and mistrust of them?

Thus a narrative approach is very different from traditional approaches to the assessment of mental health states. Less specific questions that not only elicit unique outcomes but also aid goal-setting include:

- How did the problem seduce you into thinking that way, or going along with it?
- What influences led to your enslavement by the problem?
- What prevented you from resisting it? What were the restraints?
- Does it really suit you to be dominated by it?
- What effect or influence does the problem have on your life, or on those close to you, on your relationships, self-image?
- What effect do you have on the life of the problem?
- Given a choice between life with the problem and life free of the problem, which do you choose?
- Tell me about the times you made Anxiety wait.
- How long has Temper been making your life miserable?
- Tell me about a time you didn't fall for the story Anorexia has been telling you?
- (When there are unique outcomes), what are the implications for the sort of person you are when you refuse to cooperate with the problem's invitations?
- What does it say about your ability to undermine the problem?

Note that these last two questions are reflecting on the qualities of the person rather than on their actions. White (1988) refers to this as adding to the *landscape of consciousness/identity*, enriching a possible alternative story through a *language of action*. The language is the language of resistance and liberation, and it is used to understand how the client submitted to the problem's ways and how these ways are neither liberating nor ideally suited to the client's preferred way of living. This involves looking back at the past to some extent, before going on to becoming future and solution-orientated. But it is not a blaming look at the past or a search for deficits, it is empowering in that it develops a sense of the client being intrinsically okay, as *not being* the problem, but as being oppressed by it and sometimes colluding with it. Thus the explanation that is developed is not one that seeks the cause of the problem in the person, but one that seeks to understand how this, basically okay, person became ensnared by the problem's invitations.

Externalising the internalised story

It is not enough to simply externalise the problem as this neglects the context in which it is storied (White and Epson, 1990; Roth and

Epston, 1996). Frequently part of a client's enslavement to a problem is caused by societal attitudes, such as attitudes that suggest that the consumption of alcohol is socially necessary or that women should be the main carers in families. More accurately, people are *restrained* in these ways from resisting the problem or from taking responsibility in various ways. A narrative style, storying the separate lives of the person and the problem, encourages a sense of ownership of one's life; a sense that the client and counsellor can co-author a future story, breaking away from the performance of the past unhelpful story and thus experiencing the capacity to create change. New narratives yield a new vocabulary and construct a new meaning, new possibilities and new self-agency. White has found that more clients than expected are able to re-author their lives, and we cannot assess their capabilities to do so until we afford them the opportunities created by narrative promptings.

Externalising conversations thus aid the development of alternative stories and encourage the service user to take action against the problem. They emphasise context, deconstruct the objectification of people, and challenge dominant stories through which 'disorders' and 'pathologies' are constructed; what Epston refers to as a 'spy-chiatric gaze' (1998, p. 127). Externalising conversations invite people to take up a position toward the problem and consider whether they want to continue living with it. In the case of violent or other oppressive behaviour on the part of a client, accountability is not minimised; instead the beliefs and attitudes supporting the violence are externalised, *externalising the internalised story*, enabling other ways of responding to situations to be discovered. Here the work of Jenkins (1990, 1996) is particularly useful; he suggests that much male violence is supported by dominant stories about 'being a man' in which the need to 'be someone' is exaggerated and extreme. He invites men to take responsibility for their behaviour by asking questions which externalise this internalised story, the 'blueprint' of his marriage for example. The man is invited to externalise patriarchal restraints and consider their influence in his life and the extent to which he has slavishly and blindly followed a set of oppressive and unhelpful beliefs:

- If a man takes this recipe on board, what sort of marriage is he going to be building?
- Is he going to want his wife to be her own person with her own ideas or his person with his ideas?

- Is she more likely to respect him more if he tries to get her to be his person or if he allows her to be her own person?
- If she was just doing what she is told, would she be more likely to give out of love and desire or out of duty? (Jenkins, 1990, p. 82).

As stories about how to do 'being a father' are not well-developed in our society, clients are more likely to have internalised mothering stories so it is an essential part of narrative assessment work to make fathering stories more visible by raising the issue of gender as a possible context for behaviour. For example, Elliott (1997) asks:

- What ideas about mothering have you been recruited into?
- How have these ideas directed you to act in relation to others?
- How have they directed you to act in relation to your partner?
- Who else have you watched behaving in this fashion?
- Would they be supportive of your way of acting in relation to your partner?
- How did your mother handle these issues?
- How did your father handle the same issues?
- Do you think you should be responsible for setting limits on your behaviour?
- Have you been recruited into certain ideas about relationships that involve you being the gatekeeper for other people's behaviour?

Narrative approaches dovetail well with feminist family therapy (Gosling and Zangari, 1996) and, for women clients, narrative counsellors also question stories about the all-nurturing nature of mothering (Milner and O'Byrne, 2002a):

- Who comes first in your family? Second? Third? (And so on).
- Does it feel comfortable always to be at the bottom?
- How can you put yourself a little higher without being selfish?
- Are your expectations of your mothering reasonable? Attainable?
- How much responsibility can a mother realistically take for her family's behaviour?

It matters little what sort of blueprint people develop for living in their families as long as this story works equally well for all family members. Narrative questioning does not aim to push a particular story or suggest that a person is thinking distortedly; it aims only to assist a person to tell a different story if they discovered that 'habitual, significantly limiting discourses, derived from . . . history and from 'assumed truths' in contemporary society, no longer made sense' (Payne, 2000, p. 59). There are important differences between the cognitive distortions of cognitive-behavioural and narrative therapy, although there is some blurring where the former is based on Beck's ideas, as we have seen in Chapter 6. A major difference is that cognitive-behavioural therapists are largely concerned with cognition and behaviour, whereas a narrative therapist is interested in experience. As one of our respondents said, 'rather than seeing a child *with* a cognitive distortion, we see it as a distortion that is *given to* them'. Externalising the internalised story also differs from the insight giving of psychodynamic approaches in that ways of interacting with others are not revealed as maladaptive attachment patterns. This is only another (psychological) story; one that has become embedded in contemporary stories about attachments, commitment and 'being there' for friends. We find that many young women have internalised this story and then struggle with friendships that do not meet their expectations. They tell us that they think there is something wrong with themselves but, rather than assess them for deficiencies in intimacy, we ask them questions about their story of friendship:

- What is the most important thing you get from your friends? Support when you are troubled? Having a laugh? Someone to go out with?
- Can all your friends do all these things?
- Can a person expect the same level of commitment from all their friends?
- Which friends are you closest to?
- What is the difference between your supportive and unsupportive friends?
- Are some of your friends supportive and others social friends?
- Perhaps there are different sorts of friends – silver, gold and platinum?

Another totalising and restricting story we frequently interrogate is the story of 'low self-esteem'; one which is popular with both counsellors and clients. As we have said earlier, narrative therapists see self-esteem as fluid and dependent on different contexts. We are not coherent wholes, although we may perceive ourselves as such:

> our culture (Western, technologically advanced) is so individually oriented that we are taught to experience our-self and others in this individual

manner. We tend to embrace a dominant identity and seem blind to the way it is dependent on our current interactional network, which in turn is shaped by dominant cultural knowledges. We tend not to make sense of the other versions of our-selves that occur with less frequency in other social contexts. (Zimmerman and Beaudoin, 2002)

Thickening the counterplot

The dominant 'individualism' story of much counselling practice has the effect of centering all meaning on the individual with the result that clients attribute problems to themselves rather than see them as context-specific. Concentrating on problems in assessment means that counsellors are likely to hear only what narrative counsellors refer to as a *thin* story; one that allows little space for the complexities and contradictions of life, allowing little space for people to articulate their own particular meanings of their actions and the context within which they occurred. This leads to thin formulations, which obscure people's skills, knowledges, abilities and competencies; thin descriptions and formulations support and sustain problems. The key question for narrative counsellors is how to assist people to break away from thin conclusions and generate *thick* stories that do not support or sustain problems (Freedman and Combs, 1996). Assisting clients to reexamine their lives and focus on their own local, experiential knowledge can have a counterbalancing effect, producing richer descriptions of their lives, perhaps remembering positives that have been edited out of their story, what narrative counsellors call *thickening the counterplot* (see, also, Payne, 2000, pp. 33–4). However, thin stories can be powerfully maintained by counsellors' expert diagnoses and commentaries:

> Problematic stories have an advantage. They've been around for a while. Their plot is thick. Like a snowball, they have packed together certain incidents and episodes in the family's life, finally freezing them into a solid mass. The once innocent snowball becomes a force with which everyone has to reckon. These problem-saturated stories can become very pervasive. The trouble is that their effects are negative and discouraging. (Freeman *et al.*, 1997, pp. 94–5)

Thus the alternative story, the counterplot, needs strengthening. Juxtaposing the plot and counterplot thins the plot and thickens the counterplot, and this is done in assessment by specific questioning:

- What kind of alternative story would be required if the client/family/counsellor were to tell another version at odds with the problem's story?
- How might the client/family/counsellor look and act in an alternative story different from the way the problem's story told them to look and act?
- How might the anomalies, irregularities and strangenesses that lie outside the predictive reach of the problem's story be considered meaningful events in the life of the client and powerful antidotes to the problem?

An additional way to thicken the counterplot when there is no-one in the client's life to tell the new story to is to use narrative metaphors which emerge in externalising conversations. Also aiding thickening of the counterplot is asking the client's permission to broadcast the news (for a fuller description, see Epston, 1998). The main intention is to thicken the emerging alternative story by asking the client what advice they would give to people with similar problems to their own. Thus they have to explain how they intend to, or have, overcome the problem, and how they spotted its sneaky ways of setting them up for a slip back. These additional ways of thickening the counterplot intertwine between assessment and ongoing therapy.

Narrative feedback

Written narrative feedback differs from the more usual formal assessments that distance the counsellor from the client when the former becomes the expert author of the latter's life. White and Epston (1990) argue that such an author has a 'library of terms and descriptions that have been invented by and considered the property of this particular domain of knowledge' (p. 188). This 'expert' knowledge, combined with the invisibility of the author, creates the impression of the possession of an objective and detached point of view that does not actually exist, one that bolsters a view of the counsellor as benevolent expert, with the moral assumptions implicit in their specialised narrative hidden by their construction of the subject. Permitting the client to read such an assessment report does not allow them the scope to do more than disagree with factual errors; the meaning-making (interpretation) being the counsellor's.

Narrative approaches challenge this view of recording by providing clients with written feedback which uses their own words and explanations: what Epston (1998) considers to be the work of a conscientious scribe: 'who faithfully notes down the proceedings for posterity and makes available a client's history, capturing on paper the particular thoughts and understandings with which they make sense of their lives' (p. 96). This provides a check on the counsellor's accuracy of perceptions, reduces power imbalances between the counsellor and client, and encourages co-authorship. Epston writes long letters which include the metaphors people use to tell their stories and any unique outcomes, commenting on these as a means of expanding the externalising conversation. Letters need to be adapted to the reading and concentration levels of clients; for example, children with learning needs may need a pictorial record of any unique outcomes. Letters are also unsuitable for most agency records, particularly where the assessment is risk-focused. A form of written feedback that is appropriate for clients and agency records can be found in Milner and O'Byrne (2002a).

Evaluating the narrative process

As narrative assessments are collaborative, the client plays a significant part in mapping out the direction of the therapeutic journey. Most counsellors check out their understanding of what the client is saying in various ways – trial interpretations, summarising and so on, but Morgan suggests that a narrative counsellor seeks to understand what is of interest to clients and how the journey is suiting their preferences, so narrative counsellors also ask if their *questions* are appropriate too:

• How is this conversation going for you?
• Should we keep talking about this or would you be more interested in . . . ?
• Is this interesting to you? Is it what we should spend our time talking about?
• I was wondering if you would be more interested in me asking you some more about this or whether we should focus on . . . ?

For an excellent example of how a narrative conversation is guided and directed by the interests of the person consulting and how a thick description of knowledges and skills can be generated see White's (2000, pp. 154–71) verbatim account of a supervision session.

The initial assessment is checked out with the client in two more ways: by *evaluating the interview* at the end of the assessment session, and the provision of *written narrative feedback* as described above. The former consists of simply asking the client at the end of the interview if the session had been what they expected, whether or not it had been helpful, and whether they felt understood. The solution-focused question 'what would I have been doing differently if I had been more helpful?' is a useful one here.

Definitional ceremonies

Much of what has been said about assessment so far refers to assessing individual clients or, at most, considering them within the context of their families and schools or work. Narrative therapy has, however, a long tradition of working with larger groups who share a common problem (or have had a common problem ascribed to them), and has developed particular ways of undertaking a narrative assessment with larger groups and communities. White (1995, 2000) has developed the notion of a definitional ceremony which provides an opportunity for people and communities to re-define their lives and identities according to their preferred values and ideals. Definitional ceremonies consist of three distinct stages:

1 *The initial telling*: a community gathering is facilitated through which participants are given an opportunity to meet in small groups to talk about themes in their lives. These themes form the foundation for inquiries into the alternative stories of people's lives, their particular knowledges and skills of living, and the histories of these. Problems can also be interrogated, such as racism in schools (McMenamin, 1999), bullying in colleges (Lewis and Cheshire, 1999), drugs (Moss and Butterworth, 1999), and HIV (Browde, 1999). Members from a *listening team* join each small group to assist conversations to explore themes decided on through a prior consultation process. These listening team members have a special responsibility to note any special skills and knowledges.
2 *A re-telling*: the listening team members sit at the centre of a circle of all participants, re-telling what the small groups gave them permission to share. The primary focus is the re-telling, although listening team members invite each other to locate their re-tellings in their own experience to note what was significant to them and resonates with their own experiences. Particularly, they comment on how what they have heard will influence their lives and work. This is often experienced as powerfully acknowledging by those

who have spoken in the small groups in stage one, being a most effective form of empathy.

3 *Returning to the wider circle*: after the listening team have spoken, everyone joins into a single circle where all participants have the opportunity to reflect on what they heard in the re-telling. This includes responses and images about life in general, their own lives in particular, or any realisations or reflections. During the three stages of the gathering, people have an opportunity to tell stories about their own lives that relate to the themes they have identified to be important to them. These stories are powerfully acknowledged and further thickened.

The listening team members fulfil the role of assessment for whole communities, thickening thin stories. The principles involved include: refusing to generalise, allowing people to define themselves, questioning the idea of unity (particularly where people are totalised as problems due to similar ethnicity or 'illness'), and identifying common ground (most usually the common ground of caring and having something to offer). This enables the skills of community members to be built upon, getting counsellors away from notions of charity and paternalism to facilitate partnership and fair exchange. Reporting on a community health initiative – Latino Health Access – Bracho (2000) adds that such an approach makes evaluation and accountability simpler:

> We believe we have to be able to say how and why something is working. We may not be able to predict at the beginning where we will end up, but we can demonstrate clearly the journey we have been on, who has come with us, and the real effects of this journey.

All counsellors ought to be able to demonstrate the same responsibility towards accountability.

Implications for assessment

Selection

Intake focuses on the client's story, on whether there are any possible signs of an ability to resist the problem and change the problem-saturated story. If the client finds the line of questioning useful or interesting, counselling can proceed. Apart from basic considerations of safety, no-one who can have some sort of conversation (not necessarily verbal) is rejected.

Formulations

Formal formulations are avoided unless there is an agency imperative, in which case the therapeutic relationship would be threeway: the counsellor, client, and the 'given goal'. An informal formulation would consider:

- How was the person recruited into the problem story?
- What influences or invitations contributed to this recruitment?
- What influence does the client have on the problem, making it welcome, for example?
- What effects does the problem have on the client's life?
- Are there any unique outcomes?
- Can the client handle externalisation?
- What are the meaningful metaphors for this client?

Reviews/ongoing assessment

Reviews consist of conversations about how useful and relevant the process is and when it can end; for example, asking regularly: 'is what we are talking about helpful to you?, can I just check that we haven't drifted off what you wanted to talk about?'

Endings

These are negotiated with the client. Does the client feel able to live the new, more satisfactory story?

Advantages and disadvantages

Narrative therapy has a wide range of applications. The type of problem does not limit its use; it is effective with clients of limited intellectual capacity, including elderly people who are muddled in their thinking, people with learning needs, and those who might be storied by others as having major mental illnesses. It can be used with individuals, families and groups, including support groups for people with 'anorexia' or 'schizophrenia', community groups of aboriginal people tackling problems of diabetes that are partly the result of poverty, and groups of AIDs workers in villages in Malawi, for example. In larger group work, externalising conversations have been shown to lead to an exposé of the problem that empowers the taking of community and political action.

However, although we find it difficult to think of any major disadvantages, this may be because we have a strong personal preference for 'third-wave' approaches to counselling and caution the reader not to be carried away by our enthusiasm; we are aware that we must not push our agenda. The main disadvantage for counsellors trained and experienced in other approaches is the very real difficulty of deconstructing their own stories and being prepared to not only make these explicit, but also abandon cherished theories about the nature of people. Also the emphasis on using the clients' own language does run the risk of colluding with male metaphors of control; the notion of resistance readily lends itself to 'fighting talk', thus linguistic oppression must always be guarded against in narrative assessments.

Outcomes

Research into narrative approaches is in its infancy, yet Gorer, Thyer and Pawluk (1998) found that where there is a 'mutual client–worker strategizing' to change an external target 'the prevalence of moderate to large interventive effects may be fivefold greater' compared with cognitive-behavioural approaches. They found that when the problem is defined as transcending the individual, 'that is the problem does not reside 'under the person's skin' the work is very effective' (p. 274). They add that practice based on anti-oppressive theories has 'possible greater effectiveness' compared with traditional problem-solving approaches; for example, in work with survivors of abuse.

We are also aware of the work of Fisher, Himble and Hanna (1998) in studying the externalisation of problems in work with compulsive adolescents where the problem was made 'the enemy'. They found that 11 of 15 participants who provided follow-up data showed significant improvement following a seven-week programme. Similarly, Milner and Jessop's (2003) evaluation of a domestic violence programme showed that a combined solution-focused and narrative approach resulted in both significantly lower drop-out rates and recidivism than other programmes at 18-month follow-up. Jacob (2001) reports that combining these approaches is effective with clients with eating disorders, and Selekman (2002) found such a combination effective with young people who self-harm.

Summary

Narrative counsellors think in terms of stories – dominant stories and alternative stories – linked together over time; past, present and future stories that have powerful effects on people's lives. Thus narrative assessments take care to ensure that clients are considered as experts in their own lives; problems are seen as separate from clients, who are assumed to have many skills, competencies, beliefs, values and abilities that will help them change their relationship with problems; and that the client plays a significant part in determining the directions taken. Additionally, the counsellor retains a curiosity and willingness to ask questions to which they genuinely don't know the answers (and get worried if they think they do know the answers to questions), and that there is no single correct direction a narrative conversation can take.

9

The Solution–Focused Approach: A Navigator's Map

This chapter presents the second of two theoretical maps that belong to the third wave of counselling theory. Like the narrative approach, it eschews pathology and problems. It shares some of the values of the humanist models of counselling and has some features in common with cognitive behavioural therapies in that it uses cognitive and behavioural questions and frequently leads to tasks to be carried out (although the range of questions used is much broader, encompassing narrative, experiential and systems dimensions of clients' lives). However, the focus is quite different. As its name implies, this approach focuses on understanding *solutions*, maintaining that it is not necessary to understand a problem in order to understand its solution. Any link between the problem and the solution may be nominal. This approach begins at the end (the solution) and works back from there, rather like a navigator plotting a sea journey, pinpointing the destination first and then drawing a line back to the present position.

Solution-focused theory

This approach originates mainly from work developed at the Milwaukee Centre for Brief Therapy by Steve de Shazer and his colleagues. In a succession of publications over the past 17 years, de Shazer (1985, 1988, 1991, 1994) set out the solution-focused approach, which can be described as postmodern and constructionist. His philosophy is largely based on the psychotherapeutic ideas of Milton Erickson (1959), and on the theories of language and meaning of Derrida (1973) and Wittgenstein (1980). This philosophy is set out more fully in Parton and O'Byrne (2000) and Milner and O'Byrne (2002a). The image of the person in the social-constructionist approach is that of the person as a social agent, who has to be seen in a cultural context. This leads solution-focused counsellors to:

> explore not what is *within* (intrapsychic) people, as if there was an inner world divorced from a cultural, anthropological context, but to examine what lies *between* people, i.e. an interactional perspective. Feelings, thoughts and actions always take place within the linguistic negotiations in which people engage. Meanings are always open for renegotiation. (O'Connell, 2001, p. 29)

Psychoanalysts such as Elliott (2002) would consider this to be a post-modern intellectual sleight of hand in that it ignores unconscious drives which, they maintain, cannot be created in discourses. At its simplest, solution-focused practitioners hold an unwavering belief in the capacity of service-users to discover their own, workable solutions to their problems.

De Shazer looked at problem patterns and how attempted solutions often served to maintain these, becoming interested in the inconsistencies of problem behaviour. However serious or chronic a problem, it was never possible to obtain a truly accurate picture because nothing ever remained quite the same. Thus whatever the problem behaviour there will always be exceptions, times when the problem is less apparent or even absent altogether. Examining in great detail 'what worked', de Shazer's team perfected a set of economical techniques that form the foundation of the approach. Many of the techniques will be familiar to counsellors adopting different approaches, particularly the Socratic questioning of Frankl's (2000) logotherapy or Beck's cognitive therapy (for a more detailed discussion, see Colledge, 2002), but solution-focused workers use these techniques to explore clients' futures, not to understand past events. Solution-focused counselling also has a strong foundation in research, testing its assumptions and discarding anything that is not backed up by the evidence. Over 30 outcome studies have been published between 1991–2000 (see outcomes section), so we can say that the theory grew out of effective practice. None the less, the practice itself is atheoretical in that it uses the local knowledge of clients (which is theoretically limitless), rather than depending on professional knowledge; that is, it adopts the Socratic stance of ignorance (for a fuller discussion, see, Annas, 1998). This means that in order to ask useful questions, solution-focused counsellors are required to develop their listening skills, curiosity and humility; the theory may be simple but the practice is far from simplistic. Solution-focused counsellors do not engage in hypotheses because, however well constructed, they do not necessarily shed light on what the client needs to do to make progress. They also have the potential to close down or deter the client from making changes, so they are to be avoided (O'Connell, 2001). As one of our respondents commented:

> I make no assumptions at all. We have a referral meeting and grade clients from A – like an overdose, to E – a consultation. Whereas my colleagues will not take certain complexities, I'll take anything. In the first session, I find out if it's useful. I don't make an assessment of whether the case is complex or not.

Thus solution-focused counselling embraces one-half of the evidence-based practice development – effectiveness, remaining cautious about the evidence-based practice which makes generalisations about the nature of people. It is deeply sceptical about the ability of the 'grand' modernist theories and explanations to deliver truth, holding instead to a plurality of truths, including those contained in the 'local' theories of clients. It avoids any form of diagnostic labelling and sees professional categorisation of people as disempowering. For example, the Finnish psychiatrists Furman and Ahola (1992) reframe 'depression' as 'latent joy', and 'borderline personality disorder' as 'a search for a new direction in life'. As clients are viewed as essentially capable, there is a constant search for competencies; for example, a client who may be considered to suffer from an obsessional, compulsive disorder in some counselling models, is viewed from a solution-focused point of view as being a person with many strengths – tenacity, conscientiousness, concern for possible harm to others, and so on, all of which can be used in solution finding.

Solution-focused counselling takes a *not knowing* stance towards people's problems, preferring to remain *curious* about people's stories and views, about their strengths and potential, about occasions when the problem was less, and about how that happened – curious about the seeds of solution. Rather than seeking to understand (based on some grand theory), it merely seeks *more helpful* 'misunderstandings'. There is a preoccupation with *difference*, with what was different when things were better and what needs to be different for them to be better again. As de Shazer comments, 'It is so easy to forget feeling good compared to how easy it is to remember that you feel bad' (SFT email list, 2002). It utilises each problem-free aspect of the person and engages in *problem-free talk*, engaging the person, rather than the problem. This includes questions such as:

- I know very little about you apart from a little about what brings you here. What would you feel happy to tell me about yourself?
- What are you interested in?
- What do you enjoy?
- What are you good at?
- [for relatives of the client] What does [client] do that makes you proud of him/her?

Sharry, Madden and Darmody (2001) say that though this may resemble social chitchat, problem-free talk is a skilled process involving the counsellor in always looking for client strengths and resources that may be helpful in resolving the problem, however tangential they may at first appear.

Solution-focused counselling sees the problem as outside the person: the person is not the problem; the *problem* is the problem. The counsellor joins with the client *against* the problem and thereby gets a different story. Therefore this approach seeks not to be pathology-based, and thus its assessments are not based on identifying deficits. This is particularly so in the assessment of danger, solution-focused workers finding it easier to assess safety, which is measurable, than risk, which resists quantification. In other words, it is easier to assess the presence or start of something, safety, than it is to assess the absence or cessation of something, risk.

This solution-focused approach seeks to find the seeds of solution in the client's current repertoire, seeking those occasions or *exceptions*, however small or rare, when the problem is less acute in order to identify when and how that person is doing or thinking *something different* that alleviates the problem. This involves listening carefully to, and then *utilising*, what the person brings to the encounter, focusing on problem-free moments, constructing an envisaged future when the problem is no longer there, and getting a very detailed description from the client of what will be different then and whether any of that is already beginning to happen. In partnership, the client and the counsellor build a picture of a possible future without the problem. Emotions are not ignored; as Sharry *et al.* comment,

> Sensitivity to the unique client should be the guiding principle, rather than the need to ask solution focused questions . . . it would be insensitive to ask newly bereaved clients about times when they don't feel any grief without first hearing and acknowledging their pain. (2001, p. 31)

One of our respondents stressed the danger of having a blind spot to such situations, 'It can leave clients struggling with parts of their lives that they can't bring to the conversation. So we need to be sensitive to their need, perhaps say that something is untoward.'

Validation of emotions in solution-focused counselling differs from rather more traditional ways of expressing empathy in that it has what O'Hanlon (1995) calls a 'twist', adding a word that implies a possibility of difference. For example, if a client says she feels suicidal, the counsellor would reply, 'that must be scary, have you felt suicidal *before*?' If the answer is affirmative, the follow up question would be, 'how did you recover *last time*?' Or with a client talking about deeply experienced grief, 'I'm sorry that things are so difficult for you at the moment and I'm wondering what your *hope* is for coming here?' (Lipchik, 1994; Sharry *et al.*, 2001). The client needs to be heard but, rather than attempting to understand clients' emotional experiences as separate, emotion, cognition and behaviour are viewed as interdependent and the focus is on *engaging* at an emotional level (Lipchick and Turnell, 1999). Hence the client is asked how they *do* depression, happiness, and so on, rather than how they *feel* them.

Talk (language) is seen as powerful enough to construct life; talk of life with the problem constructs a problem-laden life; talk of life without the problem constructs a problem-free life. Talking in detail of what will be happening, what people will be saying, what effect this will have on relationships, and so on, provides the *experience* of a glimpse of that life; that life then becomes a *possibility* and the person experiences a sense of personal agency in setting out to construct it. The new story can even include a changed or different self, especially an accountable self. Assessments that fix people's identities, conflating the person and the problem, are avoided as new possibilities become visible. From this assessment process, messages and tasks emerge for the client to consider between sessions.

This approach thus has a view of assessment different from most others. Rather than assuming that information about a problem will help to find its solution, the assumption is that we can understand a solution without necessarily knowing a great deal about the problem. Searching for an understanding of a problem usually leads to a laundry list of deficits or negatives, whereas this approach says that what is needed is a list of positive strengths and *exceptions* to the problem. Lists of deficits often risk overwhelming both the client and the counsellor, engendering hopelessness and a tendency on the part of the counsellor to use such expressions as 'unmotivated', 'resistant' or 'not ready to change'. In solution-focused assessments, 'resistance' is regarded as an inability on the part of the counsellor to recognise the client's *unique way of cooperating* and an indication that more careful listening needs to happen. For example, Iveson (1990) says that when people repeatedly shout about their complaints, or complain in other ways we find difficult to hear, they are invariably people who are not being heard. To hear them we must accept their language as rational and meaningful, even when it appears irrational, unreasonable or perverse. The solution-focused approach can be summed up as helping an unrecognised difference become a difference that makes a difference (de Shazer, 1988).

As Durrant (1993) puts it, psychological assessment tends to assume that qualities are measurable entities, that there are 'normative' criteria for determining healthy functioning and that we need to identify deficit and fault before planning intervention. He contrasts this with the solution-focused approach, which assumes that the meaning of behaviour and emotion is relative and constructed; that psychological and emotional characteristics are partly a product of the observer's assessment and interpretation; that intervention need not be directly related to the problem; and that counsellors should build on strengths rather than attempt to repair deficits. This approach therefore develops an apparently 'atheoretical, non-normative, client determined view' (Berg and Miller, 1992, p. 5) of difficulties in which change is regarded as constant and inevitable. As a result, it makes sense to find what bits of positive change are happening and to use them to develop a solution. If counsellors do not look carefully for what the client is doing when the problem is not happening, or is not perceived to be a problem, these exceptions will go unnoticed. The most striking example of this is the 'pre-session change' question. Because de Shazer's team believe that change is constant, that no problem, mood or behaviour happens all the time or to the same degree, new clients are asked what has changed since the appointment was arranged. The team found that a considerable proportion of people reported some change. By then asking 'How did you do that?', they quickly got a solution-focused assessment under way.

Philosophical assumptions

The assumptions that underlie solution-focused thinking can be expressed as follows:

- Problems do not necessarily reflect a deficiency.
- The future is more significant than the past; an understanding of what will be happening when the problem is ended avoids the need to understand the cause of the problem. Or, as one client put it, 'what's the use in digging in the graveyard when there are fields to be ploughed?'
- If the counsellor assumes that there may be underlying meanings to problems, then it becomes increasingly difficult to 'listen' to the client. Rather, the explanation for events is they just happen; blame for what has happened is avoided but responsibility for what happens in the future is encouraged.
- Change is constant and inevitable – there are always exceptions.
- Meanings and changes are constructed by talk.
- Staying on the surface of the words is important in hearing what the client is saying – looking beneath the surface is looking at one's own theory and, thus, finding what the counsellor expects to be there.
- Unless there is a goal that is salient to the client there will only be confusion and drift – for a yacht without a destination port, no wind is a good wind. The counsellor has no other goal than that formulated by the client.
- As long as the goal is legal and morally acceptable, no limits are put on client aspirations for a joyous future.
- Counselling should be as brief as necessary so that it can be minimally intrusive but only the client can know when the work is finished and whether the work has been helpful.

Techniques

The main techniques are simple questions, the 'miracle' question, the 'pessimistic' question, scaled questions and coping questions.

The *miracle question* is helpful in developing goals with people who are not sure what their goals are or who find it difficult to believe in a better future:

> Suppose tonight, while you are asleep, a miracle happened and the problems you have today are gone in a flash, but because you were asleep you don't know this has happened. What would be the first difference you would notice in the morning?

This is followed by gentle prompts about new behaviours, new attitudes and new relationships, followed by 'Is any little bit of this happening already, sometimes?' So the miracle question helps to get a picture of the future without the problem, and the follow-up searches out small exceptions to the problem. When these are found the key question then is '*How did you do that?*' This is not only a compliment, but it presupposes personal agency and builds up possibilities of repeating what they are able to do at least once. With some small exceptions, a minimum of motivation and a little imagination, when we use constructive questions the possibilities are boundless and the client can get ready for change without analysing the problem – being able to 'describe what they want without having to concern themselves with the problem and without traditional assumptions that the solution has to be connected with understanding or eliminating the problem' (de Shazer, 1994, p. 273).

Pessimistic questions. The miracle question can also be asked in reverse, as a *nightmare question.* This has been found to be particularly helpful for mandated clients, for people who are very worried about impending events, and those pessimistic clients who enjoy catastrophising.

> Suppose that when you go to bed tonight . . . a nightmare occurs. In this nightmare all the problems that brought you here suddenly get as bad as they can possibly get . . . But this nightmare comes true. What would you notice tomorrow that would let you know you were living a nightmare life?' (Berg and Reuss, 1998)

This question is used only after the miracle question has been tried. Like the miracle question, it is followed by questions to elicit greater description, only in reverse. 'What will your wife notice about your drinking?' 'What will you notice that is different about how she feels then?' 'Are parts of the nightmare happening already?' 'Who is interested in preventing the nightmare?' Problem talk is being used to make a small start at building a solution the client can consider or live with.

Although it is the experience of solution-focused counsellors who work with suicidal clients that dying comes across as a means to an end rather than an end in itself, and future-oriented questions identify what the client wants to be different, the nightmare question can also be asked in a different version with those suicidal clients who can think of no exceptions to their misery:

> Let us suppose you went for the last option and actually died. You are at your own funeral as a spirit looking down from about 10 feet at the mourners

below. What might you be thinking about another option you could have tried first? At this funeral, who would be most upset among the mourners? What advice would they have wanted to give you regarding other options? (Hendon, 2002)

Scaled questions are used in a particular way in this approach. They can be directed at clients' estimations of the severity of their difficulty, at their level of confidence about reaching their goal or at their willingness to work hard to make progress. A scaled question is usually put like this: 'Suppose we had a scale of 1 to 10, with 1 being the "pits" and 10 being "there is no problem", where would you put yourself on that scale?' This scale is set up 'in such a way that all numbers are on the solution side' (de Shazer, 1994, p. 104), but it is impossible to be sure about what any number really means, even for the client. They and we know that 5 is better than 4 and less good than 6, so answers provide a way of grading progress – or its lack – for both counsellor and client. But, more importantly, scaled questions and their answers help to make concrete what is not concrete, making it easy to describe what is hard to describe.

Numbers get their meaning from the scale to which they belong; they are content-free in so far as only the subject has any idea what they mean. But when we ask 'How will life be different when you move from 5 to 6?' and 'What will important people in your life notice that is different?', these future-orientated questions help the client to begin constructing progressive change. Scaled questions also make it much easier for a client to talk about behaviour that either embarrasses them or reminds them of failure and censure. In discussing a problem such as depression, scaled questions help us to get away from the idea that one is either depressed or not, as if depression had an on–off switch. Suppose a counsellor asked, 'So if 1 is how depressed you were when you asked for help and 10 is when you will be unaware of any depressing feelings, where are you now?', any reply above 1 would indicate that the depression was less bothersome now and that things are already moving towards the goal (de Shazer, 1994).

Kral (1989) produced an assessment device, the 'solution–identification scale' (S-Id), to aid this process (see Parton and O'Byrne, 2000). Referrers are asked to score 39 different strengths as not at all, just a little, pretty much and very much, examples of strengths being such details as 'sleeps OK', 'is happy', 'is considerate', 'tells the truth' and 'shows honesty'. While this helps to focus attention on strengths, and allows weaknesses to be acknowledged, it also ensures that progress is not ignored, thus providing a better chance that the location of steps towards solutions can be found. It has the added advantage that it can be completed by clients as well as by referrers, giving tangible evidence of a partnership approach. Kral also suggests four basic questions at the initial assessment stage:

1 To estimate self–concept, he asks 'Think about the best person you could be and give that person 100 points. Now tell me how many points you would give yourself these days'. Most people without serious problems give themselves between 70 and 85. If a client says, for example, 60, this would influence the second question.
2 'On a scale of 1 to 10, how much are you satisfied with your score of 60?' If highly satisfied, the person is not considered likely to be a good 'customer' (a term that will be explained shortly). Equally it could mean that the client considers they are doing the best they can in adverse conditions.
3 'When you move from 60 to 70, what will be different that will tell you that things have changed?' or 'Have you been at 70 before and if so what was happening then?' or 'What is the highest you have ever been and what was going on then?' Although these variations of the same question ask nothing about the problem, they open the door to finding exceptions, in which will lie the seeds of solutions. They also clarify for the client what change is within their control.
4 'What are the chances, on a scale of 1 to 10, that you could do that again?' This question hints that the person should make such a change, thus helping to estimate commitment and pave the way for a task assignment.

Clearly, these questions have nothing to do with why the problem is happening. They are about goals, where people are positioned in their situations and what the client is doing that is different when there is less of a problem or no problem. They are about 'putting difference to work' (de Shazer, 1991): the questions explore what is different when the problem is not happening. They enable clients to identify well described goals that are associated with good outcomes; that is, goals that are positive (what is wanted rather than not wanted), small, concrete and observable, significant to the client, realistic, recognised as involving hard work, and beginnings rather than endings.

Coping questions. A distinction can be made between problems and unhappy situations. 'Problems' relate to patterns of behaviour, attitudes, beliefs and moods; 'unhappy situations' relate to losses (for example, loss of work, of a person, or a resource) and to environmental events (for example, the weather). While there are solutions to problems, many unhappy situations have to be coped with. In this case, *coping questions* are important, such as 'How do you manage to get by?' 'Are there times when you can cope better?' 'What helps?' Other questions that can be asked at the assessment stage include:

- *Resource questions*:
  - So what did it take to do that?
  - How did you do that?
  - What helped you achieve that?
  - Did you know that about yourself?
  - What did you learn about yourself managing to do all that?

- *Shifting from negatives to positives*:
  - When you are no longer depressed, what will you be doing *instead*?
  - When you are not thinking about food all the time, what will you be thinking about *instead*?
  - What did you used to do together before you started shouting at each other?
  - How did you make this happen?
  - When you are not shouting at each other, what will you both be doing instead?
  - What have you done in the last couple of weeks that has made a difference to this terrible situation you are in?
  - What has stopped you taking your life up to this point?

- *Shifting from the general to the specific*:
  - How will you know that you are happier?
  - What will you be doing that will tell others that your confidence is returning?
  - Who will be the first person who will notice that you are moving forward in your life?

- *Eliciting small exceptions*:
  - When was the last time that you woke up and thought 'I might just go out today'?
  - Tell me about those days when you think, even fleetingly, that 'the tide might be beginning to turn'. What is different on those days?

- ○ What about those days when you have a little bit of hope and optimism? What is different about them?

As solution-focused counselling aims to be as brief as possible, endings questions are also asked at the assessment stage, such as:

- How will you know when you don't need counselling any more?
- What will people notice differently about you when you don't need counselling any more?
- How will you know when you have drowned your sorrows enough?
- How will you know when you have talked about the problem enough?
- What will I notice differently about you when you don't need counselling any more?

One of our respondents commented that he looked out for what the client was saying after two or three sessions that added up to 'the problem isn't a problem any more' and would then ask, 'so what does this mean for counselling?', adding something like 'you must be feeling very confident then?' to ensure that the work remains as brief as possible.

Meeting client, family and referrers' needs

An important part of a solution-focused assessment is in accommodating differences in willingness and motivation to change; not all clients are willing clients. de Shazer distinguishes between three sorts of clients: customers, complainants or visitors. A *customer* is a person who acknowledges the need to make some personal change and who wants to be helped. In these instances the work is usually straightforward. The second category, *complainant*, is rather more complex, involving as it does a person who wants the counsellor to change someone else but does not wish him/herself to change. The complainant often has a vested interest in the problem being located in the complained-about person, so they are given an observation task to help them join forces with the complained-about person against the problem. Asking complainants to do more observation, but with exceptions noted also, builds on their strengths – they are good at observing – and provides an opportunity for them to become customers. For example school teachers of disruptive pupils will have many complaints about clients, and these concerns should be listened to and taken seriously if one is to engage the teacher in a way that will be helpful. We can, however, change the information we collect by asking teachers to help in the development of a solution by listing, in detail, those times when the pupil is or was *doing better* in class. We use our own 'report card' to facilitate this process. This resembles an ordinary school report card but is two-sided. One side asks the teacher to report on what the pupil has done right in each lesson, and the other side asks them to report what the pupil has done wrong. However, there is a rider to the 'wrong' side which says 'do not write anything on this side of the card until you have written something on the other side'. We find that even the most truculent pupil will turn up for lessons, and behave, for the sheer pleasure of watching a disliked teacher write something good about them.

How counsellors and clients 'see' situations is crucial in a solution-focused approach. Once we 'see' a person as 'troublesome', we see only trouble, so we need to consider in what ways s/he is not troublesome, and we also need to consider what difference it will make when that person sees him/herself differently and is not seen to be troublesome. This involves an explicit awareness that we and referrers can suffer from 'delusions of certainty', 'rigor psychologicus', and 'a hardening of the categories' (Colledge, 2002, p. 7) in the sense that people tend to see what they believe or expect. Similarly, parents who complain about their children's behaviour are carefully listened to but they are encouraged to identify exceptions/strengths by asking them what makes them proud of their child. Selekman (2002) uses a *famous guest consultant* experiment for 'stuck' families, asking each family member to choose a famous person they admire and asking them how this famous person would approach their problem.

A *visitor* is a person who is neither a customer nor a complainant but visits the counsellor because there is no choice; for example, where contact is mandated by courts, a parent or another person in authority. For example, almost all the adults who attend our domestic-violence programme are motivated to attend by the threat or actuality of their partners leaving them. As Dobash *et al.* (2000) point out, people only change when they are ready and this point usually comes from some sort of personal crisis involving personal costs. Scaled questions with wide boundaries are useful here to enable the visitor to take some responsibility for their behaviour without being totally condemned. For example, a young woman 'brought' for counselling by a mother in despair over her eating difficulties might be asked, 'on a scale of 1–10, where 1 is "there's hardly a snowball's chance in hell" and 10 is "you'd eat fish and chips and pudding for definite" . . . ?' (Jacob, 2001, p. 30); or a man 'forced' into counselling by his wife's threats to leave him if he doesn't stop drinking might be asked, 'if 1 is a teetotaller and 10 is drunk in the gutter everyday, where would you rate your drinking?' As no person is likely to say either 1 or 10 in this example, *wherever* they locate themselves admits of some need to change or develop. Similarly, where clients and counsellors disagree about the possible levels of risk, a safety scaling question can be asked.

Task selection

With 'customers' for whom a situation is vague, a *formula* (or standard) first session (F1) task is given, asking clients to list all those things that are happening in their life that they want to continue to happen. By listing what does *not* need to change, this exercise helps the clarification of appropriate goals. Sometimes people are so overwhelmed by their problems that they say they want to change everything, and here it is useful to ask them to 'take a step in a direction that will be good for them'. This helps them take a step towards taking responsibility for their futures and, thus, a step away from victimhood.

When a client is unable to recall an exception, a *pretend* task is suggested, for example pretending to be not depressed one half of the week and noticing what is different or what other people see is different. This helps to develop and identify possible exceptions that make a difference to the problem.

Where exceptions are spontaneous or the result of other people's efforts – that is, not deliberate on the client's part or seen as outside their control – they can be asked to *predict* when spontaneous exceptions are going to happen. For example, a client who compulsively steals could be asked to predict days when the urge to steal will or will not come. It has been found that clients can improve their ability to predict this correctly with practice and, of course, when they can get a high proportion of predictions correct, the question is 'Are the exceptions really spontaneous, or do you have some control?' Where the client can identify several exceptions and how they have been achieved, they are simply asked to *do more of the same*.

Key features

1 *What does the client want?* What 'project' are they willing to engage in with us? By approaching them in a non-blaming, respectful way,

highlighting strengths via compliments and what they do that is useful, most people will work towards what would be better for them (getting rid of a problem).

2 *What can the client do?* This is to be found in the exceptions and in the part of the goal that is already happening.

3 *What else needs to happen to get to the goal?* To make life safe enough, remove someone's concern, make coping better?

Solution-focused reports, then, address the following points:

- State the difficulty without analysis; state the client's ideas about it and their rating of severity. Include your rating or that of other reports if necessary.
- What is okay – strengths and abilities?
- Is it a 'problem' or an 'unhappy situation'? If the latter, how is it being coped with on a scale of 1 to 10 (client's rating, with perhaps your comment).
- Is the person a visitor, complainant or customer?
- What do they want? Clear picture of the goal? Or of what they think others (e.g. parents) want of them? Their view and your view of what is needed, or needs to happen.
- What can they do (related to the want)? Is it spontaneous or deliberate? Is it helpful or not?
- What else needs to happen (be done)? Their view and that of significant others.
- Their level of motivation (after some work on solution construction)?
- Their level of confidence in their ability, their chance of being able to do what is required?
- Risk? The balance between signs of safety and signs of danger.

Implications for assessment

- *Selection.* Since the work focuses on understanding the solution, usually a clear goal emerges and, so long as the client can have a conversation, that is take turns in talking and remain in the session, a First Session takes place. It is left to the client to decide whether to have another session.
- *Formulation.* Notes are taken and can be used as feedback to the client. These focus on abilities and successes and may include suggestions for tasks to be attempted after the session. No diagnostic language is used unless the client uses it and finds it helpful.

- *Ongoing assessment.* This is achieved via the scaled questions that are part of every session. These will show whether there is progress, at least from the client's subjective viewpoint.
- *Ending.* This is decided by the client.

Advantages and disadvantages

Solution-focused counselling has a very wide application, the main advantage being the emphasis on listening to the client's story and focusing on exceptions, which is both anti-oppressive and empowering, seeking solutions within clients' lives rather than in the counsellor's head. It is an economical way of working and is not only the least intrusive approach, but also the most painless in that it takes the easiest route to solution-finding. It has also been found to produce less dependency and have long-lasting effects, even with clients from those socio-economic groups who do less well with other forms of psychotherapy.

A major advantage of this form of counselling is its ability to avoid making matters worse. While it may be 'good to talk', as the telephone advertisement says, problem-talk can increase problems, whereas solution-talk builds up solutions. A recent study by Professor Wessley (reported by Baxter and Rogers, 2003) speaks of the 'toxic effect' of much of the counselling on offer for post-traumatic stress disorder (PTSD) – at best it was useless, at worst it made people more likely to suffer PTSD. What was needed was to focus on how to get on with life rather than dwell on tragedy. Those who can suppress the worst memories did best, in this study, whereas it was found that reliving the experience can be harmful. A study by professor Bonanno at Columbia University (also reported by Baxter and Rogers) of the counselling provided after the 11 September disaster in New York found 'little evidence that getting people to "open-up" actually helps them. There is more data supporting the view that talking about how unhappy you are just makes it worse'. Solution-talk does not seem to have that disadvantage.

Other advantages for counsellors are that it is easier to learn than more traditional therapies. Those who use it report that they prefer it to other approaches they have used, mostly on the grounds that they find it more respectful, more effective and less stressful. Both our solution focused respondents commented on this:

> It's brief by outcome. Less stressful for me by far. I have none of the side effects of working that my colleagues have. I'm not suffering from burnout.

The energy that develops – more upbeat and positive, not just me but the client. People leave the room more confident. The energy comes from talking about what is going well, from being connected with their own solutions. It's empowering. I also like the results.

We find it difficult to think of any major disadvantages, although some older people who are very muddled in their thinking are not usually able to answer scaled questions. The approach is intrinsically anti-oppressive because of its central emphasis on empowerment, respectful uncertainty and minimum intervention, but feminists have argued that the emphasis on competence and strengths tends to overlook gender and power differences (Dermer *et al.*, 1998). Gender differences are discussed by several solution-focused writer/practitioners (see, for example, Letham 1994; Berg and Reuss, 1998; Dolan, 1998; Milner, 2001); the main implication being that tracking the client's language runs the risk of ignoring the reality that much language is constructed by men and does not always allow for a full understanding of women's experience.

Because the approach involves a complete change of emphasis from those traditionally used by counsellors there is a danger that the technique might be too hastily applied or used uncritically, neglecting the philosophical basis. It is essential for counsellors hoping to employ the approach to get into the habit of reframing situations and listening carefully to clients. Although the approach creates a good flow to the work, it still requires careful analysis. Using it well is not as easy as it sounds. The notion of understanding a solution without understanding the problem could be misread for finding a solution before knowing anything about a problem. If this latter reading were taken out of context, it could result in the counsellor adopting a solution forced approach rather than solution focused one (O'Connell, 2001).

Outcomes

Solution-focused approaches have been evaluated more extensively than most other approaches. The European Brief Therapy Association (EBTA) publishes a full list of studies on the internet (www.ebta.nu/news.html); some of the main studies are listed in Parton and O'Byrne, 2000. The results show that solution-focused therapy is as effective or slightly more effective than other psychotherapies. Benefit is not limited to any specific client group or problem type, the outcome research showing that it has been used effectively with traditionally poor outcome problems, such as anorexia and chronic alcohol/drug use, regardless of learning ability, age or socio-economic status. There is beginning evidence that drop-out rates from solution-focused counselling may be lower than more traditional approaches (see, for example, Milner and Jessop, 2003), but this remains an area where much research is still needed.

Summary

Assessment focuses on trying to understand the client's *solutions* that make a difference. Iveson's (2002) summary is brief but comprehensive:

> Solution-focused work is an exploration not of present problems or past causes, but of current resources and future *hopes*. Assessment therefore focuses on four main questions:
>
> 1 What is the client hoping to achieve by coming?
> 2 What will be the details of her desired life after the problem?
> 3 What is she already doing that might contribute to this? Here the counsellor moves from eliciting exceptions to discussing what the client is *already doing* that is helpful.
> 4 What will be different when she takes one very small step in that direction?

As regards motivation, all the counsellor needs is that the client wants something different. The assessment process is thus summed up by Iveson (2002) as in Figure 9.1.

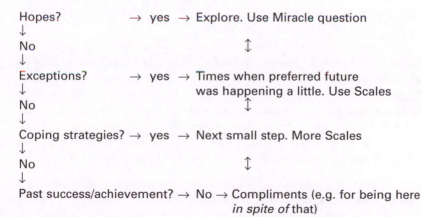

Hopes? → yes → Explore. Use Miracle question
↓
No ↕
↓
Exceptions? → yes → Times when preferred future
↓ was happening a little. Use Scales
No ↕
↓
Coping strategies? → yes → Next small step. More Scales
↓
No ↕
↓
Past success/achievement? → No → Compliments (e.g. for being here *in spite of* that)

Figure 9.1 Solution-focused flow chart (from Iveson, 2002)

10

Integrative Models. Mixed Metaphors

In this chapter we examine how theory and practice intertwine and how this influences both the purpose and form of assessment. Although all counselling practice emphasises increasing clients' responsibility for their lives by helping them make choices that will help them feel, think and act effectively, formulations that counsellors develop – their working hypotheses – are highly dependent on their theories about the nature of people and their problems. As we have seen in the preceding 'maps' chapters, the sorts of questions asked vary enormously, depending on the particular theoretical orientation of the counsellor. The qualities of the therapist will also be different, and thus the 'coherent narratives' offered to clients can be very different. Counsellors develop a sense of 'fit' with their own practice theory, probably based on their own learning style; that is, how comfortable they are with feelings, thought or actions. This may not match clients' learning styles and, where the counsellor has adopted an eclectic approach, there are further possible tensions.

We discuss the implications for assessment of counselling practice based on a single model, eclectic approaches and integrationist models, and the implications of this in terms of training, personal therapy and supervision. We also assess the outcomes research into non-specific factors in counselling effectiveness, asking how much does it matter what theory-base counsellors use and suggest some possible ways in which client choice and counsellor effectiveness can be increased when assessment processes are made more explicit.

Single-theory assessment practice

In theory each counselling theory is incompatible with all the others. As we outlined in the preceding 'maps' chapters, each theory focuses the assessment in a particular direction, depending on the theoretical understanding of how problems occur, where they are located and what forces sustain them. Thus a psychodynamic counsellor would explore in depth the client's inner world, searching for links between childhood experience and adult problems. Although interested in the client's current situation, the assessment would be unlikely to include family members, there being much more interest in the transference relationship with the counsellor. Thus the emphasis throughout the assessment would be on feelings. A cognitive-behavioural counsellor would have little interest in these issues, being primarily concerned about the client's current functioning, thinking processes, existing reinforcements and capacity for change. Although primarily 'feelings-focused', many person-centred counsellors eschew formal assessment at all costs, hoping instead to develop a therapeutic relationship and avoid the labelling implicit in both psychodynamic and behavioural assessment.

What these theories about the nature of people and their problems have in common is that they are all problem-based so the counsellor, regardless of orientation, would be assessing the problem as much as the person. Conversely, the solution-focused counsellor's assessment ignores all this, searching instead for embryonic solutions. The narrative counsellor, whilst broadly accepting this theory of the nature of people and their competencies, would spend some assessment time deconstructing problems.

These differences in assessment processes are not quite so stark in practice, being largely a matter of an emphasis that will focus the assessment rather than fundamental issues as the theories have considerable overlap. This is mainly because each new theory draws on the work of other theories, particularly the 'middle'-period theories such as TA and person-centred counselling. Both these models encompass ideas from psychoanalysis, existential and behavioural psychology. And these theories have drawn on other, much earlier, theories; for example Colledge (2002) points out that Ellis owed much to the Stoic philosophers in his development of cognitive-behavioural therapy and Frankl uses Socratic philosophy in his development of existential counselling theory as well as drawing on the ideas of Heidegger, Nietsche, Kierkegaard and Sartre. Solution-focused brief therapy acknowledges the influence of Wittgenstein, and we could perhaps also see the influence of Socrates who, too, was interested in how the 'virtues' could be utterly transparent in a rationally articulated form. Similarly, the postmodern assumptions of narrative counselling echo

Plato's warning that written words are dead and cannot answer back, whereas true philosophy is always a live activity and interchange of thought (for a brief but lucid account of Socratic and Platonic philosophical thinking, see Annas, 1998, pp. 231–9).

As there is little that is new in counselling theory, it is not surprising that counselling practices are rarely distinctive. Counsellors 'add on' to their basic theories elements of others which seem most suitable to meet the cultural changes affecting clients, the particular blend of practical and existential difficulties that people encounter at different times. Thus the single-theory counsellor is a relatively rare bird: we venture to suggest that even more counsellors are eclectic or integrationist than the research indicates (the percentage varies from 30–55 per cent, see McLeod for an overview, 1998, pp. 204–5). We make this claim on the basis of our small-scale research into how counsellors assess their clients. Only four counsellors identified themselves as using a single theory, three psychodynamic and one solution-focused, although two counselling psychologists interviewed used only CBT. The other respondents adopted varied degrees of eclecticism or integration. The most eclectic were those who viewed themselves as predominantly TA or person-centred; incorporating a very wide range of ideas and techniques from older and newer models. The cognitive-behavioural counsellors spoke of using some person-centred principles, whilst the solution-focused and narrative counsellors integrated ideas from each therapy. The movement towards eclecticism tended to have followed an 'add-on' of 'newer' ideas to existing theories encountered at initial training, but one respondent had moved the other way, abandoning TA for psychodynamic counselling – although retaining some ideas from Gestalt counselling.

This was a small consultation exercise and could not be said to be particularly representative of counsellors in general; certainly all the counsellors we interviewed were atypical in that they were all very experienced. What the overall results do not show is perhaps more significant; that is, the difficulties we encountered in attempting to identify counsellors who were in any way representative of a particular school of counselling. This is not surprising in the case of TA and person-centred counselling, but we were surprised not to be able to find a single cognitive-behavioural 'purist' in counselling, as opposed to counselling psychology, despite making determined efforts. Time and again recommendations about particular counsellors were made, people known to other counsellors to be cognitive-behavioural specialists and who accepted referrals on this basis, but, when approached for interview, these counsellors said that they *did* some cognitive-behavioural counselling but this was not how they predominantly viewed themselves. One did view himself in that way but we detected significant narrative influences in his work. Cognitive-behavioural therapy seems to exist as a single-theory model, and is regularly researched on this basis with good outcomes reported, but we have come to the conclusion that it exists only in *form*. The cognitive-behavioural counsellors use a wider range of theories in actual practice. We ought not to have been so surprised at the extent to which the counsellors we interviewed used an eclectic approach; the 'map' is not, after all, the territory in most cases.

Eclectic assessment practice

Eclecticism has been much discussed in the counselling literature (see, for example, O'Sullivan and Dryden, 1991; Dryden, 1992; Garfield, 1995; Feltham, 1997; Palmer and Woolfe, 2000; Colledge, 2002). Colledge identifies two types of eclecticism; unsystematic, where the portfolio of techniques adopted by counsellors has no consciously coherent rationale; and systematic or technical, where counsellors use a particular technique or theory but also borrow from other approaches. He suggests that the latter more closely resembles integrationism, as does McLeod in his suggestion that this is a deliberate effort on the part of the counsellor to select the most appropriate ideas and techniques to meet the demands of clients. He adds that it emerges from the way theories are used in practice in that counselling has an oral tradition as much as a written one, and that the implicit knowledge of the former strongly influences practice.

We suspect that Colledge's two types of eclecticism are not so distinct, or that the oral tradition is as strong as McLeod suggests. Our small survey revealed a body of counsellors who were constantly reflective in both traditions, reading extensively (even where theories did not 'fit' with their current ideas) and checking the oral tradition against the written tradition. The 'two types' probably reflect different stages of personal development on a trajectory that is impelled by the need to do something different when stuck, or respond to a newly emerging set of problems, or to 'touch base' after exposure to newer thinking in order to confirm an original theoretical perspective.

Not surprisingly the most eclectic counsellors in our survey were those who described themselves as predominantly TA, person-centred, or cognitive-behavioural. These middle-wave practice theories have borrowed the most extensively from earlier theories, and from each other including large amounts of psychoanalytic, existentialist and behavioural theory, so we were not surprised that our person-centred respondents were as likely to use rational-emotive therapy or sand-tray therapy as they were to be non-directive and non-diagnostic. Similarly, TA is eclectic in that, despite its basic simplified Freudian ideas about the nature of people, it has a rich repertoire of techniques ranging from Gestalt ideas about challenging, confronting and creativity to behavioural techniques. In the latter there was much use of cognitive-behavioural ideas about irrational thinking as this 'fits' with ideas about script formation and racket systems. Still current in much of the TA literature is Korzybski's (1933) postulation about the 'abstract' models of the world that we carry around inside our heads, and our tendency to 'misevaluate' when we react to models rather than events; this 'fits' with concepts of transference and counter-transference, script formation and irrational thoughts. The cognitive-behavioural and solution-focused counsellors were eclectic to a much lesser degree, an interesting dimension being a lasting allegiance to the 'core conditions' of person-centred counselling where this had been a previously preferred form of practice.

The therapeutic qualities required of the humanist tradition include not only a commitment to the core conditions, but also an expectation that they have depth of experience because the counsellor should explore no further than she has, herself, done. The counsellor must also secure the trust of the client, develop intimacy so clients can reveal their deepest levels of experiencing, increase mutuality and use hunches and intuition, therefore the counsellor can self-disclose as the relationship develops and deepens. The basic assumption is that being listened to enables clients to listen to themselves. The purpose of this sort of relationship is 'that of providing deep understanding and acceptance of the attitudes consciously held at this moment by the client as he explores step by step into the dangerous areas which he has been denying to consciousness' (Rogers, 1951, p. 219). This runs contrary to the assumptions underlying cognitive-behavioural or solution-focused counselling, but the notion of a warm, genuine, empathic relationship is deeply seductive. Although Masson says that 'no real person really does any of the things Rogers discusses in real life' (1989, p. 232), therefore genuineness can never be attained, eclectic counsellors aspire to underpin their techniques with a strong therapeutic alliance or, when they find the therapeutic alliance on its own is insufficient, they add on techniques.

There are obvious paradoxes here, not least being muddle over whether the counsellor is for or against diagnosis, or does both at the same time, but we must ask the question: do they matter very much? Eclectic counsellors have strong support for their stance from the outcome research which suggests that counselling has similar success rates across models (Luborsky *et al.*, 1975), non-professionals are as effective as professionals (Hattie *et al*, 1984), only 15 per cent of variance in client outcome is attributable to the model used (Lambert and Bergin, 1994), and non-specific factors rate higher than specific techniques (Llewelyn and Hume, 1979). Of the non-specific factors, the human qualities communicated by the counsellor (warmth, openness, genuineness, empathy and care) are what clients report to be the most helpful (Frank, 1974; Smith *et al.*, 1980; Grencavage and Norcross, 1990; Mahoney and McRay-Patteson, 1992; Garfield and Bergin, 1994; Beyebach *et al*, 1996; Beyebach and Carranza, 1997; Beyebach and Rodrigues Morejon, 1999). Similarly, where counsellors are able to instil hope and expectancy, this too contributes to successful outcomes (Grencavage and Norcross, 1990; Snyder *et al.*, 1999; McDermott and Snyder, 1999; Duncan and Miller, 2000).

There is therefore consistent evidence that the Rogerian concept of the therapeutic relationship is the single most important factor in effective counselling. So, why does the person–centred counsellor, the one with the most explicit faith in the centrality of the therapeutic relationship, turn out to be the counsellor who is most likely to be eclectic? Could it be that her relationship is so finely tuned that she can determine exactly when to shift models and utilise the 15 per cent variable that can be attributed to different models? Actually it is neither so simple nor so complex; not only does the therapeutic relationship not exist as separate from theories, but there are other non-specific factors involved.

These non-specific factors include extra therapeutic ones that strongly influence effectiveness, such as resilience factors, clients' unique coping strategies, client-generated precounselling changes, and chance events (Hubble *et al.*, 1999; Duncan and Miller, 2000). Most models assess for resilience and coping strategies, the literature being particularly rich with 'suitability for counselling' factors: Jacobs

lists 12 features that indicate unsuitability for either counselling or
psychotherapy, including narrowly defined problems, chronicity and
no desire for change (1988, p. 53), similarly, McDermott and Snyder
(1999) demonstrate how poorly defined goals combined with low-
hope clients are associated with poor outcomes. Psychodynamic
models tend not to value client-generated precounselling change,
viewing it as flight into health, although solution–focused and narrative approaches welcome it. Equally these models aim to increase
hope and expectancy in low-hope clients through the use of presup-
positional questions (O'Hanlon and Weiner-Davis, 1989; Selekman,
1993, 1997). These extra-therapeutic factors are, then, relevant in
assessment as some theoretical models use them to determine which
clients are unlikely to benefit from counselling, while other models
see them as indicators requiring specific intervention techniques.

Non-model-dependent specific therapeutic relationship factors
intertwine with theory and technique in a complex manner. For
example, Frank (1973, 1974) found that it was not just the creation of
a supportive relationship that was influential on outcomes, but also
the provision of a rationale by which the client can make sense of
problems, and the participation by both client and counsellor in healing rituals. Similarly, where clients perceive techniques as sensible,
practical and having the potential for success, the client is more likely
to cooperate with counselling (Reimers *et al.*, 1992), and the rationale
provided by the counsellor needs to be in line with clients' own views
of their problem situations (Conoley *et al.*, 1992).

It is clear from this that both the use of theory and the personal
qualities of the counsellor are important, and thus there are potential
difficulties as well as benefits in eclectic practice. The intention to
select the most appropriate ideas and techniques for the specific needs
of each client is an excellent one, but it requires a sound knowledge
of how theory works. McLeod (1998) suggests that while there is no
problem in counsellors using lower-level, observational constructs
that carry little in the way of theoretical baggage, higher-level theoretical constructs and concepts cannot be taken out of their parent
model. It might seem reasonable to import a technique that has
proven successful in some context and therapeutic model, but 'One
should bear in mind that any given technique, developed in a particular context and under different theoretical premises is probably
transformed into a different technique when used under different
circumstances' (Lazarus and Messer, 1991). For example, any counsellor can use scaling questions but the rationale will depend on the

parent model used. Thus a person–centred counsellor would use them to assess the severity of a problem, whereas a solution-focused counsellor would use them as a means of eliciting exceptions and solution-building. The skill of the predominantly person–centred eclectic counsellor must surely be a way of communicating to the client the reasons for a shift in techniques and the rationale for this, particularly a shift from bringing long-buried material to consciousness in a non-directive way to a focus on a more directive behavioural assessment of what is happening here and now.

There are even more possibilities for theoretical confusion for the predominantly TA eclectic counsellor. Although TA *is* eclectic in nature, not everything 'fits', not least of which is the 'addition' of ideas from Gestalt counselling. As McLeod points out, Gestalt counselling can be thought of as a source of practical techniques for exploring current awareness, but it does have a theoretical framework of its own; it is essentially existential rather than interpretative, which carries a very different view of the person than that of TA counselling. A further potential difficulty with eclectic practice is that the counsellor trained in a single model is unlikely to have themselves experienced the sort of counselling they are 'adding on'.

We next look at integrationist models as these seem to be the logical outcome of a personal development trajectory through unsystematic eclecticism to a thoroughly systematic and integrated model of practice.

Integrative assessment practice

Integrative counselling includes a great variety of approaches and divergencies of methodologies (see, for example, Goldfried, 1991; Norcross and Newman, 1992), all of which describe an attempt to develop counselling that makes the most of successful models to include what works best, although not all of them have theoretical consistency. In this section we outline two models that integrate assessment techniques within a coherent theoretical framework: Lazarus' multimodal counselling (Palmer and Lazarus, 1995) and Beyebach's integrative solution-focused brief counselling (Beyebach, forthcoming). Other integrative models attempt to identify those higher order constructs that can be combined without transforming techniques out of context. We will briefly outline three of these trans-theoretical models: the skilled–helper model developed by Egan (1998), and two stages–of–change models (Prochaska *et al.*, 1982; Stiles *et al.*, 1990).

Multimodal assessment

Multimodal assessment was developed by Lazarus in response to the restrictions and limitations of traditional counselling. It can be described as eclectic in that it places emphasis on selecting the best techniques to suit the unique needs of each client, it does have a full theory of how people develop, and it adopts the theories and frameworks of others (Colledge, 2002). However, it is technically integrative in that it is underpinned by a consistent social cognitive learning theory and avoids the pitfalls of the eclectic approaches described earlier through the use of a systematic assessment framework, explaining the rationale to clients and using bridging procedures to accommodate shifts of emphasis in technique selection.

Most counselling assessments are trimodal, looking at feeling, behaviour and cognition, whereas Lazarus' multimodal assessment framework includes also interpersonal and imagery modalities (Palmer, 1997, p. 138). Lazarus identified seven modalities in all that are in a constant state of reciprocal interaction and flux, interconnected by complex sequences of behaviour and other psycho-physiological processes. People develop tendencies that favour some modalities over others, thus assessing these tendencies is important if counselling is to be tailored to fit different client learning styles. The seven modalities extend other, more simplified, notions of learning styles, such as Honey and Mumford's (1992) division of people into activists, reflectors, pragmatists and theorists.

The seven modalities, known by the acronym BASIC ID, are comprehensively assessed by the completion of a 15-page Multimodal Life History Inventory. This can be completed by the client at home or the questions can be asked over a period of time by the counsellor (for a useful list, see Palmer, 1997, pp.139–41). Individual functioning within the seven modalities provides the sub-goals of long-term individual functioning:

- **B**ehaviour: taking effective action to achieve realistic goals.
- **A**ffect: acknowledging, recognising and clarifying feelings; enhancing positive feelings and coping with negative ones.
- **S**ensation: being in touch with and enjoying one's senses.
- **I**magery: using coping images and being in touch with one's imagination.
- **C**ognition: having adequate and accurate information, and thinking realistically.

- **I**nterpersonal: having good relating skills such as conversational and assertion skills, plus a capacity for healthy interdependency.
- **D**rugs/biology: taking proper care of one's physical health, and eating and drinking alcohol in moderation (*source*: Colledge, 2002, p. 262).

There are two parts to the first comprehensive assessment: a structural profile and a modality profile. The modality profile serves as a working hypothesis, albeit one that is always provisional and tentative. Techniques are then selected for intervention in discussion and negotiation with the client. A structural profile is also completed which looks at client *learning styles*:

- **B**ehaviour: how much of a doer are you?
- **A**ffect: how emotional are you?
- **S**ensation: how 'tuned in' are you to bodily sensations?
- **I**magery: how much are you into mental images and pictures?
- **C**ognition: how much of a 'thinker' are you?
- **I**nterpersonal: how much of a 'social being' are you?
- **D**rugs/biology: to what extent are you health conscious? (source: Palmer, 1997, p. 153).

Clients are asked to rate subjectively on a scale from 1–7 how they perceive themselves in relation to these seven modalities, so that a 'desired' structural modality can be contemplated. Palmer makes the important point that these modality scores do not necessarily reflect an area that needs change simply because they are high or low. A client may be happy with being a 'doer' with a score of seven, whereas another client may decide that a score of seven indicates 'doing too much' or doing too much of the wrong tasks, and other clients may be happy to keep a low score. Client perception of the subjective scores is the important factor in assessment. It is also important to ask clients what they think counselling is about, how long they think it should last, and what personal qualities they think the counsellor should ideally possess (Colledge, 2002, p. 266).

This last question is important as the multimodal counsellor adapts the therapeutic relationship by matching the client's style, whether this be a businesslike approach or the more traditional warm and empathic approach. The relationship continuum ranges from formal to tight bonding, and can be cold, warm or tepid; gentle or tough; and highly directive or highly supportive. Four modes of supportiveness–directiveness are described and an effective multi-modal counsellor will use all four, as and when necessary. Shifts in these modes will also occur when a second-order BASIC ID assessment is made to deal with specific problems or particularly resistant problems that emerge during counselling (Palmer and Dryden, 1995). In multimodal counselling, authenticity has been appropriately described by Lazarus (1993) as the counsellor as 'authentic chameleon'.

Although seemingly laborious, time-consuming and potentially rigid (most counsellors quail at the thought of completing a 15-page questionnaire), multimodal assessment conforms to all the tenets of sound assessment, aspiring to high levels of ethical practice. The counsellor adapts to fit clients with different problem solving styles, it offers choice through ongoing negotiation over goals and appropriate techniques, and the process is transparent. As we saw earlier, client confidence in techniques chosen is a substantial factor in successful outcomes in counselling (Lazarus, 1973; Reimers *et al.*, 1992; Conoley *et al.*, 1992).

Integrative solution-focused brief counselling

The development of solution-focused brief counselling in America and narrative counselling in Australasia meant that, despite them both belonging clearly to the 'third wave' of counselling, they tended to be used mainly as single-theory assessment models. Whilst this remains largely the case with narrative counselling, a number of solution-focused counsellors have combined the two approaches (see, for example, O'Hanlon and Weiner-Davis, 1989, O'Hanion, 1993; Furman and Ahola, 1992; Dykes and Neville, 2000; Saggese and Foley, 2000; Shilts and Reiter, 2000; Milner and O'Byrne, 2002a); others have retained elements of family therapy, which is linked historically and conceptually with solution-focused counselling (see, for example, Dolan, 1991, 1998: O'Connell, 2001). The movement from radical 'purism', via a period of eclecticism when the model is departed from through the addition of techniques from other models, to integration has been most clearly described by Beyebach and Morejon (1999). Counselling is only truly integrative when eclectic practice is *thought* about 'in the context of the vast literature on integration in psychotherapy' (Beyebach, 2002). He outlines a model of technical solution-focused integrative practice to extend counselling to those clients for whom a 'purist' model is not working (for a fuller discussion see O'Connell,

2001, chapter 6), to improve 'fit' with clients, and to provide non-solution-focused short-cuts by utilising solidly established intervention strategies. Central to Beyebach's integrated model is a fundamental adherence to the philosophy of solution-focused counselling and collaborative assessment.

Where a 'purist' approach is not working, Beyebach recommends a careful reexamination of both counsellor and client goals. If they are agreed, achievable, small and specific but there is no progress, he suggests that a process of sequential integration is embarked upon. The techniques which can be 'added on' without compromising basic solution-focused philosophy would include: small problem-pattern modification (for further details, see O'Hanlon and Weiner-Davis, 1989); externalisation (see, for example, Jacob, 2001); interruption of problem-maintaining attempted solutions (Fisch *et al.*, 1982; Shoham and Rorhbaugh, 1996); psycho-educational interventions and structural interventions.

Similarly, Selekman (1997) expands the model in his work with young people when parents change their ideas but their behaviour towards the child does not change; where parents' goals are achieved but they do not consider the changes in their child significant; and where there are several professionals involved who are pessimistic about change. In the first instance he uses play and art therapy with the family, and visualisation and cognitive work with the child. In the second and third instances he concentrates on taking the parents and professionals seriously, ensuring that their concerns are listened to fully. Durrant (1993) provides a useful outline of how both pessimistic parents and professionals can be made to feel part of the change process in the difficult area of counselling in residential care.

Like the multimodal assessment model, Beyebach also gives consideration to client learning styles in order to increase 'fit' (see also, Tohn and Oshlag, 1995; O'Connell, 2001). For example, clients who demand expert advice or to know 'why' can become frustrated with patient and persistent solution-finding, experiencing this as solution-forced. In the former case, he would recommend 'adding on' psycho-education to provide 'outside' clarity so that goals can be agreed. These would include: thought stopping (see also O'Connell, 2001; Selekman, 2002); replacing negative imagery (Dolan, 1998 provides a comprehensive range of possible exercises); relaxation training and meditation (Dolan, 1991; Selekman, 2002); and cleansing rituals (Dolan, 1998; Milner, 2001; Selekman, 2002). In the latter case he is prepared to offer possible explanations but, unlike the multimodal counsellor who favours the high–direction–high–support mode when involved in an educational process (Colledge, 2002, p. 263), possible explanations and techniques are proposed rather than imposed so that the client can evaluate them for 'fit'. Where explanations are acceptable to the client, techniques are always tailored through exploration and negotiation with the client so that they 'fit' the unique needs of each client. Another way of increasing 'fit' is via externalising problems, as proposed by narrative counselling. Externalising the internalised story is viewed in the integrative solution-focused model as developing 'disputation skills' in which clients' beliefs are challenged in a much less direct way than the confrontational style of the cognitive counsellor (O'Connell, 2001, pp. 105–6), or 'decatastrophising' (Selekman, 2002, p. 94).

Non-solution-focused short-cuts are recommended to make use of techniques that are well-defined in both practice and research as effective ways of tackling specific problems. These would include all problems where diminution of symptoms actually enhances self-consciousness, such as tics, phobias, eating distress, and drug misuse. Here behavioural ideas could be used to underpin exception-finding; psycho-educational approaches used for family members; and drugs such as Antabuse contracts. Where problems are seemingly intractable anything from previous counselling that worked is utilised, regardless of the model from which it stemmed, although Beyebach always aims to get back as soon as possible to the solution-focused basics. He also uses motivational interviewing techniques for clients who are 'visitors' (Miller and Rollnick, 1991), and paradoxical injunctions for those clients who are particularly resistant to change. When assessing 'visitors' and negotiating goals, Beyebach suggests that it is useful to identify the existence of a three-way relationship which includes counsellor, client *and* the 'given' goal. Acknowledging a 'given' goal enables the counsellor to deal with high-risk situations by providing escape plans for potential victims, or actively persuading clients to consult a psychiatrist; for example in cases of domestic violence, psychosis or severe eating difficulties.

The advantages of an integrative solution-focused approach to assessment is that the model can be extended to hard-to-reach clients, but it does raise the potential danger of promoting diagnostic thinking and the counsellor working harder than the client. Beyebach suggests safeguards against this: sticking to simplicity, using non-solution-focused techniques in a solution-focused way, maintaining an open mind, and getting back on a solution-focused track as quickly as possible.

Transtheoretical models

The integrative models described so far are based on single-theory models, utilising techniques from other models to increase the range of applicability and improve 'fit' with clients' learning styles only where the departures from the underpinning theoretical assumptions fulfil one of three criteria: they are transparent in that they are explicitly negotiated with the client; they are brief, temporary departures; or they can be used in conjunction with the single-theory techniques without compromising theoretical coherence. They constitute, therefore, no more than technical integration. As theory is strongly influenced by cultural change, they cannot be said to be universally applicable. There has been a search in counselling for a model that integrates theories in a way that is appropriate for our postmodern, multicultural society with its many images of the person. Integrating at a theoretical level involves identifying higher-order constructs that can account for change mechanisms beyond individual theories, there being several models that aspire to be transtheoretical. We outline three of them briefly below before discussing some of their limitations.

The skilled-helper model

Egan's (1998) model of the skilled helper, who need not necessarily be a professional counsellor, is based on an image of the person as a potent human being who has both the resources and will to act. His key integrating concept is *problem management*, viewing counselling as a means of assisting clients to take an active part in tackling their problems. The client is encouraged to take the lead in problem management, persist in doing so, and make links between behaviours and their results. The counsellor is viewed as a hired servant who helps people to be more effective at living, but running the business remains with those who hire the skilled helper. Thus the helper is a mere passing support system, although Egan suggests that problem management is furthered by increasing the helper's expertness and attractiveness so that they are more influential. The helper will help people manage their lives through a three-stage framework: exploration, interpretation, and goal setting/action, drawing on ideas from a range of theories such as the empathy and congruence of person-centred counselling and insights from psychodynamic counselling. The qualities required of a skilled helper are:

- Basic intelligence and respect for ideas.
- Knowledge and competent use of theory.
- Evaluation skills.
- Common sense and social adeptness.
- Easiness with others.
- The ability to feel at home in the social and emotional world of others as well as their own.
- The ability to respond effectively to a wide range of human needs.
- Lack of fear of deep human emotions, both their own and those of others, and a willingness to work at the level of distress.
- A willingness to explore their own feelings and behaviour and to work at recognising and integrating all aspects of the self.
- The ability to interpret non-verbal messages (*source*: Colledge, 2002, p. 1).

The advantages of Egan's model are that it is practical and pragmatic and has utility over a very wide range of situations. Its limitation is that it is transtheoretical only within the modernist, problem-based paradigm, the image of the person as a potent human being corresponding closely to Roger's concept of the 'authentic self'. Rather than transcending theories, it tends to ignore theoretical assumptions about the nature of people in favour of concentrating on the nature of the relationship. This makes it more difficult for the skilled helper to make explicit to the client the basis on which a coherent narrative is offered.

Stages-of-change models

Prochaska and Di Clemente (1984; Prochaska 1999) take an area of commonality across theories to develop their transtheoretical formulation of the stages of change: precontemplation, contemplation, determination, action and maintenance. It might seem obvious that a client would not attend counselling sessions if there was nothing they wanted to change, but such an assumption is rarely born out by experience. A client may well want life to improve without having to make change, having a great need to hang onto behaviours that may be destructive but offer a measure of safety due to their familiarity. Or they may want others to change. A stage theory of change has therefore great potential in the assessment stage of counselling, particularly affecting how goals are agreed and appropriate tasks set.

Clients at the precontemplation stage may be reluctant to attend counselling and doubtful that it will work, or they may have been coerced by others into seeking help although they do not accept that there is a problem. The counsellor would therefore negotiate an agreed goal, perhaps to work on an area in which the client is willing to make changes, waiting for the 'main issue' to emerge later, or make a decision that the client is not yet ready for counselling. Jacob (2001) illustrates how identification of the precontemplative stage in clients with eating distress can aid assessment of those clients who can be eased into counselling and those who are so much at risk that re-referral is essential to ensure safe and ethical practice. Clients at the contemplative stage are not fully committed to counselling but can recognise that some change is needed and can talk about it to some extent. Recognising this stage enables the counsellor to help the client move on; for example, the psychodynamic counsellor would work with the ambivalence and resistance, offering tentative interpretations, whilst the solution-focused counsellor would identify discrepancies between the client's present situation and preferred future, negotiating easily achievable goals to increase the client's experience of solution-finding. The last three stages of change are to some extent self-explanatory, but recognising that clients rarely progress evenly through the five stages enables the counsellor to select the most appropriate therapeutic approach and aids regular reassessment.

Identifying the client's stage of readiness for change is useful in all forms of counselling, but is, perhaps, most used by counsellors whose work is brief by theoretical orientation or agency restrictions on the number of sessions available. Counsellors in the latter situation may use the formulation of stages to make the decision not to work with clients in the precontemplative stage at all – it would not be helpful to move a client on to the contemplative stage and then have to tell them they are not entitled to any more sessions or must be referred to another counsellor for long-term work. Identification of clients at the contemplation stage is essential in brief counselling; the most appropriate approach being an exploratory one in which the counsellor takes time to understand the client's hopes and expectations. It is, of course, important not to waste a great deal of time exploring these issues with clients who are at the action stage as this frustrates their decision to take action (for a fuller discussion, see Dryden and Feltham, 1992, pp. 51–4). Assessing a client's stage and level of change is not a traditional part of intake interviews, but could be usefully incorporated.

A rather different way of looking at how change occurs is the *assimilation model* (Stiles *et al.*, 1990; Barkham *et al.*, 1996). This fits even more neatly with developmental counselling approaches than Prochaska and Di Clemente's model, in that it uses Piagetian developmental psychology – particularly the concepts of cognitive schema. This model outlines a series of stages but emphasises that change is assimilated and accommodated most significantly in relation to problematic experiences. This model provides the counsellor with a framework from which not only to understand where the client is at and identify stuckness, but also provides guidance on the different therapeutic techniques most appropriate to each stage. For example, assessment of a client at the first, *warded off*, and second, *unwanted thoughts*, stages suggests that psychodynamic ideas about the unconscious will be useful, whilst the client who is at the stage of *vague awareness* will benefit from person-centred ideas about gently working through emotions in a climate of acceptance, behavioural ideas not becoming useful until the client has reached a much later stage of *application/working through*.

This model is useful in helping the counsellor make more conscious decisions about appropriate therapeutic style and interventions than occurs in the more intuitive eclectic approach. Like Egan's skilled-helper model, it is only transtheoretical in terms of problem-based theories, so, although it has obvious utility in situations of grief and loss, it has little to offer in ways of understanding structural power relations that may severely limit client movement through the change process.

Implications for training and supervision

As we discussed in Chapter 1, assessment is regarded as a hotly debated subject on most training courses, but the debate is about the advantages and disadvantages of assessment models linked to single theories; that is, formal or informal, formulation or anti-diagnosis, problem or solution-based (see, for example, Carswell, 2002; Spurling, 2002). And those courses which recommend their students to undertake personal therapy usually only provide one model of therapy. As counselling is not just a set of techniques but a continuous learning process, this leaves a large gap for the counsellor who develops a more eclectic way of working. Trainees would be better prepared to take advantage of their reflective practice if they were offered a range of personal-counselling opportunities. This would not only give them experiences similar to those of their later clients, but as, unlike clients, counselling trainees cannot vote with their feet if they do not have positive experiences of personal therapy, it might go some way towards reducing the ill effects of personal therapy. Such effects are estimated at 15–40 per cent of all counselling trainees (Macaskill, 1988), although there is no information on the effects of the 'newer' forms of counselling. Solution-focused and narrative counsellors are expected to incorporate the underlying philosophy into their personal lives, but there is a dearth of evidence on personal experiences of behavioural counselling.

The role of supervision is even more important as this is mandatory and continuous. The literature on supervision promotes three basic functions: educational (or formative), supportive (or restorative) and management (normative), but it is the latter two functions which are paid most attention. This is supported by the research; for example, Greenberg (1980) found that supervisees' expectations include access to support, affirmation of practice, personal growth and an opportunity to evaluate strengths and weaknesses; Webb (2001) also identified a high level of affirmation needs. Our respondents, too, all said that they would take stuck cases to supervision or when they needed reassurance. Our respondents who were also supervisors mentioned the problem of supervisees deselecting clients for discussion, an issue identified also by Corbett (1995). How much of this is due to experiences of being supervised from a model of supervision developed out of a preferred way of 'doing' counselling? How does a supervisor adapt his or her model to meet the specific needs of each supervisee, including their learning styles (frustration with constant 'reflecting back' is a common complaint of supervision), and how do they help supervisees develop a coherent eclecticism or integrationism when this may well run counter to the supervisor's preferred style of counselling practice? For example, one of our supervisor respondents said that her baseline was Rogerian, 'the three core conditions, then I draw on other models, TA and rational-emotive brief therapy', whilst another said 'psychodynamic theory underpins all my work. I may not overtly use the method but it would inform my thinking even if I am not engaging in interpretation or using transference'. And how does it utilise the oral tradition of counselling?

There is perhaps a case to be made for supervision to abandon its direct link with personal counselling and embrace a more distinctive educational role, one that provides challenges and opportunities for the supervisee to think through the implications of using techniques from other models. This would not preclude the functions of supportiveness and management. The implicit benefits of the one-to-one tradition of supervision could also be usefully reevaluated; planned use of small group peer supervision would enable counsellors to better utilise the informal oral tradition of counselling as this is a rich source of new ideas.

Summary

We hope this brief overview of how counsellors mix metaphors highlights the careful thought that needs to given to how a counsellor can remain logical and able to explain to clients when shifts of model are made. There are numerous advantages in integrative assessment – so long as it thought out. An integrative assessment will look like a combination of some of the models described in the previous chapters, perhaps along with some we have not described, and thus such an assessment would involve the use of questions drawn from the models used unless counsellors confine themselves to a model such as multimodal practice.

Assessment, however, involves making up one's mind about a case, and therefore in the next and final chapter we revisit the problems of keeping an open mind, the issue of risk as opposed to safety assessment, the special problems of disadvantaged clients, and the power of records. These are discussed in terms of the decisions counsellors make to continue working with a client, to refer on for specialist help, or assess as unsuitable for counselling.

11

Assessment Decisions

Assessment is a crucial element in the power relations between counsellor and client. Whether or not a counsellor makes a formal assessment, he or she makes an important decision – to proceed or not. If the decision is to proceed with counselling, an assessment has been made that the counsellor understands the client well enough to calculate the likelihood of therapeutic success. If not, the counsellor decides either that the client will not benefit from counselling or refers the client to another counsellor or agency – most usually for specialist help. Thus the counsellor controls who has access to counselling, who will undertake it, what form it will take, and how long it is likely to last. Clients have no power over these issues, other than the power to vote with their feet. There is considerable evidence that clients do vote with their feet: drop-out rates from counselling have been estimated at approximately one-third (McLeod, 1998). This gives the client some say over how long counselling will last, but it does not give the client any power over access. As we saw in Chapter 2, clients with longstanding, intractable problems and those with multiple socio–economic difficulties are the least likely to be accepted for counselling; it is therefore possible that assessment as unsuitable for counselling may further oppress the most needy clients.

This chapter will explore factors that have the capacity to hinder accurate assessments in all three decision-making choices. These factors include: common individual decision distortions that limit our capacity to keep an 'open mind'; issues around risk assessment, and allied intra- and inter-agency distortions; issues around confidentiality in report writing and recording; and difficulties in matching clients with counsellors. We conclude each section with some suggestions about how these difficulties can be minimised so that clients receive the most expeditious and effective help.

Deciding to proceed with counselling

Counsellors have to assess needs, evaluate risks and allocate resources in a way that is as equitable as possible for both clients and agencies. Inevitably, the rights and entitlements of some people will be restricted. Keeping an open mind during this process is problematic because all people are liable to be biased in all their assessments of each other; goodwill and well-meant activity are no guarantee of impartiality. Social psychology suggests that we are all 'cognitive misers' in that we do not use fresh eyes each time we assess another person because we simply lack the time that this would involve, so we use quick and 'dirty' cognitive processes to move information speedily through our system of organised social knowledge (Forsyth, 1986). As we saw in the previous chapter, counsellors' social knowledge is most likely to have been informed by a single model learned during basic training, thus adding to the 'cognitive miserliness' which affects us all. Below we outline some of the more common decision-making distortions that bias assessments.

Selective attention

Although we all probably pride ourselves on our objectivity, research shows that we commonly weight some evidence from our assessments more heavily than others. Traits that have extreme value carry more weight than those with moderate value. Traits with extreme value include intelligence and verbal fluency; two factors in particular that have the potential to influence a psychodynamic assessment of likely 'fit'. The psychodynamic counsellor will be looking for the client's ability to face their feelings and look beyond the surface, deciding that clients who are unable to do this may benefit more from cognitive-behavioural approaches (Aveline, 1993, 1997) despite the fact that clients may simply be unable to express their feelings in words (Kearney, 1996). Similarly, there may be cultural constraints that influence the expression of feelings, and constraints that influence the counsellor's assessment too – for example, the value we ascribe to various traits is influenced by factors such as race; black physicality, for example, might have more extreme value than white physicality (Denney, 1992). Also, we have a tendency to give more weight to negative and less to positive information. This is particularly evident in the emphasis on *problem* identification in much of counselling knowledge.

There are also two other effects of selective attention: vivid, distinctive or unexpected data are perceptually more salient; and primacy effects overwhelm recency effects, giving truth to the old adage about the need to make a good first impression. The subjects of counselling assessments are most likely to encourage these effects, the reason for their referral usually being one which is distinctive. As they will initially be seen when they are at their 'worst' (an overload of negative information), they will then present the assessing counsellor with an initial impression that is difficult to dislodge. Thus there is an inbuilt bias towards discounting client reports of improvement as 'flight into health', and a tendency to think in terms of lengthy counselling being needed.

The most effective check against biases arising from selective attention is the creation of a good therapeutic environment in which the client is prepared in the best possible way for the beginning of a therapeutic relationship. For example, the broader therapeutic context in which counselling takes place is as important as the therapeutic relationship in delivering a service for adolescents (Everall and Paulson (2002), and has been found to play a significant role in people's recovery from eating disorders (Mearns and Thorne, 2000; Marchant and Payne, 2002). Providing a warm, relaxed welcome where the counsellor can engage in problem-free talk before beginning the more formal session allows the client to settle into the new surroundings and present their competent as well as troubled selves. Introductions that include asking clients what sort of help they want, what help they have found most useful in the past, and how they have previously overcome difficulties all aid empowerment and act as a check against selective attention effects.

Stereotyping

Data collection risks being oversimplified by stereotyping effects that permit the classification of people into ready-made compartments so that responses are prepared for particular persons. Unfortunately, there can be some truth in stereotypes — indeed, people give strong signals by the ways in which they present themselves, indicating the categories to which they consider themselves to belong. The danger is that information on which categorisation is made may be faulty because of the selective attention errors mentioned above, or because differences from a stereotype that indicate a person's uniqueness may be ignored. For example, a counsellor with a stereotype of Asian families to do with the importance of family networks assessed an Asian woman as depressed due to social isolation because she had no links with her extended family. This completely ignored the fact that she had made a conscious decision to move away from her family, whom she saw as the cause of her problems in the first place.

Primacy effects work on stereotyping in a peculiar manner. If the first impression is a good impression – which will be weighted heavily for both salience and primacy effects – a halo effect can sometimes operate in which a person's very positive characteristics colour perceptions of their various other characteristics. This is quite different from picking out positives as well as negatives in assessment work, and can have grave consequences for clients who may be expected to cope with responsibilities that are unreasonable and unachievable. Another inherent danger in stereotyping is that it tends to produce negative as well as positive self-fulfilling prophecies about people. Putting people into erroneous categories tends to perpetuate myths about them, as has been amply demonstrated by research into social class, race and gender effects on educational achievement. The most effective check against both negative and positive stereotyping effects is for counsellors to ask themselves 'how is this person similar to others – how might they be categorised?' and then ask 'how are they *different?*'

Attributional bias

All of us wish to make sense of social interactions so that we can control and predict events (Heider, 1958). That is, if we can decide why someone has done something, it will help in deciding our own behaviour towards them, as well as being able to predict what they will do. We are biased towards looking for causes and making inferences (attributions) that are subject to a range of irrational biases (for a fuller discussion, see Nisbett and Ross, 1980). The attribution process is switched on whenever people attract our attention through the selective-attention effects mentioned above, and when events and actions do not meet our expectations and need an explanation that fits with our ideas about the nature of people.

By and large, we attribute our successes to our own efforts and our failures to events outside ourselves; however, we judge other people oppositely. This is called an attributional bias. The first part of this, attributing positive outcomes to stable, personal factors and negative outcomes to unstable, external factors, is called a self-serving bias (see, for example, Miller and Ross, 1975). This is actually a healthy bias because it helps us to make sense of unexpected events, and protects our self-esteem and public image. For example, if you get a cold, you are likely to think that this is the result of being surrounded by cold germs at work, whereas if you are the only person at work who escapes getting the cold, you are likely to attribute this to something you have done – such as taking vitamin C or not smoking.

The tendency to attribute causes oppositely when observing other people is called 'fundamental attribution error'. This arises from over-attribution and defensive attribution, both of which can serve to insulate observers from anxiety. If other people are considered *personally* responsible for their misfortunes, then the same fate cannot befall the observer. This means that we are all predisposed to victim-blaming – even where the 'victim' is clearly constrained and controlled by situational factors. Thus it can be seen that we have an inbuilt tendency to prefer counselling interventions that locate the problem within the subject. It is not only that it is easier to 'work' on the subject rather than social circumstances, it also makes us each feel more individually secure. Thus as we switch from teaching victims of domestic violence to accept responsibility for the perpetrator's actions to challenging abusers, we create 'an "us" and "them" mentality, a delusion which is particularly seductive for therapists working with abuse. This delusion can mask the continuum of abusive behaviour in our own experience and the general community.' (Jenkins, 1996, p. 121). To counter this tendency, Jenkins recommends that counsellors self-monitor, reflect and debrief to check against a possible 'inner tyrant' operating from a position of self-righteous superiority.

Sensory distortions

Not only do we make judgements about people as a result of the mental processes outlined above, we also make inferences about people's whole characters simply from the way they look, smell and speak. This 'cognitive miserliness' may help us to take short cuts in assessment, but it is rarely accurate. The most obvious sensory distortion in personal perception is the effect of physical appearance on assessments. Good-looking people are usually ascribed positive personality traits – a factor that belies the saying that beauty is only skin deep. Physical appearance is, of course, the most 'salient' and 'primary' impression we receive.

We mentioned linguistic oppression in Chapter 2 but there are obvious gender and ethnic biases that operate with regard to *speech* as well as the actual words used. Many apparently natural aspects of men's and women's voices cannot be explained simply in terms of anatomical differences between the sexes, but are acquired as speakers learn the cultural norms of feminine and masculine behaviour (Graddol and Swann, 1989). Speech reflects gender divisions, a masculine tone being regarded as the voice of authority. Clients are unlikely to be able to afford the voice coaching that Margaret Thatcher used to lower the tone of her voice. Indeed, their voices are likely to lack 'authority' as a result of the stress of their circumstances making them more shrill than usual.

Clients who conform verbally with counsellors are the most likely to form positive relationships, but the counsellor also has a responsibility to conform verbally with the client. Jacob (personal communication) says that she keeps two buckets of words, one full of counselling terms for talking with professionals and an empty one for talking to clients. This allows her to listen to the client's words and use them when reflecting back. Another way of counteracting sensory distortion effects is to ask 'What characteristics do I dislike about this client's presentation?', 'Can a list of positive qualities be drawn up to counter balance them?'

Deciding to refer

The respondents in our small study rarely made the decision to refer a client to another counsellor on the basis of insufficient psychological-mindedness. Much more common was the decision to stick with the client: 'I will err on the side of proceeding'; 'try harder', 'be open and honest about stuckness', being the more common answers to our questions about what to do when stuck. The decision to refer was most frequently made on pragmatic grounds. These fell into two main categories: the amount of time available in the agency to carry out the counselling, and assessment that the client needed more specialist help. In the first, there is the obvious bias towards assessing for lengthier counselling than the client will actually want. In the second, the main issue is accurate risk assessment. Accurate risk assessment is always problematic for counsellors because it often involves breaching confidentiality – the keystone of counselling practice.

Risk assessment tends to be influenced by the counsellor's experience with clients presenting risks and the quality of supervision available (Bond, 1993), and agency protocols. Agencies are most likely to have strict protocols with regard to child protection, although the complexity of the law means that the situation for counsellors is not crystal clear. This is due to differences between responsibilities and rights in national and European legislation, and the impact of subsequent case law. Previously counsellors were able to make a balanced assessment of the likelihood of harm depending on whether the child met the Gillick competence test, whether the abuse disclosed was historic or current, and whether other children were at risk, but the situation is now more complex. Hamilton (2001) sums up the possibilities and restrictions for counsellors, the main points being:

- Article 8 of the European Convention on Human Rights states that while everyone has a right to respect for their private and family life, this is not an absolute right. Disclosure may be necessary to protect the health, morals or the freedom of others.
- Case law has imposed restrictions on Gillick competence so the right of children to have counselling without parental consent where they are sufficiently competent to consent on their own behalf is not automatic.
- Where the counsellor considers the child incompetent, counselling should not proceed *but* counsellors still owe a duty of confidentiality to the child and should not inform the parent that the child sought counselling, unless the child agrees.
- Because of the importance of child protection, no agency or individual should offer any child complete confidentiality and the limits to confidentiality should be made clear from the start.
- Only social services are required to investigate situations where they suspect a risk of significant harm. There is no corresponding duty to pass information to them, but Hamilton considers that there is a *moral* duty to do so – even against the child's wishes.
- S. 47(9–11) of the Children Act requires various, as yet unspecified, 'authorised persons' to assist social services in carrying out investigations, but not 'where doing so would be unreasonable in all circumstances of the case'. Hamilton believes that breaching the confidentiality of a 'competent' child would be unreasonable and a counsellor would be justified in refusing to provide confidential information.
- In general, confidential information should only be shared where the child consents or where it is necessary for their protection.

It can be seen from this that the counsellor retains a wide degree of discretion about when to refer a child to social services, but case law offers them no protection from any consequences of their decisions; there is no provision made for acting in good faith. Counsellors are left, therefore, with the risk of losing a client when they decide to inform social services of possible risk against a child's wishes. This, in turn, reduces the child's access to a confidential service and possible source of help.

Bond (1993), although writing about suicidal clients, has experi-ence of the dilemmas facing counsellors in deciding when to breach confidentiality. He recounts client distress at counsellors adopting a policy of telling GPs of suicidal intent when counselling has not been able to 'persuade' the client to do this themselves. Clients often have good reasons for not telling their doctors, he says, so autonomy should not be violated unless the client lacks the capacity to make her own decisions, there is substantial risk, and the counsellor can do some-thing that has a reasonable chance of averting the risk. This latter condition is perhaps the most helpful one; the counsellor may feel that breaching confidentiality is the 'safest' option, but it does have the capacity to cause harm to the client. Decisions about the likelihood of risk are also best dealt with by the individual who is counselling the client, and in discussion with the supervisor (for a fuller discus-sion, see Henderson, 2001), as there is substantial evidence that case conferences have the capacity to increase rather than reduce risk.

Much of the drive towards interagency meetings as a check against individual errors in assessment work comes from the child protection field, although the notion of the 'professionals' meeting' has now become popular in other areas of counselling. The case conference is generally thought to be particularly effective in assessing risk (see, for example, Home Office, 1991). We query the wisdom of viewing the case conference as an effective check against individually-biased assessment. We do not believe that two heads are necessarily better than one, and we support our argument with generic psychological explanations of group and individual decision-making processes.

One popular explanation of reasons for defective decision-making in groups is the concept of *groupthink*. This describes decision-making in groups under stress where a group engages in particular types of behaviour. When Janis and Mann (1977) studied several disastrous policy decisions, they found that these behaviours include shared rationalisations to support the first apparently adequate course of action suggested by an influential group member, a lack of disagree-ment between group members and a consequent high level of confi-dence in the group decision. This concept of groupthink has already been aired in the child protection literature, and suggestions for improving case–conference performance with reference to making corrections to the symptoms of groupthink have been promoted in training packs (Lewis *et al.*, 1991). However, there are two fundamental problems with the application of correctives. First, the concept of groupthink itself suggests that once a group is subject to its symptoms, it will be too deeply entrenched in its behaviour to see a need for reevaluation or change. Second, it may be the case that an individual can exert far more influence on the decisional direction of the group due to *framing effects*.

Whyte (1989, 1993) suggests that rather than alter the original framing of the problem, a group would be subject to the effects of *group polarisation*, and this would *accelerate* the tendency to risk or caution of the original framing, group polarisation effects demonstrating that people in a group take a more extreme position than they would as individuals (Moscovici and Zavalloni, 1969). This, suggests Whyte, means that rather than act as a countercheck to any unwarranted optimism, if the decision is framed in terms of losses the group will commit resources to a course of action initially agreed on by the group, even when it is failing. Group members will bolster this decision by self-justification, such as 'the plan needs more time to work' or 'we need more resources'. The group then has the potential to become so risky that there is always the possibility for a decision fiasco. This group behaviour is not only found in counselling assessments of risk; as Leiss and Chociolko comment on industrial risk assessment: 'the significance of an event's probability tends to decrease as conceivable consequences increase, until what is possible becomes more feared than what is probable' (1994, p. 31).

Kahnemann and Tversky (1979) offered an explanation of how individuals make decisions that tend towards the direction of risk or caution depending upon whether or not the initial choice is framed in terms of options that involve gains or losses. If the possible options are framed in terms of gains, individuals will be risk–averse, that is they will opt for a certain, although perhaps smaller, gain as opposed to another larger gain that is uncertain or risky. In other words, they will be less likely to gamble or risk losing the certain gain. However, if the options are framed in terms of losses, individuals will be more risk-seeking and will tend to avoid a certain, although smaller, loss in favour of another, larger loss that is uncertain. They will be more likely to risk the gamble, exposing themselves to a potentially greater risk. Positive framing leads to caution, and negative framing to risk-taking. Because of the importance of maintaining the therapeutic relationship, the various options open to counsellors are often all unattractive, desired outcomes usually having a low probability and less desirable outcomes having a high one. All the options can usually be framed either positively or negatively, and this will affect riskiness in decision-making.

The risk to a client always exists within a complex and uncertain social situation, so sound group decision-making can be enhanced by involving the client in all the discussions, consulting all the stake-holders, careful framing of the decision situation, making a systematic choice between options, and retaining individual responsibility. Whether or not the counsellor is making a decision individually or in consultation with a group, it is important to recognise that risk eludes quantification as one can never know when it has ceased to exist. Safety approaches avoid these dilemmas by inviting abusive people to take responsibility for their own behaviour, for example the no-harm contracts used in TA counselling. Effective safety plans based on solu-tion-focused and narrative approaches have also been developed in the fields of severe mental illness (White, 1995), eating disorders (Jacob, 2001), domestic violence (Jenkins, 1990, 1996; Milner and Jessop, 2003), and child abuse (Berg, 1992; Turnell and Edwards, 1999), An example of a safety approach to the assessment of suicidal clients is listed below:

- *Key points to cover*

  - Always take suicidal ideas seriously.
  - Be sincere and genuine in relating to the client's pain.
  - Show deep empathy.
  - Don't show fear of the worst scenario.
  - Acknowledge and validate feelings and thinking.
  - Together, generate possibilities.
  - Ensure that the client understands that they are responsible ulti-mately for any decisions they make.
  - Compliment them for being here now and for talking it through.

- *Sample questions to elicit suicidal intent*

  - It seems like you are having quite a time of it at the moment . . .
  - When everything comes at once, sometimes it can seem to get on top of one . . .
  - At this point, how much more do you think you can cope with?

- How far is all this getting you down right now?
- How often, recently, have you felt at the end of your tether?
- I expect sometimes you feel you have had your lot ...
- At the moment, how far do you feel able to go on?
- How close do you feel, right now, to ending your own life?
- If you decided to go ahead with the last-resort option, what method would you use, how prepared are you should you decide?
- On a scale of 1–10 (where 1 is 'not at all well' and 10 is 'very well'), how well do you feel you are coping at the moment?

- *Sample questions after suicidal thoughts have been established*

  - Tell me about a time last week when you felt least suicidal?
  - Before you were feeling as you do at the moment, what did you do in the day that interested you?
  - What has stopped you taking your life up to this point?
  - On a scale of 1–10, how suicidal do you feel right now; how suicidal were you before you decided to seek help; what would you be doing/thinking about/feeling to be another point higher?
  - What have you done in the last week/couple of weeks that has made a difference to the terrible situation you are in?
  - On a scale of 1–10, how determined are you to give options (other than suicide) a try first?
  - What would have to happen here today in this counselling session, for you to think it was worthwhile coming?
  - Let us suppose you went for the last-resort option and actually died. You are at your own funeral as a spirit looking down from about 10 feet at the mourners below. What might you be thinking about another option you could have tried first? At this funeral, who would be most upset among the mourners? What advice would they have wanted you to have about other options?
  - Suicide is the last resort. What other ways have you tried so far to crack this problem?

More details of this safety approach, including graveside and death-bed scenarios are available from John Hendon Associates (JHendon@aol.com). We have also adapted these questions to assess homicidal intent; for example, the question about how close the client feels to ending their own life is asked as 'how close do you feel, right now, to doing something so awful to your partner that the thought scares you?' Often we find that being open in this way about dangers is a great relief to clients, and it does help us to be clear about when we need more specialist help.

Deciding not to proceed

As we mentioned earlier in this chapter, this is the rarest decision. By and large, counsellors are more likely to persist in the face of difficulties or refer clients for more specialist help. However, there remains a significant number of clients who are refused counselling either at the outset or after progress is judged to be too slow to fit the agency timescale. These include what one our consultants referred to as the 'hot–potato' client:

> I wouldn't take on a client if what they presented needed a lot more time than I can give them within the remit of the agency I'm working for. I think that can be particularly true of hot-potato clients – those that get passed on from one agency to another, to get rid of them or seem to be doing something.

Clients who are poor at keeping appointments, who appear to be poorly motivated, or are veterans of counselling (which they report has been helpful but without any obvious evidence of significant improvement) are the most likely to be assessed as unsuitable for counselling. Clients with these behaviours make us feel failures, although we have a tendency to justify our decisions not to proceed with rationalisations about 'readiness' for counselling. Holding notions about readiness sets the parameters for acceptance for counselling: 'Readiness for counselling also requires that individuals recognise, if only in a small way, that they contribute to their difficulties' (Ruddell and Curwen, 1997, p. 73):

> Leaving well alone may be the right course when the counsellor judges that the client's inner world is so fragile that any change would be for the worse or that the client has insufficient personal resources to make major developmental moves. (Aveline, 1993)

This means that counsellors need to be clear about what their own, and other, therapies can achieve, and their limitations (Aveline, 1997). This is not only to aid matching of client and counsellor, but to endure that we do not deny clients access to counselling. In assessing clients as sick enough to need counselling but well enough to bene-fit from it, we are in danger of denying help to those very people who are also most likely to be rejected by more specialist agencies. And, when we do reject a client, how careful are we to explain the reasons for this openly and honestly? Or do we hide behind the time–limit constraints as a handy excuse when we are actually holding pejorative judgements in our heads? And do we accept that we, as counsellors, have a responsibility for increasing a client's motivation?

Matching clients with counsellors is facilitated where clients are consulted about their own preferences. As Aveline (1993) points out, if they have been on a waiting list for some time they may feel they have little choice. It is difficult to assess learning style so it may be easier for the client to be permitted to change counsellor until they find one they feel at ease with. This may seem an unnecessary luxury in busy agencies, but would cut down the number of missed appoint-ments. O'Connell (2001) recommends that we recognise therapeutic diversity in order to improve match between counsellor and client, but this is not as easy as it sounds. When we began our consultation exercise, we found that counsellors were rarely what colleagues thought they were. One way round this is to reevaluate and re-search our clinical experience together more (see, for example, Lees, 2001). Aveline (1993) recommends coordinating different forms of coun-selling in sequence to improve matching, a process which would facil-itate the development of local knowledge communities. A sequence of counselling need not necessarily consist of counselling *per se*; it may be that the 'hot-potato' or poorly motivated client who misses appointments would benefit from a planned therapeutic environment which prepared them for the rigours of the therapeutic relationship. For example, after feeling more like a referee than a counsellor, one of us assessed a warring couple as 'unready' for counselling but the woman made use of the excellent therapeutic environment where we work to spent an hour 'telling her side of the story' to the counselling coordinator. Two weeks after the experience of being listened to, without any attempt being made to offer help, this woman booked a counselling appointment where she demonstrated a readiness to discuss the changes she hoped to make. We have also found that, sometimes, the socially isolated client simply needs a cup of tea with ancillary staff rather than a formal hour with the counsellor. It has not been our experience that such 'needy' clients become unduly depen-dent on the agency.

Recording decisions

Recording is often problematic for counsellors. Not only is it a chore that detracts from the 'real business' of the therapeutic relationship, but it has the capacity to violate client autonomy when courts seek access to records. Whether or not the counsellor has to prepare a progress report for the funding agency, a referral report, or simply make a brief note on the case file, the client's narrated story becomes a written one. The client may never ask to see the case file but, where they are aware of its existence, it is very important to them. Research in other branches of the helping professions shows that people are very anxious to know what had been written about them (see, for example, Prince, 1988; Kagle, 1991). Once something is written down, it gains authority. White and Epston (1990) suggest that the invention of the case file enabled individuals to be captured and *fixed* in writing:

> In our world, language plays a very central part in those activities that define and *construct* persons, and if written language makes a more than significant contribution to this, then a consideration of modern documents and their role in the redescription of persons is called for. (White and Epston, 1990, p. 188)

The therapeutic relationship involves two people striving for an equal partnership but this partnership can dissolve when the counsellor starts recording. The *subject* and the *author* of the document have very different access to power. White and Epston argue that the author has 'a library of terms of description that have been invented by and considered the property of this particular domain of expert knowledge' (1990, p. 188). This expert knowledge, combined with the invisibility of the author, creates the impression of the possession of an objective and detached view that does not actually exist, increasing the likelihood of biases and inaccuracies creeping in.

The problem is that counsellors are fluent in at least two languages – the verbal language of the client and the written language of the profession. For example, the Diagnostic and Statistical Manual of Mental Disorders (DSM-1V) and the International Classification of Diseases (ICD-10) are designed to provide a common language for professionals so that the terms they use have a common meaning rather than individuals using their own unique (or clients') definitions. Whiston (2000) argues that this uniformity aids effective communication, whilst others see this as a set of punitive labels which provide, at best, 'thin' descriptions of people (White, 1995). Counsellors are often stuck with these labels when funding agencies demand that clients are categorised so they can decide how much counselling they will pay for, or when other agencies require a 'diagnosis' to make assessment for special needs – few counsellors will not have experienced the need to 'diagnose' depression so that a client might succeed with a housing application; or to diagnose 'lasting trauma' to support a compensation claim. This storying of the client as deficient is contrary to the counselling aim and some counsellors get round the issue of client autonomy by showing the client the official diagnosis list and allowing them to choose the category they feel best describes them, or the one with which they are most comfortable (see, for example, Selekman, 2001).

Reports are also subject to distortions where they have the purpose of persuading the reader to accept a recommendation as well as informing and explaining. For example, a report that seeks to refer a client for specialist help will not only use the expert language of the reader, but also contain a 'pitch' (Emerson, 1969). This involves the writer 'recycling the evidence' (Aronnsen, 1991) in an attempt to individualise or victimise the subject, using such words as 'unfortunately' and 'however' to cast doubt on statements of fact. Similarly, where the writer has decided not to offer a counselling contract, the report will contain a 'denunciation'. This will use similar words to the 'pitch' but give then a negative connotation. This is fundamentally dishonest in that it obscures differences of opinion (we have some trepidation in making such a strong statement as we look back at all the 'howevers' in this book!).

The simplest way to avoid recording distortions, which may have the capacity to damage the client when used in other forums, is to use the client's own words and avoid editing these to fit the 'expert' language, what Epston (1998) refers to as the 'spy-chiatric gaze'. Records can be co-authored with clients so that they remain experts in their own lives. Epston, for example considers his principal role as a sort of 'scribe who faithfully notes down the proceedings for posterity and makes available a client's history, capturing on paper the particular thoughts and understandings with which they make sense of their lives' (Epston, 1998, p. 96). He does edit his recordings for possibilities though, rather than dwell on problems and deficits. It is possible to prepare such notes of each session that are suitable for both the case file and for client feedback (for a fuller discussion and examples, see Milner and O'Byrne, 2002a). We have found that recording in this way also saves time as clients have their own records to submit to other agencies or courts. This not only aids client choice, but also protects us from fears that our records could be used by a third party to disadvantage a client.

Summary

Social psychology tells us that it is not easy to make objective assessments in *any* social situation. And the human tendency to make attributions, develop stereotypes and increase risk-taking in groups is such robust behaviour that exhortations to keep an 'open mind' can be quite worthless. Perhaps we don't keep our minds open at all, although we may sometimes pretend that our decisions are non-judgmental. We have suggested some checks you can use to improve the accuracy of your assessment-making, summarised below:

- First, by all means consult with all the people in your professional system, but do not hand over the responsibility for the decisions you make. Accept the individual responsibility for your own assessments. This is not to say that your supervisor or intra-agency group has nothing to offer you in terms of resources and management of the individual decision. Neither is it to say that you need not listen carefully to clients, but at the end of the day you must state your decision and note differences of opinion.
- Second, be aware of the importance of your first assessment because this will underpin all your subsequent decisions and may hinder the process of evaluation. The only way in which you can reasonably engage in evaluation of your assessments, we suggest, is by ensuring that you have multiple frames at the outset. Consider the maps outlined earlier even where they do not fit comfortably with your theories about people. These frames need to be written down in terms of possible hypotheses to provide the means by which you actually evaluate your outcomes or else you will engage in the self-justification efforts described earlier.
- Third, test each frame by checking your hypotheses against the outcomes by seeking your client's opinion. Continuous bridging of the gap between counsellor and client will assist this process.
- Finally, check your records and reports for language usage that pathologises rather than individualises the subject and make these available to your client for scrutiny and amendment.

Concluding Remarks

Counselling is a process of constructing meaning within the 'real world' conditions in which we live, a reinterpreting of how things are for each and every client. In an increasingly available world of great diversity, we can hardly expect any one map to fit every client; we need many metaphors and vocabularies, perhaps many theories. There is a growing awareness that there has, perhaps, been too much focus on pathology: 'Psychology is also about strength and potential' (Seligman and Csikszentmihalyi, 2000), and how to understand and mobilise these qualities in clients. Those authors say that counselling is not just about fixing what is broken; it is about nurturing what is best: opportunity development. Assessment is therefore, at least in part, working out with the client what needs to be made better and how best that can be done, but also looking at what is going well and at how the client does that. But as no theory is a transcript of reality, even though it has something useful to say, no assessment can write the 'truth' about another person's problems; only, at best, a storied version of things that may be useful in making progress. It may summarise old 'facts' or lead to new ones. We need, therefore, to focus on what will work for the client, not on explaining the world – however interesting that might for the counsellor, it is an unnecessary intellectual excursion.

Invitation to structure

We have attempted throughout this book to discuss the complexities of practice without making practice even more complex, and so, because the options are so numerous and the potential data so huge, and the purposes so diverse, we invite you now to look again at the ideas in Chapter 3 on holistic assessment, at the comprehensive lists of questions suggested and at the outline frameworks for *Intake Assessment* and for *Formulations*. Look also at the 'map' chapter that you favour, for further questions to help with your formulations. Then write your own selective list of questions and set out a framework to suit your own practice and to fit comfortably in your theoretical 'home'. When this book has helped you to arrive at such a structure we will be delighted.

207

References

Alexander, F. and French, T.M. (1946) *Psycho-Analytic Theory: Principles and Applications* (New York: Ronald Press).

Annas, J. (1998) 'Classical Greek Philosophy', in J. Boardman, J. Griffin and O. Murray (eds), *Greece and the Hellenistic World* (Oxford: Oxford University Press), ninth impression.

Ashcroft, R. (2001) 'What's the Good of Counselling and Psychotherapy? Developing an ethical framework', *Counselling and Psychotherapy Journal*, 12: pp. 10–2.

Atkinson, R.L., Atkinson, R.C., Smith, E.E. and Bem, D. (1993) *Introduction to Psychology* (London: Harcourt).

Audini, P. and Lelliott, B. (2001) *Are there Groups of the Population Sectioned More Often than Others? An Analysis of Mental Health Act Assessment Data* (London: Department of Health).

Aveline, M. (1993) 'Advising on the Most Suitable Counselling Arena', in W. Dryden (ed.), *Questions and Answers in Counselling in Action* (London: Sage).

Aveline, M. (1997) 'Assessing for Optimal Therapeutic Intervention', in S. Palmer and G. McMahon (eds), *Client Assessment* (London: Sage).

Baker Miller, J. (1973) *Towards a New Psychology for Women*. Boston MA: Beacon Press.

Barden, N. (2001) 'The Responsibility of the Supervisor in the British Association for Counselling and Psychotherapy's Code of Ethics and Practice', in S. Wheeler and D. King (eds), *Supervising Counsellors. Issues of Responsibility* (London: Sage).

Barkham, M., Stiles, W.B., Hardy, G.E. and Field, S.D. (1996) 'The Assimilation Model: Theory, Research and Practical Guidelines', in W. Dryden (ed.), *Research in Counselling and Psychotherapy: Practical applications* (London: Sage).

Barret-Kruse, C. (1994) 'Brief Counselling: A User's Guide for Traditionally Trained Counsellors', *International Journal for the Advancement of Counselling*, 17: pp. 109–15.

Bayne, R., Horton, I., Merry, T. and Noyes, E. (1994) *The Counsellors' Handbook* (London: Chapman & Hall).

Baxter, S. and Rogers, L. (2003) 'Stiff Upper Lip Beats Stress Counselling', *Sunday Times*, 2 March.

Beck, A.T. (1967) *Depression: Clinical, Experimental and Theoretical Aspects* (London: Hoeber).

Beck, A.T., Rush, A.J., Shaw, B.F. and Emery, G. (1997) *Cognitive Therapy of Depression* (New York: Guilford Press).

Beck, A.T. and Tomkin, A. (1989) *Cognitive Therapy and Emotional Disorders* (London: Penguin).

Beck, A.T., Weissman, A., Lister, D. and Trexler, L. (1974) 'The Measurement of Pessimism. "The Hopelessness Scale" ', *Journal of Consulting and Clinical Psychology*, 42: pp. 861–5.

Berg, I.K. (1994) *Family-based Services: A Solution-Focused Approach* (New York: Norton).

Berg, I.K. and Miller, S. (1992) *Working with the Problem Drinker: A Solution-Focused Approach* (New York and London: W.W. Norton).

Berg, I.K. and Reuss, N.H. (1998) *Solutions, Step by Step. A Substance Abuse Treatment Manual* (New York: W.W. Norton).

Bergin, A.E. and Garfield, S.L. (1994) *Handbook of Psychotherapy and Behaviour Change* (New York: Wiley) 4th edn.

Berne, E. (1964) *Games People Play* (New York: Grove Press).

Berne, E. (1978) *A Layman's Guide to Psychiatry and Psychoanalysis* (London: Penguin).

Beyebach, M. (forthcoming) 'Integrative brief solution-focused therapy: a provisional roadmap' in M. Selekman and S. Geyerhofer (eds) *Beyond Solution-Focused Brief Therapy* (Chicago: Zeig & Tucker).

Beyebach. M. and Escudero Carranza, V. (1997) 'Therapeutic interaction and drop out: measuring relational communication in solution-focused therapy', *Journal of Family Therapy*, 19: pp. 173–212.

Beyebach, M., Rodrigues Morejon, A., Palenzuela, D.L. and Rodrigues-Arias, J.L. (1996) 'Research on the process of solution-focused therapy', in S.D. Miller, M.A. Hubble and B.L. Duncan (eds), *Handbook of Solution-focused Therapy* (San Francisco: Jossey Bass).

Beyebach, M. and Rodrigues Morejon, A. (1999) 'Some thoughts on integration in solution-focused therapy', *Journal of Systemic Therapies*, 18: pp. 24–42.

Beyebach, M., Rodrigues Sanchez, M.S., Arribas de Miguel, J., Herrero de Vega, M., Herandez, C. and Rodrigues Morejon, A. (2000) Outcome of solution-focused therapy at a university family therapy centre', *Journal of Systemic Therapies*, 19: pp. 116–28.

Blackburn, I. M. and Davidson, K. (1989) *Cognitive Therapy for Depression and Anxiety* (Oxford: Blackwell).

Blair, M. (1996) 'Interviews with black families', in R. Cohen and M. Hughes, with L. Ashworth and M. Blair (eds), *Schools Out: The Family Perspective on School Exclusions* (London: Family Service Units and Barnados).

Bond, T. (1993) *Standards and Ethics for Counselling in Action* (London: Sage).

Booth, T. (1993) 'Obstacles to user-led services', in J. Johnson and R. Slater (eds), *Ageing and Later Life* (London: Sage, 1993).

Bornat, J. (ed.) (1999) *Biographical Interviews. The Links between Research and Practice* (London: Centre for Policy on Ageing).

Bowlby, J. (1988) *A Secure Base: Clinical Implications of Attachment Theory* (London: Routledge).

Bracho, A. (2000) *An Institute of Community Participation* (Dulwich Centre website. www.dulwichcentre.com.au).

Bravesmith, A. (2001) 'Book Review: Anna Bravesmith on Paul Goldman's Face-to-Face: therapy as ethics', *Psychodynamic Counselling*, 7: pp. 508–10.

Bromley, E. (1983) 'Social class issues in psychotherapy', in D. Pilgrim (ed), *Psychology and Psychotherapy. Current Issues and Trends* (London: Routledge).

Browde, P. (1999) 'An HIV story: secrets and surprises', in *Narative Therapy and Community Work: a conference collection* (Adelaide: Dulwich Centre Publications).

Burnham, J. and Harris, Q. (1996) 'Emerging ethnicity: a tale of three cultures', in K. Dwiyedi and V. Vanna (eds), *Meeting the Needs of Ethnic Minority Children. A Handbook for Professionals* (London: Jessica Kingsley).

Burns, D.D. (1992) *Feeling Good. The New Mood Therapy* (New York: Avon Books).

Burton, M. and Suss, L. (2000) 'Psychodynamic (Freudian) Counselling and Psychotherapy', in S. Palmer (ed), *Introduction to Counselling and Psychotherapy. The Essential Guide* (London: Sage).

Cameron, H., Gawthrop, D., Warwick, K. and Webster, L. (2001) 'Children with sexually problematic behaviour: suggestions for child centred practice', *Youth Justice Matters*, March: pp. 9–12.

Carswell, C. (2002) 'The Good, the Bad and the Integrative', *Counselling and Psychotherapy Journal*, 13: pp. 14–17

Colledge, R. (2002) *Mastering Counselling Theory* (Basingstoke: Palgrave Macmillan).

Coltart, N. (1988) 'Diagnosis and suitability for psychoanalytic psychotherapy', *British Journal of Psychotherapy*, 4: pp. 127–34.

Coltart, N. (1988b) 'Psychological Minded or Borderline Personality', *British Journal of Psychiatry,* 153: pp. 819–20

Conoley, C.W., Ivey, D., Conoley, J.C., Schmeel, M. and Bishop, R. (1992) 'Enhancing consultation by matching the consultee's perspective', *Journal of Counseling Development*, 69: pp. 546–9.

Corbett, L. (1995) 'Supervision and the mentor archetype', in P. Kugler (ed.), *Jungian Perspectives on Supervision* (Einsiedeln: Daimon).

Corey, G. (2000) *Theory and Practice of Counselling and Psychotherapy*, 6th edition (Belmont, CA: Wadsworth).

Cordery, J. and Whitehead, A. (1992) 'Boys don't cry: empathy, collusion and crime', in P. Senior and B. Woodhill (eds.), *Gender, Crime and Probation Practice* (Sheffield: Pavic Publications).

Cox, M. (2000) 'The equal relationship in psychotherapy: roles, rights and responsibilities', *ITA News*, 56: pp. 17–20

Crain, W.C. (1985) *Theories of Development: Concepts and Applications* (Englewood Cliffs, N.J: Prentice Hall), 2nd edn.

Crowe, M. and Ridley, J. (1990) *Therapy with Couples* (London: Blackwell Scientific Publications).

Curwin, B. (1997) 'Medical and psychiatric assessment' in S. Palmer and G. McMahon (eds.), *Client Assessment* (London: Sage).

Davies, D. (1999) 'Homophobia and heterosexism', in D. Davies and C. Neal (eds.), *Pink Therapy. A guide for counsellors and therapists working with lesbian, gay and bisexual clients* (Buckingham: Open University Press).

Denman, C. (1995) 'What is the point of formulations?' in C. Mace (ed.), *The Art and Science of Assessment in Psychotherapy* (London and New York: Routledge).

Denney, D. (1992) *Racism and Anti-Racism in Probation* (London: Routledge).

Department of Health (2001) *Treatment Choice in Psychological Therapies and Counselling: Evidence-Based Clinical Practice Guideline* (London: HMSO).

Dermer, S.B., Hemesath, C.W. and Russell, C.S. (1998) 'A Feminist Critique of Solution-Focused Therapy', *American Journal of Family Therapy*, 26: pp. 239–50.

Derrida, J. (1973) *Writing and Difference*. Chicago: Chicago University Press.

De Shazer, S. (1985) *Keys to Solutions in Brief Therapy* (New York and London: W.W. Norton).

De Shazer, S. (1991) *Putting Difference to Work* (New York and London: W.W. Norton).

De Shazer, S. (1994) *Words Were Originally Magic* (New York and London: W.W. Norton).

De Shazer, S. (1998) *Clues: Investigating Solutions in Brief Therapy* (New York and London: W.W. Norton).

De Shazer, S., Berg, I.K., Lipchik, E., Nunally, E., Molnar, A., Gingerich, W. and Weiner-Davis, M. (1986) 'Brief Therapy: focused solution development', *Family Process*, 5: pp. 207–21.

Dobash, R.E., Dobash, R.P., Cavanagh, K. and Lewis, R. (2000) *Changing Violent Men* (London: Sage).

Dolan, Y. (1991) *Resolving Sexual Abuse: Solution-Focused Therapy and Eriksonian Hypnosis for Adult Survivors* (New York and London: W.W. Norton).

Dolan, Y. (1998) *One Small Step: Moving beyond Trauma to a Life of Joy* (Watsonville, CA: Papier–Mache Press).

Dryden, W. (1990) *Rational-Emotive Counselling in Action* (London: Sage).

Dryden, W. (ed.) (1992) *Integrative and Eclectic Therapy* (Buckingham: Open University Press).

Dryden, W. (1997) *Reason and Therapeutic Change* (London: Whurr).

Dryden, W. and Feltham, C. (1992) *Brief Counselling. A Practical Guide for Beginning Practitioners* (Buckingham: Open University Press).

Dryden, W. and Feltham, C. (1994) *Developing the Practice of Counselling* (London: Sage).

Dryden, W. and Feltham, C. (1998*) Brief Counselling. A Practical Guide for Beginning Practitioners* (Buckingham: Open University Press) (reprinted edition).

Dumonte, F. and Lecomte, C. (1987) 'Inferential processes in clinical work: inquiry into logical errors that affect diagnostic judgement', *Professional Psychology: Research and Practice*, 18: pp. 433–38.

Duncan, B.L. and Miller, S.D. (2000) *The Heroic Client: Doing Client-directed, Outcome-informed Therapy* (San Francisco: Jossey-Bass).

Durlak, J.A. (1979) 'Comparative effectiveness of paraprofessional and professional helpers*, Psychological Bulletin*, 86: pp. 80–92.

Durrant, M. (1993) *Residential Treatment. A Cooperative, Competency-Based Approach to Therapy and Program Design* (New York and London: W. W. Norton).

Dykes, M.A. and Neville, K.E. (2000) 'Taming trouble and other tales: using externalized characters in solution–focused therapy', *Journal of Systemic Therapies*, 19: pp. 74–81.

Egan, G. (1998) *The Skilled Helper* (Belmont, CA: Brooks Cole), 6th edn.

Elliott, A. (2002) *Psychoanalytic Theory. An Introduction* (Basingstoke: Palgrave Macmillan), 2nd edn.

Elliott, H. (1997) 'En-gendering distinction: postmodernism, feminism and narrative therapy', *Gecko. Journal of deconstruction and narrative ideas in therapeutic practice*, 1: pp. 52–71.

Ellis, A. (1962) *Reason and Emotion in Psychotherapy* (New York: Lyle Stuart).

Ellis, A. (1987) 'The impossibility of achieving consistently good mental health', *American Psychotherapies*, p. 42.

Ellis, A. (1993) 'Reflections on Rational-emotive Therapy', *Journal of Consulting and Clinical Psychology*, p. 61.

Ellis, A. (2001) *Overcoming Destructive Beliefs, Feelings and Behaviours* (New York: Prometheus Books).

Ellis, A. and Harper, R.A. (1998) *A Guide to Rational Living* (New York: Wilshire Book Co.).

Emerson, D. (1969) *Judging Delinquents* (Chicago: Aldine).

Epston, D. (1998) *Catching Up with David Epston: a collection of narrative-based papers*, 1991–1996 (Adelaide: Dulwich Centre Publications).

Erikson, M.H. (1959) *Hypnotherapy: An Exploratory Casebook* (New York: Irvington).

Evans, J. (1995) *Feminist Theory Today* (London: Sage).

Everall, R.D. and Paulson, B.L. (2002) 'The therapeutic alliance: adolescent perspectives', *Counselling and Psychotherapy Research*, 2: pp. 78–87.

Feltham, C. (1997) 'Challenging the core theoretical model', *Counselling*, 8: pp. 181–5.

Feltham, C. and Dryden, W. (1993) *Dictionary of Counselling* (London: Whurr).

Fisch, R., Weakland, J.H. and Segal, L. (1982) *The Tactics of Change: Doing Therapy Briefly* (San Francisco: Jossey-Bass).

Fisher, D.J., Himble, J.A. and Hanna, G.L. (1998) 'Group behavioural therapy for adolescents with obsessive-compulsive disorder', *Research on Social Work Practice*, 8(6): pp. 629–36.

Fishman, P. (1978) 'What do couples talk about when they're alone?', in D. Burthurff and E.L. Epstein (eds), *Women's Language and Style* (Akron, Ohio: L. & S. Books).

Fonagy, P. (2001) *Attachment Theory and Psychoanalysis* (New York: Other Press).

Forsyth, D.R. (1986) *Social Psychology* (Monterey, CA: Brooks Cole).

Foucault, M. (1972) *The Archeology of Knowledge and the Discourse of Language* (New York: Pantheon).

Foucault, M. (1973) *The Birth of the Clinic* (London: Tavistock).

Foucault, M. (1980) *Power (Knowledge)* (New York: Pantheon).

Foucault, M. (1984) *Space, Knowledge and Power* (New York: Pantheon).

Foucault, M. (1988) 'Technologies of self', in L. Martin, H. Gutman and P. Hutton (eds), *Technologies of the Self* (Amherst: University of Massachusetts Press).

Frank, J.D. (1973) *Persuasion and Healing: A Comparative Study of Psychotherapy* (Baltimore: Johns Hopkins Univeristy Press).

Frank, J.D. (1974) 'Psychotherapy; the restoration of morale', *American Journal of Psychiatry*, 131: pp. 272–4.

Frankl, V. (2000) *Man's Search for Meaning* (Boston, MA: Beacon Press).

Freeman. J., Epston, D. and Lobovits, D. (1997) *Playful Approaches to Serious Problems* (New York and London: W.W. Norton).

Freedman, J. and Combs, G. (1996) *Narrative Therapy: The Social Construction of Preferred Realities* (New York and London: W.W. Norton).

Freud, S. (1940) *An outline of psychoanalysis. Part III: The theoretical yield*. S. E., p. 23.

Freud, S. (1952) *Collected Papers, 1917* (Translated by J. Riviere, Vol. IV) (London: Hogarth Press).

Friere, P. (1972) *Pedagogy of the Oppressed* (Harmondsworth: Penguin).

Fromm, E. (1985) 'The mode and function of an analytic social psychology: notes on psychoanalytical and historical materialism' in A. Arato and E. Gebhurdt (eds), *The Essential Frankfurt School Reader* (New York: Continuum).

Furman, B. and Ahola, T. (1992) *Solution Talk: Hosting Therapeutic Conversations* (New York and London: W.W. Norton).

Garfield, S.L. (1995) *Psychotherapy: An eclectic-integrative approach* (Chichester: Wiley).

Garfield, S.L. and Bergin, A.E. (1994) *Handbook of Psychotherapy and Behavioural Change* (New York: Wiley).

Gergen, K.J. (1985) 'The social constructionist movement in modern psychology', *American Psychologist*, 40: pp. 266–75.

Gibbens, J. (1946) *The Care of Young Babies* (London: J. & A. Churchill), 2nd edn.

Gilligan, C. (1982) *In A Different Voice* (Cambridge, MA: Harvard University Press).

Gilligan, S. and Price, R. (1993) *Therapeutic Conversations* (New York and London: W. W. Norton).

Goldberg, C. (1992) *The Seasoned Psychotherapist: Triumph over Adversity* (New York: W.W. Norton).

Goldfried, M.R. (1991) 'Research issues in psychotherapy integration', *Journal of Psychotherapy Integration*, 1: pp. 5–25.

Goldner, V. (1992) 'Making room for both/and', *Family Therapy Networker*, 16: p. 2.

Gosling, A.L. and Zingari, M-E. (1996) 'Feminist family therapy and the narrative approach: dovetailing two frameworks', *Journal of Feminist Family Therapy*, 8: pp. 47–63.

Graddol, D. and Swann, J. (1989) *Gender Voices* (New York: W. W.Norton).

Green, J.R. (1994) *Theatre in Ancient Greek Society* (London and New York: Routledge).

Greenberg, L. (1980) 'Supervision from the perspective of the supervisee', in A. Hess (ed.), *Psychotherapy Supervision: Theory, Research and Practice* (New York: Wiley).

Greenberg, L.S., Elliott, R.K. and Lietaer, G. (1994) 'Research on Experimental Psychotherapies', in A.E. Bergin and S.L. Garfield (eds), *Handbook of Psychotherapy and Behaviour Change* (New York: Wiley), 4th edn.

Grencavage, L.M. and Norcross, J.C. (1990) 'Where are the commonalities among the therapeutic common factors?', *Professional Psychology: Research and Practice*, 21: pp. 372–8.

Halgin, R.P. and Caron, M. (1991) 'To treat or not to treat: considerations for referring prospective clients', *Psychotherapy in Private Practice*, 8: pp. 87–96.

Halliday, M.A.K. (1978) 'Antileagues', in M.A.K. Halliday (ed.), *Language as Social Semiotic: The Social Interpretation of Language and Meaning* (London; Arnold).

Hamilton, C. (2001) *Offering Children Confidentiality: Law and Guidance* (Colchester: Children's Law Centre, University of Essex).

Hanson, B. and Maroney, T. (1999) 'HIV and same-sex domestic violence', in B. Leventhal and S.E. Lundy (eds), *Same-Sex Domestic Violence* (London: Sage).

Hargaden, H. and Llewellin, S. (1999) 'Lesbian and gay parenting issues', in D. Davies and C. Neal (eds), *Pink Therapy. A guide for counsellors and therapists working with lesbian, gay and bisexual clients* (Buckingham: Open University Press).

Harris, A.B. and T.A. (1986) *Staying OK* (London: Pan).

Harris, T.A. (1973) *I'm OK – You're OK* (London: Pan).

Hattie, J.A., Sharpley, C.F. and Rogers, H.J. (1984) 'Comparative effectiveness of professional and paraprofessional helpers', *Psychological Bulletin*, 95: pp. 534–41.

Hawtin, S. (2000) 'Person Centred Counselling and Psychotherapy', in S. Palmer (ed.), *Introduction to Counselling and Psychotherapy. The Essential Guide* (London: Sage).

Hearn, J. (1996) 'Men's violence to known women: men's accounts and men's policy developments', in B. Fawcett, B. Featherstone, J. Hearn and C. Toft (eds), *Violence and Gender Relations* (London: Sage).

Heider, F. (1958) *The Psychology of Interpersonal Relationships* (New York: Wiley).

Hendon, J.H.A. (2002) Workshop handout, Jhendon@AOL.com.

Henderson, P. (2001) 'Supervising counsellors in primary care', in S. Wheeler and D. King (eds), *Supervising Counsellors. Issues of responsibility* (London: Sage).

Heppner, P.P. and Claiborn, C.D. (1989) 'Social influence research in counselling: a review and critique', *Journal of Counselling Psychology*, 36: pp. 365–87.

Heimann, P. (1950) 'On transference', *International Journal of Psycho-Analysis.* 31: pp. 81–4

Hilsenroth, M.F., Ackerman, S.F. and Blagys, M.D. (2001) 'Evaluating the phase model of change during short-term psycho–dynamic psychotherapy', *Psychotherapy Research,* 11(1): pp. 29–41

Holland, S. (2000) 'The assessment relationship: interaction between social workers and parents in child protection assessments', *British Journal of Social Work,* 30: pp. 149–63.

Holmes, J. (1995) 'How I assess for psychoanalytic psychotherapy', in C. Mace (ed.), *The Art and Science of Assessment in Psychotherapy* (London and New York: Routledge).

Holmes, J. and Lindley, R. (1989) *The Values of Psychotherapy* (Oxford: Oxford University Press).

Home Office/Department of Health/Department of Education and Science/Welsh Office (1991) *Working Together under the Children Act 1989: a guide to the arrangements for inter-agency cooperation for the protection of children from abuse* (London: HMSO).

Honey, P. and Mumford, A. (1992) *The Manual of Learning Styles* (Maidenhead: Mumford).

hooks, bell (1993) *Sisters of the Yam: Black Women and Self-Recovery* (London: Turnaround).

Hubble, M.A., Duncan, B.L. and Miller, S.D. (eds), (1999) *The Heart and Soul of Change: What Works in Therapy* (Washington DC: American Psychological Association).

Hussain, N. (2001) 'We speak the same language but do we understand each other?', *Context*, 57: pp. 15–6.

Hutnik, N. (2001) 'TA and Minorities: Do we over-pathologise?', *TA UK, 61*: pp. 15–18.

Ingleby, D. (1995) 'Professionals as socialisers: the "psy complex" ', in Spitzer,

S. and A.T. Scull (eds), *Research in Law, Deviance and Social Control* (New York: Jai Press).

Iveson, C. (2001) *Whose Life? Working with Older People* (London: B T Press), 2nd edn.

Iveson, C. (2002) 'Solution-Focused Brief Therapy', *Advances in Psychiatric Treatment,* 8(2): pp. 149–156.

Jacob, F. (2001) *Solution Focused Recovery from Eating Distress* (London: B. T. Press).

Jacobs, M. (1988) *Psychodynamic Counselling in Action* (London: Sage).

Janis, I.L. and Mann, L. (1977) *Decision Making* (New York: Free Press).

Jenkins, A. (1990) *Invitations to Responsibility. The Therapeutic Engagement of Men Who Are Violent and Abusive* (Adelaide: Dulwich Centre Publications).

Jenkins, A. (1996) 'Moving towards respect; a quest for balance', in C. McLean, M. Carey and C. White (eds), *Men's Way of Being* (Boulder, CO and Oxford: Westview Press).

Jordan, J.V. (1997) 'A relational perspective for understanding women's development' in J.V. Jordan (ed.), *Women's Growth and Diversity: More Writings from the Stone Centre* (New York: Guilford Press).

Josselson, R. (1996) *Ethics and Process in the Narrative Study of Lives* (London: Sage).

Kagle, J.D. (1991) *Social Work Records* (Belmont, CA: Wadsworth).

Kahnemann, D. and Tversky, A. (1979) 'On the psychology of prediction', *Psychological Review,* 80: pp. 237–291.

Kaplan, A.G. (1987) 'Reflections on gender and psychotherapy', in M. Braude (ed.), *Women. Power and Therapy* (New York: Haworth Press).

Kearney, A. (1996) *Counselling, Class and Politics. Undeclared Influences in Therapy* (Manchester: PCCS Books).

Kernberg, O.F. (1993) *Service Personality Disorders. Psychotheraputic Strategies* (New Haven and London: Yale University Press).

King, D. (2001) 'Clinical responsibility and the supervision of counsellors', in S. Wheeler and D. King (eds), *Supervision of Counsellors. Issues of Responsibility* (London: Sage).

Kirschenbaum, H. and Henderson, V.L. (1989) *The Carl Rogers Reader* (London: Constable).

Kitzinger, C. and Perkins, R. (1993) *Changing Our Minds: Lesbian Feminism and Psychology* (London: Onlywoman Press).

Klein, J. (1999) 'Assessment – what for? who for?' *British Journal of Psychotherapy,* 15: pp. 333–345.

Klein. M. (1976) 'Feminist concepts of therapy outcome', *Psychotherapy, Theory, Practice and Research,* 13(1): pp. 89–95.

Klein, M. (1988) *Love, Guilt and Reparation and Other Works 1921–1945* (London: Virago).

Korzybski, A. (1933) *Science and Sanity: An introduction to non-Aristotelean systems and general semantics* (Englewood Cliffs, NJ: Prentice-Hall).

Kral, R. (1989) *Strategies that Work: Techniques for Solutions in the Schools* (Milwaukee, WI: Brief Family Therapy Centre).

LaCross, M.B. (1980) 'Perceived counselor social influence and counseling outcomes: validity of the counseling rating form', *Journal of Counseling Psychology*, 27: pp. 320–7.

Lambert, M.J. (1992) 'Implications of outcome research for psychotherapy integration', in J.C. Norcross and M.R. Goldfried (eds), *Handbook of Psychotherapy Integration* (New York: Basic Books).

Lambert, M.J. and Bergin, A.E. (1994) 'The effectiveness of psychotherapy', in S.L. Garfield and A.E. Bergin (eds), *Handbook for Psychotherapy and Behavioural Change* (New York: Wiley).

Lazarus, A.A. (1993) 'Tailoring the therapeutic relationship, or being an authentic chameleon', *Psychotherapy*, 30: pp. 404–7.

Lazarus, A.A. (2000) 'Multimodal Therapy' in R.J. Corsini and D. Welding (eds), *Current Psychotherapies* (6th edn) (Itasca, Il: Peacock).

Lazarus, A.A. and Messer, S.B. (1991) 'Does chaos prevail? An exchange on technical eclecticism and assimilative integration', *Journal of Psychotherapy Integration*, 2: pp. 143–58.

Letham, J. (1994) *Moved to Tears, Moved to Action* (London: B.T. Press).

Lees, S. (1997) *Ruling Passions. Sexual Violence, Reputation and the Law* (Buckingham: Open University Press).

Leigh, A. (1998) *Referral Issues for Counsellors* (London: Sage).

Leiss, W. and Chociolko, C. (1994) *Risk and Responsibility* (Quebec: McGill-Queen's University Press).

Leventhal, B. and Lundy, S.E. (eds), (1999) *Same-Sex Domestic Violence* (London: Sage).

Lewis, A., Shemmings, D. and Thoburn, J. (1991) *Participation in Practice – involving families in child protection. A training pack* (Norwich: Social Work Department, University of East Anglia).

Lewis, D. and Cheshire, A. (1999) 'Taking the hassle out of school: the work of the anti-harassment team of Selwyn College', in *Extending Narrative Therapy: a collection of practice-based papers* (Adelaide: Dulwich Centre Publication).

Liddle, S. (1997) 'Gay and lesbian clients' selection of therapists and utilization of therapy', *Psychotherapy*, 34: pp. 394–40.

Lipchik, E. (1994) 'The rush to be brief', *Networker*, March/April: pp. 35–9

Lipchik, E. and Turnell, A. (1999) 'The role of empathy in brief therapy: the overlooked but vital context', *The Australian and New Zealand Journal of Family Therapy*, 20(4): pp. 177–82.

Llewelyn, S. and Hume, W. (1979) 'The patient's view', *British Journal of Medical Psychology*, 52: pp. 29–36.

Luborsky, L., Singer, B. and Luborsky, L. (1975) 'Comparative studies of psychotherapies: is it true that everyone and all must have prizes?', *Archives of General Psychiatry*, 32: pp. 995–1008.

Macaskill, N.D. (1988) 'Personal therapy in the training of the psychothera-pist: is it effective?', *British Journal of Psychotherapy*, 4: pp. 219–26.

Mace, C. (ed.), (1995) *The Art and Science of Assessment in Psychotherapy* (London and New York: Routledge).

Mahoney, M.J. and McRay-Patteson, K. (1992) 'Changing theories of change' in S. Brown and R. Lent (eds), *Handbook of Counselling Psychology* (New York: Wiley).

Mahrer, A.R. (1989) *The Integration of Psychotherapies: a Guide for Practicing Therapists, Research and Practice* (New York: Human Sciences Press).

Mair, D. and Izzard, S. (2001) 'Grasping the nettle: gay men's experiences in therapy', *Psychodynamic Counselling*, 7: pp. 475–90.

Malan, D.H. (1975) A *Study of Brief Psychotherapy* (London: Plenum).

Malan, D.H. (1979) *Individual Psychotherapy and the Science of Psychodynamics* (London: Butterworth).

Malley, M. and Tasker, F. (1999) 'Lesbians, gay men and family therapy: a contradiction in terms?', *Journal of Family Therapy*, 21: pp. 3–29.

Marchant, L. and Payne, H. (2002) 'The experience of counselling for female clients with anorexia nervosa: a person–centred perspective', *Counselling and Psychotherapy Research,* 2: pp. 127–132.

Masson. J. M. (1984) *Assault on Truth: Freud's Suppression of the Seduction Theory* (New York: Farrar, Straus and Giroux).

Masson, J.M. (1989) *Against Therapy* (London: Fontana).

McCallum, M. and Piper,W.E. (1990) 'A controlled study of effectiveness and patient suitability for short-term group psychotherapy', *International Journal of Group Psychotherapy*, 40(4): pp. 431–52

McDermott, D. and Snyder, C.R. (1999) *Making Hope Happen: A workbook for turning possibilities into reality* (Oakland, CA: Harbinger).

McDougal, G.M. and Reade, B. (1993) 'Teaching biopsychosocial integration and formulation', *Canadian Journal of Psychiatry*, 38: pp. 359–62.

McLean, C., Carey, M. and White, C. (eds), (1996) *Men's Ways of Being* (Boulder, CO and Oxford: Westview Press).

McLeod, J. (1998) *An Introduction to Counselling* (Buckingham: Open University Press), 2nd edn.

McMenamin, D. (1999) 'Interviewing racism', in *Extending Narrative Therapy: a collection of practice-based papers* (Adelaide: Dulwich Centre Publications).

Mearns, D. and Thorne, B. (1988) *Person-Centred Counselling in Action* (London: Sage).

Mearns, D. and Thorne, B. (2000) *Person-Centred Counselling in Action* (London: Sage).

Merry, T. (1999) *Learning and Being in Person-Centred Counselling* (Ross-on-Wye: PCCS Books).

Messerschmidt, J.W. (2000) *Nine Lives. Adolescent Masculinities, the Body, and Violence* (Boulder, CO: Westview Press).

Meyer, C. (1993) *Assessment in Social Work* (New York: Columbia University Press).

Miller, D.T. and Ross, M. (1975) 'Self-serving biases in the attribution of causality: fact or fiction?', *Psychological Bulletin*, 82: pp. 213–18.

Miller, J.B. (1973) *Psychoanalysis and Women* (Harmondsworth: Penguin).

Miller, W.R. and Rollnick, S. (1991) *Motivational Interviewing* (New York: Guilford).

Milner, J. (2001) *Women and Social Work: Narrative Approaches* (Basingstoke; Palgrave).

Milner, J. and Jessop, D. (2003) 'Domestic violence. Narratives and solutions', *Probation Journal*, 50: pp. 127–41.

Milner, J. and O'Byrne, P. (2002a) *Brief Counselling. Narratives and Solutions* (Basingstoke: Palgrave Macmillan).

Milner, J. and O'Byrne, P. (2002b) *Assessment in Social Work* (Basingstoke: Palgrave Macmillan), 2nd edn.

Milner, J. and O'Byrne, P. (2003) 'How counsellors make assessments', *Counselling and Psychotherapy Research*, 3: pp. 134–47.

Mitchell, J. (1974) *Psychoanalysis and Feminism: A Radical Reassessment of Freudian Psychoanalysis* (London: Allen Lane).

Mohr, D.C. (1995) 'Negative outcomes in psychotherapy: a critical review', *Clinical Psychology: Science and Practice*, 2: pp. 1–27.

Morgan, A. (2000) *What is Narrative Therapy?* (Adelaide: Dulwich Centre Publications).

Moscovici, S. and Zavalloni, M. (1969) 'The group as polariser of attitudes', *Journal of Personality and Social Psychology*, 12: pp. 125–35.

Moss, P. and Butterworth, P. (1999) 'Introducing mosaic', in *Narrative Therapy and Community Work: a conference collection* (Adelaide: Dulwich Centre Publications).

Nelson-Jones, R. (1993) *Practical Counselling and Helping Skills: How to Use the Lifeskills Helping Model* (London: Cassell).

Nelson-Jones, R. (1995) *The Theory and Practice of Counselling* (London: Cassell).

Nelson-Jones, R. (2000) 'Lifeskills Counselling' in S. Palmer (ed.), *Introduction to Counselling and Psychotherapy. The Essential Guide* (London: Sage).

National Children's Homes (NCH) (1994) *The Workhouse Diet and the Cost of Feeding a Child Today* (Press Release, NC: Action for Children, 1 February).

Netto, G., Gaag, S. and Thanki, M. (with L. Bondi and M. Munro) (2001) *A Suitable Space: Improving counselling services for Asian people* (London: The Policy Press) (for Joseph Rowntree Foundation).

Nisbett, R.E. and Ross, L. (1980) *Human Inference: Strategies and Shortcomings of Social Judgement* (Englewood Cliffs, NJ: Prentice Hall).

Norcross, J.C. and Newman, C.F. (1992) 'Psychotherapy integration: setting the context', in J.C. Norcross and C.F. Newman (eds.), *Handbook of Psychotherapy Integration* (New York: Basic Books).

O'Connell, B. (1998) *Solution Focused Therapy* (London: Sage).

O'Connell, B. (2000) 'Solution focused therapy', in S. Palmer (ed.), *Introduction to Counselling and Psychotherapy. The Essential Guide* (London: Sage).

O'Connell, B. (2001) *Solution-Focused Stress Counselling* (London: Continuum).

O'Hanlon, B. (1993) 'Possibility therapy', in S. Gilligan and R. Price (eds), *Therapeutic Conversations* (New York and London: Norton).

O'Hanlon, B. (1995) *Breaking the Bad Trance* (Conference on Solution Focused and Narrative Brief Therapy, London).

O'Hanlon, B. and Beadle, S. (1994) *A Field Guide to Possibility Land* (Omaha: Possibility Press).

O'Hanlon, W.H. and Weiner-Davis, M. (1989) *In Search of Solutions: A new direction in psychotherapy* (New York and London: Norton).

O'Leary, C. (1999) *Counselling Couples and Families: A Person-Centred Approach* (London: Sage).

O'Sullivan, K.R. and Dryden, W. (1990) 'A survey of clinical psychologists in the South East Thames Region: activities, role and theoretical orientation', *Clinical Psychology Forum*, 29: pp. 21–6.

Palmer, S .(1997) 'Modality assessment', in S. Palmer and G. McMahon (eds), *Client Assessment* (London: Sage).

Palmer, S. (ed.), (2000) *Introduction to Counselling and Psychotherapy. The Essential Guide* (London: Sage).

Palmer, S. and Dryden, W. (1995) *Counselling for Stress Problems* (London: Sage).

Palmer, S. and Lazarus, A. A. (1996) 'In the counsellor's chair: Stephen Palmer interviews Professor Arnold A. Lazarus', *Counselling*, 6: pp. 271–3.

Palmer, S. and McMahon, G. (eds), (1997) *Client Assessment* (London: Sage).

Palmer, S. and Woolfe, R. (2000) *Integrative and Eclectic Psychotherapy* (London: Sage).

Partington, P. (1997) 'How do counselling psychologists assess and formulate case work? A comparison of counselling psychologists, clinical psychologists and counsellors', *Thesis submitted for MSc in Psychology and Counselling* (Department of Psychology and Speech Pathology: Manchester Metropolitan University).

Parton, N. and O'Byrne, P. (2000) *Constructive Social Work* (Basingstoke: Palgrave).

Payne, M. (2000) *Narrative Therapy: an Introduction for Counsellors* (London: Sage).

Penfield, W. (1952) 'Memory mechanisms', *AMA Archives of Neurology and Psychiatry*, 67: pp. 178–98.

Piper, W.E., Azim, H.F., Joyce, A.S. and MacCallum, M. (1991) 'Transference interpretations, therapeutic alliance, and outcome in short-term individual psychotherapy', *Archives of General Psychiatry*, 48(10): pp. 946–53.

Pollard, R.(2001) 'Ethical considerations in teaching counselling theory', *Counselling and Psychotherapy Journal*, 12: pp. 14–7.

Poupeau, F. (2000) 'Reasons for domination, Bordieu versus Habermas', in B. Fowler (ed.), *Reading Bordieu on Society and Culture* (Oxford: Blackwell).

Prince, K. (1996) *Boring Records? Communication, speech and writing in social work records* (London, Bristol: Jessica Kingsley).

Prochaska, J.O. and DiClemente, C.C. (1984) *The Transtheoretical Approach* (Homewood, IL: Dow Jones-Irwin).

Prochaska, J.O. and DiClemente, C.C. (1992) 'Stages of change in modification of problem behavors', in R.M. Hersen and P. M. Miller (eds), *Progress in Behavior Modification* (Sycamore,IL: Sycamore Press).

Prochaska, J.O. Di Clemente, C.C. and Norcross, J.C. (1982) 'In search of how people change', *American Psychologist*, 47: pp. 1102–14.

Pulver, S.E. (1987) 'Epilogue' in S.E. Pulver, P.J. Escoll and N. Fisher (eds), *Psychoanalytic Inquiry, Special Edition*, 7(2): pp. 141–299.

Rapp, H. (2001) 'Working with difference and diversity: the responsibilities of the supervisor', in S. Wheeler and D. King (eds), *Supervising Counsellors. Issues of Responsibility* (London: Sage).

Ratigan, B. (1999) 'Working with older gay men', in D. Davies and C. Neal (eds), *Pink Therapy. A guide for counsellors and therapists working with lesbian, gay and bisexual clients* (Buckingham: Open University Press).

Rayner, J. (2000) 'Working cross-culturally', *Context*, 50: pp. 8–12.

Reibstein (1997) – quoted in *The Independent* newspaper's 'Tabloid', 26.02. 1997.

Reimers, T.M., Wacker, P., Cooper, L.J. and DeRaad, A.O. (1992) 'Acceptability for behavioral treatments for children; analog and naturalistic evaluations by parents', *School Psychology Review*, 21: pp. 628–43.

Rennie, D. (1998) *Person-centred Counselling: An Experiential Approach* (London: Sage).

Renzetti, C.M. (1992) *Violent Betrayal. Partner Abuse in Lesbian Relationships* (London: Sage).

Rice, L.N. (1974) 'The evocative function of the therapist', in D. Wexler and L.N. Rice (eds), *Innovations in Client-centred Therapy* (New York: Wiley).

Rich, A. (1977) *Of Woman Born: Motherhood as Institution and Experience* (London: Virago).

Rogers, C.R. (1951) *Client-Centred Therapy* (London: Constable).

Rogers, C.R. (1961) *On Being a Person* (Boston: Houghton Mifflin).

Rogers, C.R. (1980) *A Way of Being* (Boston: Houghton Mifflin).

Rose, S. (2000) 'Evidence-based practice', *Counselling*, 11: pp. 38–40.

Roth, A. and Fonagy, P. (1996) *What Works for Whom? A Critical Review of Psychotherapy Research* (New York: Guilford).

Roth, S. and Epston, D. (1996) 'Consulting the problem about the problematic relationship: an exercise for experiencing a relationship with an externalised problem', in M.F. Hoyt (ed.), *Constructive Therapies 2* (New York: Guilford Publications).

Ruddell, P. (1997) 'General Assessment Issues', in S. Palmer and G. McMahon (eds), *Client Assessment* (London: Sage).

Ruddell, P. and Curwen, B. (1997) 'General Assessment Issues', in S. Palmer and G. McMahon (eds), *Client Assessment* (London: Sage).

Rush, A.J., Beck, A.T., Kovacs, M. and Hollons, S. (1977) 'Comparative efficacy of cognitive therapy and pharmacotherapy in treatment of depressed outpatients', *Cognitive Therapy and Research*, 1(1): pp. 17–38.

Saggese, M.L. and Foley, F.W. (2000) 'From problems or solutions to problems and solutions: integrating the MRI and solution focused models of brief therapy', *Journal of Systemic Therapies*, 19: pp. 59–73.

Saunders, P. (2000) 'Mapping person-centred approaches to counselling and psychotherapy', in *Person Centred Practice*, 8(2): pp. 62–74.

Sawicki, J. (1991) *Disciplining Foucault: Feminism, Power and the Body* (London: Sage).

Segal, J. (2000) 'Psychodynamic (Kleinian) counselling and psychotherapy', in S. Palmer (ed.), *Introduction to Counselling and Psychotherapy. The Essential Guide* (London: Sage).

Segal, Z.V., Swallow, S.R., Bizinni, L. and Rouget, B.W. (1995) 'How we assess for short-term cognitive behaviour therapy', in C. Mace (ed.), *The Art and Science of Psychotherapy* (London: Routledge).

Selekman, M.D. (1993) *Pathways to Change: Brief therapy solutions with difficult adolescents* (New York: Guilford).

Selekman, M.D. (1997) *Solution-focused Therapy with Children: Harnessing family strengths for systemic change* (New York and London: Norton).

Selekman, M.D. (2002) *Living on the Razor's Edge. Solution-Oriented Brief Family Therapy with Self-Harming Adolescents* (New York and London: W. W. Norton).

Seligman, M.E.P. (1992) *Helplessness: On Depression and Death* (New York: Freeman).

Seligman, M. and Csikszentmihalyi, M. (2000) 'Positive Psychology: an Introduction', *American Psychologist*, 55: pp. 5–14

Sexton, T.L., Whiston, S.C., Bleuer, J.C. and Walsh, G.R. (1997) *Integrated Outcome Research in Counseling Practice and Training* (Alexandria, VA: American Counselling Association).

Sharry, J., Madden, B. and Darmody, M. (2001) *Becoming a Solution Detective: A Strengths Guide to Brief therapy* (London: B.T. Press).

Shilts, L. and Reiter, M.D. (2000) 'Integrating externalization and scaling questions: using "visual" scaling to amplify children's voices', *Journal of Systemic Therapies*, 19: pp. 82–89.

Shoham, V. and Rohrbaugh, M. (1996) 'Problems and perils of empirically supported psychotherapy integration', *Journal of Psychotherapy Integration*, 6: pp. 191–206.

Simon, G. (1999) 'Working with people in relationships', in D. Davies and C. Neal (eds), *Pink Therapy. A guide for counsellors and therapists working with lesbian, gay and bisexual clients* (Buckingham: Open University Press).

Skynner, R. (1997) 'Looking over your shoulder: Robin Skynner remembers', *Context*, 34: pp. 5–6.

Slone, R.B., Staples, F.R., Cristol, A.H., Yorkson, N.J. and Whipple, K. (1975) *Psychotherapy Versus Behaviour Therapy* (Cambridge, MA: Harvard University Press).

Smith, G. (2000) 'In the land of the blind, the one-eyed person is put in a psychiatric hospital', *Context*, 51: pp. 13–50.

Smith, M., Glass, G. and Miller, T. (1980) *The Benefits of Psychotherapy* (Baltimore: Johns Hopkins Press).

Snyder, C.R., Michael, S.T. and Cheavons, J.S. (1999) 'Hope as a psychotherapeutic foundation of common factors, placebos, and expectancies', in M. A. Hubble, B.L. Duncan and S.D. Miller (eds), *The Heart and Soul of Change: What works in therapy* (Washington, DC: American Psychological Association).

Spender, D. (1985) *Man Made Language* (London: Routledge), 2nd edn.

Spurling, L. (2002) 'One model is enough', *Counselling and Psychotherapy Journal*, 14: pp. 14–16

Steiner, C. (1971) 'The stroke economy' in *TAJ*, 1(3): pp. 9–15

Stern, D.N. (1985) *The Interpersonal World of the Infant: A View from Psychoanalysis and Developmental Psychology* (New York: Basic Books).

Sternberg (1992) quoted in C. Mihill and M. Tysoe in *The Guardian* newspaper, 14 February.

Stewart, I. (1989) *Transactional Counselling in Action* (London: Sage).

Stewart, I. and Joines, V. (1987) *TA Today. A New Introduction to Transactional Analysis* (Nottingham and Chapel Hill (NC): Lifespace Publishing).

Stiles, W.B., Elliott, R., Llewelyn, S.P., Firth-Cozens, J.A., Margison, F.R., Shapiro, D.A. and Hardy, G. (1990) 'Assimilation of problematic experiences in psychotherapy', *Psychotherapy*, 27: pp. 411–20.

Stiver, I.P. (1991) 'The meanings of 'dependency' in female–male relationships' in J.V. Jordan, A.G. Kaplan, J.B. Miller, I.P. Stiver and J.L. Surrey (eds), *Women's Growth in Connection: Writings from the Stone Centre* (New York: Guilford Press).

Strand, P.S. (1997) 'Towards a developmentally informed narrative therapy', *Family Process*, 36: pp. 329–39.

Stratford, J. (1998) 'Women and men in conversation; a consideration of therapists' interruptions in therapeutic discourse', *Journal of Family Therapy*, 20: pp. 383–94.

Strupp, H.H. and Binder, J.L. (1984) *Psychotherapy in a New Key* (New York: Basic Books).

Tamasese, K. and Waldegrave, C. (1996) 'Cultural and gender accountability in the 'just therapy' approach' in C. McLean, M. Carey and C. White (eds), *Men's Ways of Being* (Boulder, CO and Oxford: Westview Press).

Tantam, D. (1995) 'Why assess?', in C. Mace (ed.), *The Art and Science of Assessment in Psychotherapy* (London and New York: Routledge).

Thompson, N. (1995) *Age and Dignity. Working with Older People* (Aldershot: Arena).

Thompson, N. (2003) *Language and Communication* (Basingstoke: Palgrave Macmillan).

Tillett, R. (1996) 'Pyschotherapy assessment and treatment selection', *British Journal of Psychiatry*, 168: pp. 10–5

Tohn, S. and Oshlag, J. (1995) *Crossing the bridge: Integrating solution-focused therapy into clinical practice* (New York and London: W. W. Norton).

Turnell, A. and Edwards, S. (1999) *Signs of Safety. A Solution and Safety Oriented Approach to Child Protection in Casework* (New York and London: W. W. Norton).

Waddington-Jones, L. (1996) *Availability bias in clinical understanding* (Research School of Medicine, Department of Clinical Psychology, Leeds).

Waterhouse, R. (1993) ' "Wild women don't have the blues": a feminist critique of "person-centred" counselling and therapy', *Feminism and Psychology*, 3: pp. 55–71.

Webb, A. (2001) 'Expecting the impossible? What responsibility do counsellors expect their supervisors to take?', in S. Wheeler and D. King (eds), *Supervising Counsellors: issues of responsibility* (London: Sage).

Weir, A.L. (2002) *Irene Iveson, Woman and Campaigner* (Rotherham: CROP).

Werner-Wilson, R.J., Price, S.J., Zimmerman, T.S. and Murphy, M.J. (1997) 'Client gender as a process variable in marriage and family therapy: are women clients interrupted more than men clients?', *Journal of Family Psychology*, 11: pp. 373–77.

West, C. (1990) 'Not just 'doctors' orders': Directive-response sequences in patients' visits to women and men physicians', *Discourse and Society*, 1: pp. 85–112.

Westwood, S. (1996) 'Feckless parents. Masculinities and the British state', in M. Mac an Ghaill (ed.), *Understanding Masculinities* (Buckingham: Open University Press).

Wheeler, S. (2001) 'Supervision of counsellors working independently in private practice: what responsibility does the supervisor have for the counsellor and their work?', in S. Wheeler and D. King (eds), *Supervising Counsellors. Issues of Responsibility* (London: Sage).

Whiston, S.C. (2000) *Principles and Applications of Assessment in Counselling* (Belmont, CA: Brooks/Cole).

White, M. (1984) 'Pseudo-encopresis: from avalanche to victory, from vicious to victorious circles' *Family Systems Medicine*, 2: pp. 150–60.

White, M. (1988) Process of questioning: a therapy of literary merit?', *Dulwich Centre Newsletter*, Winter: pp. 8–14.

White, M. (1993) 'Deconstruction and therapy', in S. Gilligan and R. Price (eds), *Therapeutic Conversations* (New York and London: W. W. Norton).

White, M. (1995) *Re-Authoring Lives: Interviews and Essays* (Adelaide: Dulwich Centre Publications).

White, M. (1997) *Narratives of Therapists' Lives* (Adelaide: Dulwich Publications).

White, M. (2000) *Reflections on Narrative Practice: Essays and Interviews* (Adelaide: Dulwich Centre Publications).

White, M. and Epston, D. (1990) *Narrative Means to Therapeutic Ends* (New York and London: W. W. Norton).

Whyte, G. (1989) 'Groupthink reconsidered', *Academy of Management Review*, 14: pp. 40–56.

Whyte, G. (1993) 'Decision failures, why they occur and how to prevent them', *Academy of Management Review*, 5: pp. 23–31.

Wilkinson, I. (1998) *Child and Family Assessment: Clinical Guidelines for Practitioners* (London and New York: Routledge).

Wittgenstein, L. (1980) *Remarks on the Philosophy of Psychology* (Oxford: Blackwell).

Wolff, L. (1995) *Child Abuse in Freud's Vienna* (New York and London: New York University Press).

Woodward, K. (ed.), (1997) *Identity and Difference* (London: Sage).

Worsley, R. (2002) *Process Work in Person-Centred Therapy* (Basingstoke: Palgrave–Macmillan).

Young, M.E., Feiler, F. and Witmer, J.M. (1989) 'Eclecticism', unpublished paper at Stetson University FL.

Young, V. (1999) 'Working with older lesbians', in D. Davies and C. Neal (eds), *Pink Therapy. A guide for counsellors and therapists working with lesbian, gay and bisexual clients* (Buckingham: Open University Press).

Zimmerman, J.L. and Beaudoin, M-N. (2002) 'Cats under the stars: a narrative story', *Child and Adolescent Mental Health*, 7: pp. 31–40.

Index